Grade 4

Patricia Horne Sumner
Jean F. Bernholz

Helen G. Cappleman, Series Editor
With grateful acknowledgment to the late Anne H. Adams,
the originator of *SUCCESS in Reading and Writing.*

GoodYearBooks

An Imprint of ScottForesman
A Division of HarperCollinsPublishers

Cover illustration by Mark Mitchell.
Cover design by Amy O'Brien Krupp.
Book design by Carolyn McHenry.

Good Year Books

are available for preschool through grade 6 and for every basic curriculum subject plus many enrichment areas. For more Good Year Books, contact your local bookseller or educational dealer. For a complete catalog with information about other Good Year Books, please write:

Good Year Books
Scott, Foresman and Company
1900 East Lake Avenue
Glenview, Illinois 60025

Sumner, Patricia Horne
    Success in reading and writing. Grade 4 / Patricia Horne Sumner, Jean F. Bernholz.—2nd ed.
        p. cm.
    Rev. ed. of: Success in reading and writing. Grade four / Anne H. Adams, Patricia Horne Sumner, Jean F. Bernholz.
    Includes bibliographical references and index.
    ISBN 0–673–36004–0
    1. Language arts (Elementary) 2. English Language—Study and teaching (Elementary) 3. Fourth grade (Education) I. Bernholz, Jean F.   II. Adams, Anne H. Success in reading and writing. Grade four. III. Title. IV. Title: Success in reading and writing. Grade four.
LB1576.S89 1992
372.6—dc20t   91–23839
                                                                                    CIP

▶ Preface

Patricia Horne Sumner
and Jean F. Bernholz,
authors

SUCCESS in Reading and Writing invites teachers to use their professional knowledge and creativity to help students become thinking communicators. SUCCESS classrooms are characterized by heterogeneous, whole-group instruction. Each student reads and discusses books of his or her choice. Students read a wide range of materials to locate information. They write every day, expressing their own ideas. Students work with their peers, organizing, discussing, and sharing knowledge.

As students and teachers become co-investigators in each day's four thirty-minute reading and writing lessons, they expect that they will learn something new. SUCCESS gives everyone a chance to be surprised. The common goal of the class becomes not just to cover, but to discover and uncover the curriculum. SUCCESS is based on a philosophy that respects teachers and learners and proclaims that learning from and with others is exciting.

This revision of SUCCESS provides a clear explanation of an integrated language arts philosophy, a rationale for why this approach is appropriate, a guide for practical application, and a framework for 180 lessons. The revision comes in response to the educational research supporting a more natural way of teaching reading and writing and to the discoveries of teachers who have been using SUCCESS during the last twelve years. More attention is given to the writing process, to integration of the lessons with content-area subjects, and to the use of literature throughout the program. These changes reflect the positive experiences of teachers who have become decision makers and curriculum designers. Based on this input, the authors have attempted to preserve what works with SUCCESS and to make changes for clarity and consistency.

The basic procedures for each module have remained the same. The names of three modules have been changed to identify more clearly what takes place during each thirty-minute period. The Spelling/Phonics module has been renamed Word Study. The focus of this module is on the joy and delight of learning new words and how to use them. Composition has been renamed Writing. The writing process is presented in the lessons so that students think and behave as writers. Study Skills is now called Research. In this module, students develop the skills of researchers as they expand their knowledge. Recreational Reading retains its original name, and its emphasis remains on reading books of choice every day while the teacher has conversations with the students. There is more flexibility in the methods of conferencing, as well as more opportunities for sharing reading experiences. The value of daily reading aloud is emphasized, and suggested books are listed in each lesson.

The authors hope that these modifications will be helpful and appropriate for today's teachers and students. However, it should never be forgotten that the process of revision is ongoing. Teachers will revise from year to year what is presented today in this book. Learning about learning does not stop.

▶ Acknowledgments

SUCCESS in Reading and Writing workshop leaders, who have helped shape SUCCESS as it has developed in classrooms across the country:

Mary Armstrong	Becky Haseltine	Cam Newman
Peggy Bahr	Debby Head	Kathy Newport
Jean Becker	Paula Hertel	Ola Pickels
Patti Bell	Bridget Hill	Libby Pollett
Jean Bernholz	Tina Hinchliff	Karen Powell
Barbara Blackford	Robbie Ivers	Susan Quick
Jill Board	Connie John	Donna Rea
Elaine Bowie	Shae Johnson	Cathy Reasor
Ann Bryan	Delores P. Jones	Patty Redland
Jacqueline Buckmaster	Joanne Jumper	Mary B. Reeves
Helen Cappleman	Janice Keegan	Carole Reindl
Stacey Carmichael	Nancy Kerr	Pat Reinheimer
Kathi Caulley	Dana Kersey	Marilyn Renfro
Betty Cramer	Annie Kinegak	Janice Reynolds
Donna Croft	Barbara Krieger	Marlene Rotter
Suzie Desilet	Esther Lee	Pat Scherler
Bobbi Donnell	Sue Lippincott	Janet Schneider
Marilyn Enger	Lisa Lord	Shirley T. Scruggs
Betty S. English	Kathy Malick	Celeste Singletary
Sandra Fain	Judy Mansfield	Kathleen Smith
Debra Fetner	Howard Martin	Patty B. Smith
Neita Frank	Judy Martin	Pat Sumner
Carol George	Lila Martin	Pam Tate
Randy Gill	Nancy J. Mayhall	Donnye Theerman
Lynn Gori-Bjerkness	Becky Miller	Shirley A. Thompson
Letha Gressley	Debbie I. Miller	Jean Weaver
Andra Gwydir	Debby Miller	Beth Whitford
Carol Hall	Paul Moller	Pat Wong
Mary Harris	Cinda Lee Moon	Michael Wong
Roberta Harrison	Avril Moore	Kristin Zeaser-Sydow

For their loving support and understanding, we thank our families, friends, and colleagues, especially Blake Bernholz, Dustin Sumner, and Michael Bernholz. We also want to thank SUCCESS teachers who sent artwork and ideas from their classrooms. Our thanks to each other for the special friendship that has allowed us to examine and challenge our personal beliefs as educators. And finally, we thank our students who pushed us to find a better way.

▶ Art Acknowledgments

The following young artists have contributed to this edition of *SUCCESS in Reading and Writing,* Grade 4:

Dequita Major, Dixie, Georgia
Philip Allgeier, Louisville, Kentucky
Alicia Scott, Louisville, Kentucky
Joseph Ware, Louisville, Kentucky
Erin Johnson, Richmond, Virginia
Ella Jean Lumpkins, Louisville, Kentucky
Kendrick Waters, Dixie, Georgia
Bethany Ann Miller, Louisville, Kentucky
Zerric Backett, Louisville, Kentucky
Jason Bradbury, Louisville, Kentucky
Sarah Perkins, Louisville, Kentucky
Scott Johanningsmeier, Louisville, Kentucky
Joy Berry, Hillsborough, North Carolina
David Gowers, Louisville, Kentucky
Jennifer Perkins, Louisville, Kentucky
Leslee Pugh, Louisville, Kentucky
Katie Robertson, Louisville, Kentucky
Lori Walls, Louisville, Kentucky
Tiffany Weber, Louisville, Kentucky
Adrian Jackson, Louisville, Kentucky
Amber Powell, Springfield, Missouri
Nikki Thomas, Hillsborough, North Carolina
Ginny Jenkins, Louisville, Kentucky

Contents

Grade 4

Chapter 1   SUCCESS: The Basic Assumption

What is *SUCCESS in Reading and Writing?* SUCCESS is a student-centered instructional design based on the belief in the expertise of professional teachers to guide the development of readers, writers, and thinkers. The SUCCESS philosophy scraps jargon, eliminates stereotyping of students, and removes obstacles to the growth of communication skills and knowledge. It signals a new day of respect for what happens in classrooms.

▶ SUCCESS in Action

How does SUCCESS look in action? Open the door to a SUCCESS classroom, and you will see pairs or groups of students reading and writing, sharing and reacting. All is not quiet. The unobtrusive noise signals that students are involved and excited about what they are learning. Students are using a variety of materials to learn about specific topics. Students are making decisions about what is important to include as they collect information and organize it to share with others. The body of information keeps changing, and what they learn is spontaneous. An authentic learning community exists. Examples of students' work are displayed throughout the room. A print-rich environment is evident from shelves full of books, reference materials, magazines, newspapers, and other resources. Where is the teacher? The teacher is among the students observing, encouraging, and instructing. The classroom has a real worked-in, learned-in look. A joyous learning environment exists in SUCCESS classrooms.

SUCCESS promotes student interaction with print materials and with other learners. Students are actively involved in their learning. They are learning that reading, writing, and thinking are inseparable aspects of the process of becoming a literate person. Students make choices about how and what to learn. They accept the responsibility for their own learning.

The teacher is not viewed as the single provider of information. Two of the greatest teachers, Socrates and Plato, taught that the answers did not lie within the teacher. They suggested that true learning took place through discussion and clarification of ideas. Students learn from each other; they learn through exposure to many different materials and resources; they learn through questioning.

SUCCESS offers many opportunities for

1. improving the learner's self-image and confidence as a learner;
2. valuing the opinions and contributions of others;
3. broadening knowledge and concepts;
4. clarifying thoughts and ideas;
5. making direct and indirect association of information;
6. applying skills to make relevant connections to life;
7. strengthening communication skills;
8. discerning and organizing important information;
9. developing various group and individual techniques for sharing information;

Dequita Major

10. evaluating resources, information, products, and methods for sharing information;

11. establishing lifelong learning skills and goals.

▶ Basic Structure of SUCCESS

Four modules provide the basic structure for SUCCESS. Each module has 180 daily lessons corresponding to the length of the current school year in most school districts. Each module provides a different, yet complementary, approach to teaching reading and writing.

THE MODULES

In the fourth grade the modules are Research, Recreational Reading, Writing, and Word Study. Each lesson within these modules allows for the development of readers and writers with attention to the processes necessary to this development.

Research In the Research module students practice the processes of locating, organizing, and sharing information from a wide range of resources. It enables them to expand their knowledge base as well as their creative and critical thinking skills.

Recreational Reading Students read books of their choice and have conversations with the teacher and other students to share their growth as readers and their joy of reading.

The SUCCESS program has opened my eyes widely to teaching. It has shown me how to get the most out of our students. I can see SUCCESS being the number one teaching program in the future. It's great!! SUCCESS YES!

Dakota Holman, teacher

Writing Students write each day making choices about topics and practicing the steps of the writing process to complete and share published work.

Word Study Students expand their vocabulary and thinking as they select words they associate with a topic. They also learn to recognize spelling patterns and develop strategies.

DAILY SCHEDULES

With the daily SUCCESS schedules, students can always count on a time during the day to read, write, think, and share. A regular and consistent schedule helps students know what to expect. A predictable schedule helps eliminate confusion and allows students to plan and think ahead about what they will be doing.

The schedule allows thirty minutes for each module. The four modules may be taught in any order and at any time of the day. The decision about when to teach the SUCCESS modules rests with the teacher, who must take into consideration the needs of the students and other daily schedule demands.

The following two examples show that the order and time of day are flexible. Some SUCCESS teachers prefer devoting an uninterrupted time block of two hours to the modules:

RECREATIONAL READING	8:30–9:00
WRITING	9:00–9:30
RESEARCH	9:30–10:00
WORD STUDY	10:00–10:30

Others prefer teaching other subjects in between modules. Often students are scheduled for special classes outside the classroom, and teachers must arrange the SUCCESS schedule to accommodate these students.

WORD STUDY	8:45–9:15
WRITING	10:00–10:30
RESEARCH	1:00–1:30
RECREATIONAL READING	2:15–2:45

When teachers determine the time for each module, they post the schedule with the name of each module and the time it is taught outside the classroom door. Posting the schedule informs visitors of the time for specific modules that they may want to observe. The posting of a schedule is also an excellent way to help students learn to budget their time. Once it is posted, the teacher should adhere as closely as possible to the module schedule each day, although it may be impossible to stay exactly on the thirty-minute target.

At the beginning of the year, students may need more than thirty minutes per module (except for the Recreational Reading module) until they learn the format and procedure for each. Thirty minutes may be too long at the beginning of the year for some students to read library books silently dur-

Philip Allgeier

ing Recreational Reading. Teachers may wish to start with fifteen minutes for this module and gradually build to thirty minutes.

Teachers who do all four modules daily have a balanced and complete language arts program. When modules are omitted, important segments of SUCCESS are lost to the students. SUCCESS lessons are designed to help students move forward each day. In all fairness to the teacher, to SUCCESS, and especially to the students, all four modules should be taught each day. Chapters Two through Five explain how to teach each module.

▶ The History of SUCCESS

A NEED FOR CHANGE

SUCCESS in Reading and Writing was born from the need for change. The late Dr. Anne H. Adams describes the beginning of the program in the original edition of *SUCCESS in Beginning Reading and Writing (1978):*

> Although I did not realize it at the time, research for this book began in 1964 when I found myself under contract to teach 36 first graders, none of whom could read. It was one of the most frustrating years of my professional life; however, through those experiences I began to identify some of the major problems and concerns expressed orally or in the literature with specific reference to beginning reading instruction. My approach was direct. I tried to analyze each problem as a springboard for an exploration of alternatives that might eliminate or alleviate the problem. Part of the analysis was my doctoral dissertation, in which I researched the concept of correlated language arts in the first grade without use of basal readers.

Until 1976, the contents of this book were in the form of a rough draft and had become one of those things "I would finish one day soon." Matters were expedited that year when I was asked to work with 17 first-grade classes in the Durham (North Carolina) City Schools. . . .

The reader should be aware that the program described in this book was not initiated under ideal conditions. It should have been difficult enough to ask teachers of 17 classes to stop doing what they had been doing and start a different program the next day. Most of the teachers, however, were willing to give it an honest try because they were neither satisfied with the way things had gone nor content with the reading/writing abilities of many of their students in the past. One teacher said she "boxed up things I'd been using for 20 years" and started this program the day after our first meeting. It took a few of the other teachers longer to break the traditional spells; however, as the program gradually unfolded, they, too, discarded some methods and materials in favor of this approach, and each added her own expertise to its dimensions.

Durham City Schools is an inner-city school district, supposedly populated with scores of youngsters destined for, if not already in, remedial classes. According to the proposal submitted by the Durham City Schools for the Right-to-Read grant, approximately 50 percent of all the students in grades 3 to 11 were below the 23rd percentile achievement level on the Science Research Associates reading test. Because such large numbers of black and white parents had put their children in private schools or had moved to other school districts, the Durham City Schools' 1969 enrollment of 14,101 had dropped to 9,389 in 1975. Of those who remained, approximately 80 percent were on government-subsidized lunches. Under these conditions, the program was begun in mid-October 1976, in approximately half of the first-grade classes. . . . At the end of the year, the teachers reported the total absence of nonreaders in their classes. No longer could the blame be placed completely on variables such as the students' homes, parents, vocabularies, and/or socioeconomic conditions.

IMPLEMENTING CHANGE

Many teachers quickly embraced the ideology of Dr. Adams. They were trained, caring, and dedicated professionals who believed they could make a difference in the learning of their students. They believed their students could learn to read and write, but with a different approach from what had proven in too many cases to be unsuccessful.

When the authors of this text first learned of the SUCCESS program, Dr. Adams had only written the first-grade manual, *SUCCESS in Beginning Reading and Writing.* We were team-teaching a fifth-grade class and were frustrated because many of our students did not enjoy reading and writing. Like many teachers, we were searching for a better way.

By chance, we discovered Dr. Adams and sought to learn of the new ways she advocated for teaching. She responded immediately to our needs. She believed that the same basic principles outlined for first-graders could apply to our students in fifth grade. We worked with Dr. Adams to develop lessons for our class during the 1977–78 school year and were invited to be co-authors of the fourth- and fifth-grade editions in the spring of 1978.

▶ SUCCESS Today

*M*y students are teachers. SUCCESS changes attitudes and expectations about students—and that makes all the difference!

Kathy Folsom, teacher

The reasons that SUCCESS has survived and is constantly being embraced by more and more teachers are the same as the reasons that led us to try this new promising approach. The keys to teaching reading and writing have always been and will always be (1) the teacher and (2) what is taught.

At first, teachers were attracted to SUCCESS because what they were using was not working; both they and their students were bored with more traditional methods.

Research now exists to support the principles of SUCCESS: Students should be taught to read and write using materials, such as newspapers and real books that are now available to them and will be in the future. Students should have choices about their reading and writing. They should have the opportunity to write every day and develop the ability to think and make associations and connections to real life through their reading and writing. Research has further helped us to identify the steps in the writing process and to expect that there is a natural development of this process when students are given opportunities to use these steps. The growing body of research also supports cooperative learning and the noncompetitive support of peers as meaningful ways to facilitate learning.

Everything that we have learned from research and from teachers has strengthened our basic belief in the foundations of SUCCESS.

Most SUCCESS teachers are receptive to new ideas and philosophies that offer better learning and teaching opportunities. They are, however, not willing to change from one way of teaching to another if they do not think this will lead to improved learning. They also want learning to be fun and enjoyable. They are interested in educating, not schooling, their students.

WILLINGNESS TO CHANGE

SUCCESS offers hope for those who are ready for change. It offers a more natural, spontaneous, and supportive structure for teaching language arts. It provides an alternative. The number of teaching hours and days could possibly change in the future, but the most important change must be what happens in classrooms during those hours and days.

What will it take to make the change? People must recognize the need for change and must want to make a change. Teachers must believe that a change will be in the best interest of their students. Teachers who decide to change should not be overwhelmed by the process. Dare to take the risk and accept the challenge.

PROMISES OF CHANGE

What is different in a SUCCESS classroom? What will change? Many SUCCESS teachers have shared the following observations with us:

Group learning activities are based on student interest, student needs, and student choice. These choices include topics, partners, directions for exploration, and methods of sharing.

Teaching students in three to six ability groups is eliminated with the SUCCESS program. Students are not to be grouped for reading instruction according to their standardized tests scores. Trying to identify artificial "reading levels" is of little importance. Labels such as *high, medium,* and *low* are eliminated.

Materials and resources are as open and varied as the imagination allows. Academic textbooks are only one type of reference material. Creating and using a print-rich environment becomes a major goal and focus of the SUCCESS teacher.

Clerical chores, such as checking boxes on student skill sheets; parroting questions and other ideas from "canned" teacher's guides; or any other robotlike activities are eliminated. Instead, the teacher becomes the facilitator of myriad learning activities.

The students' writing, thinking, and reading about anything in print and their opportunities to discuss and validate their thoughts are the foci of learning.

For some teachers and students, change is embraced with enthusiasm and energy. For others, change is an evolutionary process. Both need support and encouragement.

Whether teachers decide to read further and use SUCCESS, they are still faced with a decision. What will they do with their students this year to best facilitate their learning?

> The bottom line is, America's fight for long term competitiveness ultimately will be won or lost not in the halls of Congress . . . not in the boardrooms around the world . . . but in America's classrooms.[1]

---

[1]John L. Clendenin, CEO, BellSouth Corporation; Chairman, U.S. Chamber of Commerce

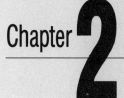

Chapter 2   The Research Module

"Bouillabaisse! Yes, that's it. The perfect dish for my dinner party."

A novice cook selecting a new recipe for a dinner party reads over the list of ingredients. "Saffron? What's that? Calls for only one tablespoon. It must be a spice."

She calls her friend, a much more experienced cook: "What is saffron?"

"It's an orangish colored spice used to flavor fish and rice dishes. It's very expensive."

Later at the grocery story, she asks, "Why is this so expensive?"

"It does cost a lot for such a little bit. Wonder why?"

Stopping by the library to return an overdue book, the cook says to herself, "While I'm here, I'll find out more information about saffron."

On the evening of the dinner party, a guest comments, "This is delicious fish stew. What's the spice?"

"Funny you should ask . . . ," and so the hostess shares her new knowledge. "Saffron is a spice that comes from the crocus flower. . . ."

Do you think this person is a researcher, an inexperienced cook, a lifelong learner, or all of these?

Recent research findings indicate that some problems of student motivation and achievement are related to the lack of relevance of classroom instruction and activities to real life. Often students ask, "Why do I need to know this?" Too often comes the reply, "It will be on the test." Educators must ask themselves, "What is important for students to learn: facts for a test or how to learn and process new information?"

▶ The Rationale

In our current age of rapidly changing information and knowledge, students, to be successful, must know how to process information and make meaningful connections. It is learning how to learn that will produce and sustain lifelong learners. Lifelong learners are always questioning and seeking new knowledge. Even trying a new recipe can engage a person in the pursuit of knowledge, not because it is necessary for the bouillabaisse to taste good, but because the desire to learn has been stimulated. Learning is fun! Satisfying a desire to know something is a pleasurable experience.

The Research module gives students the opportunity to ask questions, find answers, and work together as a learning community to share knowledge. For thirty minutes each day, students read, write, and share information about a selected topic. They practice the research process and become familiar with many resources. Through small group and class research projects, students discover new information, decide how to share the information, and learn valuable group interaction skills.

Chapter 2

Alicia Scott

▶ Becoming Lifelong Learners

The Research module is designed to help students develop and use skills for forming questions and finding the answers to what they want to know, when they want to know it. This module establishes the practice of personal inquiry as the foundation for the lifelong learner. Students learning with and from each other, expanding their knowledge, and discovering how to learn are the building blocks of this foundation.

STUDENTS LEARN WITH AND FROM EACH OTHER

Students work with a partner, a small group, or with the whole class during the Research module. Because there is always a shared purpose or goal (Research Project), it is important for students to value the opinions and contributions of others. Often the group must choose a topic, subtopics, resources, what facts to include in the final presentation, and how to organize and share their information. This requires the students to be active listeners, as well as participants, in the decisions that must be made in order to reach the goals of the group. Each student becomes a valued member in a community of learners.

STUDENTS LEARN NEW INFORMATION

During each Research lesson students are engaged in activities that allow them to expand their knowledge in several different directions. They may gain a new understanding of group processes as they plan a report. The new knowledge may be something they learn and share about the research topic. It may be finding out how to use a new resource. Students are free to explore a topic in depth by using a wide range of materials. This freedom encourages discovery of new information.

The integration of the Research module with content areas reinforces and expands the curriculum. Most fourth-graders study machines. Lessons 11 through 16 are designed to broaden students' knowledge beyond what may be found in their science textbook. Students can choose to work by themselves or in teams to do in-depth research and study of a machine they want to learn more about. After locating and organizing the information they discover, they write and share reports with the rest of the class. Through the use of resources other than a textbook, students might find that the study reveals much about the history and early development of machines that are now taken for granted. Students become aware of a world of information through their unlimited use of resources.

STUDENTS LEARN HOW TO LEARN

When students attach meaning to a learning task, they apply the skills and strategies needed to accomplish the task. Students must decide where to look for information, which resources are most appropriate, and how to use those resources. When the students select a topic, such as the telephone, they discuss what subtopics (who invented it, where, when, why, etc.) to investigate, and where they will look for the information. The students might choose encyclopedias, social studies textbooks, books about communications, and fiction books. As they look for information, they become adept at using glossaries, indexes, tables of contents, chapter outlines, headings, and subheadings. The connections between their need to know and how to find out become apparent. Students learn through repeated practice that they can make decisions about what is important to learn and how to best learn it.

RESEARCH AND REALITIES

If this sounds idealistic, teachers should consider what research has demonstrated. Students learn best when the following takes place:

- interaction with print materials and other learners
- reading, speaking, and writing are accepted as inseparable aspects of the learning process
- students are actively involved in their learning
- students are given choices for how and what to learn
- the responsibility for learning belongs to the student

A consideration of realities leads to this question: What specific changes will promote these learning conditions in the classroom? The following alternatives should be examined:

- Instead of students working independently and silently, pairs or groups of students read and write, share and react to information they discover through their research. The activity and talking mean real learning is taking place.
- Instead of copying facts word for word from reference materials or from teacher's notes on a chalkboard, students figure out for themselves what information is important to collect and how to organize it to share with others.
- Instead of the teacher lecturing at the front of the classroom, he or she moves among the students, from one group to another, questioning, guiding, assisting, and learning with them.
- Instead of the teacher relying on textbooks as the primary source of one set of facts to be learned by the students, the students use a variety of materials to learn about specific topics. They are not limited in their learning but encouraged to explore topics as they choose.
- Instead of the teacher working diligently to cover a mandated curriculum, the curriculum becomes a guide but does not dictate or limit how and what the students will learn. What to learn keeps changing.
- Instead of fill-in-the-blank questions as the source of the teacher's assessment of students' knowledge, teachers are observers of the total learning process. This enables them to evaluate their students' abilities to ask questions and select appropriate materials for answers, make connections to real life, and share the information.

Probably nowhere is it more necessary for teachers to be flexible and open to different approaches than in the Research module. Teachers must recognize that students learn by discussing and clarifying their ideas with others; that they learn through exposure to many different materials and resources;

that they learn through questioning themselves, their peers, and the information found in the resources they select.

▶ Prepare for the Research Module

Creating an environment conducive to research and preparing oneself and the students to become active researchers is important.

GATHERING THE MATERIALS

Here are the basic things teachers will need to do to assemble the materials for the Research module.

1. Provide a file folder for each student to be stored in a permanent file drawer or box somewhere in the classroom.

2. Gather the basic resource materials: a variety of textbooks, fiction books, nonfiction books, maps, newspapers, magazines. Other materials needed for lessons include such things as pamphlets, schedules, contest forms, sweepstakes forms, tax forms, product labels, catalogues, and telephone books.

3. Discuss arrangements with other teachers and media specialists/ librarians for using and sharing encyclopedias, atlases, subject/content area media kits, videos, records/tapes, etc.

4. Ask parents, doctors, lawyers, and others to donate magazines.

5. Arrange for students to be instructed in using video and other audio-visual equipment.

SUCCESS saved me! After spending fifteen years teaching a traditional program, I was suffering badly from burn-out. SUCCESS rejuvenated me—and my children! Sparks came from children who had not shown them before and lights came on in eyes that I had not previously seen. These sparks were contagious. The children motivated me, which encouraged me to continue motivating them. We became a team—me in charge, them in control.

Carol J. George,
principal

6. Form close ties with the public library. If possible, arrange for regular Bookmobile stops at the school.

7. Obtain a schedule of educational TV programming and plan lessons that use TV as a learning resource rather than entertainment.

8. Become familiar with the growing resources for Research in technology products—from telecommunications-based software to laser videodiscs (see Chapter 6).

CLASS MANAGEMENT

Once the materials are assembled, teachers must establish ground rules with the students for group activity. Working in groups and sharing resources and information might require thinking about different classroom arrangements. Desks, tables, and chairs should be arranged to allow for easy movement into small- and large-group configurations. Resource materials are more readily accessible to students if they are labeled and kept visible.

▶ How to Teach the Research Module

The three sections of the Research module are the Lead-in, Research Project, and Sharing.

LEAD-IN: INTRODUCING THE RESEARCH PROJECT (5–10 MINUTES)

During the Lead-in, the teacher introduces the topic and focus and the resource(s) to be used. The class shares ideas or directions for beginning the Research Project. The directions to the class should be very short and very specific. Many students will understand the assignment and will be ready to begin work immediately; others will need additional explanation and some assistance.

As the students begin their work, the teacher should move immediately from student to student, helping as many as possible on an individual basis.

In many of the lessons, suggestions are made for class structure. If students are working in groups, the teacher may decide how the groups are to be structured, or students may select their partners and/or group members. Students should always understand the ground rules under which the groups operate. The Lead-in might go like this:

> **Teacher:** Today you will be reading in a <u>newspaper</u> for <u>words relating to transportation</u>. You will first make a list of transportation words. Then you will make a chart to put these words into categories.
>
> Quickly volunteer some words you are finding related to transportation.
>
> **Student:** Truck.
> Mercedes Benz.
> Cadillac.
> Convertible.
> Automobile.

Teacher: How would you categorize this list?

Student: Cars could be one category.

Student: You could break cars into American and foreign made.

Teacher: I think you have the idea for this lesson. I'll be checking to see how you are doing with your list of transportation words and the categories you put them in.

(The teacher moves around the room monitoring student progress and offering assistance as needed.)

RESEARCH PROJECT: READING AND WRITING (15–20 MINUTES)

As students begin to read and find words related to transportation, the teacher moves among groups to help them with the assignment and to listen to their discussions. This student-to-student and teacher-to-student interaction identifies who needs help, who grasps new ideas quickly, and how students think and process printed information.

Students who are noisy or not on task should be dealt with quickly. The teacher will remind them of the topic and focus, answer questions, and channel behavior in the desired directions. If two students are engaged in an animated discussion, the teacher might ask, "Are you discovering ways to classify your words? Tell me what you are finding." The teacher may need to give more direction and perhaps some specific examples using the words they have selected. If the students understand the assignment but have gotten off task because of an argument about which car costs the most, the teacher redirects their attention to the purpose of the lesson: locating words for their charts. Both behavioral and instructional help is most effective when given individually, rather than to the whole class.

The classroom will not be silent, nor should it be chaotic. Students and teachers will decide on the level of activity that allows them to be most productive and how to achieve and maintain a comfortable learning environment. Some classes and teachers will require more structure than others, depending on learning and teaching styles.

The teacher continues to move around the room, stopping to talk with as many students as time allows. Each student will be at a different point in his or her assigned task. Near the end of the time for reading and writing, the teacher should remind the students that they have three minutes until the sharing begins.

SHARING (5–10 MINUTES)

A Sharing time is built into each Research lesson. Most lessons suggest a method for sharing; however, the teacher should decide whether or not this is the most appropriate method for the class. The teacher might introduce sharing by saying, "Today you are going to share with a partner the words you have located. When you are sharing, read from your papers the list of words and how you have categorized them."

After five minutes, he or she might bring closure to the sharing time by asking students to share with the entire class how they categorized their transportation words.

Joseph Ware

Sharing is an integral and enjoyable part of the module, but students will need guidance on how to use the time effectively. At the beginning of the year they are excited about the freedom to talk, explain, and even debate main ideas. Teachers will need to work with students to help them focus their sharing on the information and listening to others. Before students share, basic rules and respect for others should be discussed. The teacher should evaluate how sharing time is being used with the students and revise methods and rules if necessary.

At the close of each lesson, students are to write their name and the date on their papers before they are filed in the Research folders.

A REVIEW OF THE STEPS

What happens during this thirty-minute Research module? Every day students will be locating and organizing information about a topic using the following procedures:

1. The teacher introduces the Research Project: topic and focus, resources, and group structure (5–10 minutes);

2. students read to locate and write information they associate with the Research Project (15–20 minutes);

3. students share their information with other students (5–10 minutes);

4. students date and file papers in Research folders.

▶ Introduce Research Skills

One of the first things students need to learn in order to think and behave as researchers is that information is organized for easy access. The first five lessons of the Research module introduce and/or review alphabetical order. Students locate words relating to one topic—people—from a variety of resources and practice listing their words in alphabetical order. The next five lessons introduce students to a variety of reference materials, indexes, glossaries, etc., with alphabetized arrangements of information. Finally Lessons 11 through 15 provide opportunities for the students to use these skills as they do a research project on machines. Throughout the year this format is repeated. The students are learning new material as they acquire the skills of a researcher.

The purpose of these lessons is to establish the concept that a broad base of information is available to learners and that learning about a topic is enriched by using a variety of materials. The students are also learning that reading and writing are connected and that conversations about what they are learning can stimulate thinking about other possible connections. Rather than emphasizing the product of research, the lessons focus on the process of researching to prepare students for the tasks ahead.

Erin Johnson

After the first fifteen lessons, students will be introduced to a variety of study skills from notetaking to making comparisons. As these skills are learned, there is an opportunity for application through integrated five-day lessons and six- to ten-day Research Projects. Throughout the year, students will continue to be introduced to new research skills and techniques for interpreting information as they collect data on a given topic. The continual application and practice of the skills in context enable the student to locate information successfully.

SELECTING TOPICS

The teacher presents a topic, such as countries. Students brainstorm countries of the world that they might like to learn more about. Teams of students decide which country they will research. They decide what they want to know about the country and where they might locate the information.

LOCATING INFORMATION

Students read to locate information and write the important information they find pertaining to the research topic. At the end of the period, students meet, share, and discuss information located. This step is repeated for several days as the lessons show; it can be extended or shortened depending on the amount of time the teacher feels is needed to complete the Research Project.

ORGANIZING INFORMATION

Students compile their information and decide how best to share and present information to the class. The students gather materials and prepare research project presentations.

PRESENTING AND EVALUATING

Each student or group presents the Research Project. The other students respond by identifying strengths of the presentation and suggesting improvements.

▶ Presenting

Presentations have three main ingredients: preparing the audience, sharing the information, and responding to the presentation. Some lessons suggest that the students prepare the listeners for their presentations by forming two or three questions that they think will focus attention on the main concepts to be shared. The presenters may write the questions on the board, and when the presentation has ended, ask the audience to respond, either orally or in writing. Finally, the class might discuss the answers given and whether or not the presentation provided enough information to answer the questions. Some general evaluative questions might include:

Was the information clear and easily understandable?

What techniques were the most helpful?

Can you suggest ways to improve the presentation?

If you were doing this report over, how would you change it?

Although students are usually their own harshest critics, helping them make improvements should be the main objective of this evaluation time. Simple rules of respect enable students to help each other without being hurtful.

GROWING AS PRESENTERS

New SUCCESS teachers need to be prepared! When students begin making their presentations—no matter how much preparation time they have had—some will be disastrous: the students involved in the presentation, the audience, and the teacher will all agree that it just didn't work. The teacher should be patient and allow students time to try out new presentation ideas and methods. They will grow as self-evaluators and communicators only if they have the opportunity to see for themselves how best to share what they know.

As the year progresses and students gain skill and recognize their own strengths, the reports will improve in clarity and content. The teacher should let the students know that improvement is expected and that the whole class is working to help each one become a more effective learner and teacher. Students appreciate a job well done, and the spontaneous outburst of applause that greets a particularly engaging report is genuine.

In order for students to experiment and gain presentation skills, they will need to be introduced to a wide variety of reporting modes and to know that they can make choices and change their minds if they feel the format is not right for their project. Working together to solve problems and assign duties is a crucial part of the presentation planning stage.

TECHNIQUES FOR PRESENTATION

In the course of the year, the following reporting techniques and formats may be included in the lessons. Teachers will find this is only a partial list and will add many ideas from their students.

Charts of main ideas	Letters, journals, or diaries
Tape-recorded information	Graphs, charts, and maps
Books of facts	Surveys and questionnaires
Written reports	Newspaper articles
Oral reports	Bulletin boards and posters
Videotaped reports	Files for authors, presidents, etc.
Interviews	Directions and lists
News broadcasts	Plays, skits, and commercials
Quiz shows	Calendars and time lines
Dramatic role playing	

Sometimes teachers will need to allow extra time (or even days) for presentations or for sharing at the end of lessons. It is important to develop a time structure and help students work toward meeting their deadlines. Guard against letting sharing time run on and on without focus or closure or allowing the information-gathering time to cut short the sharing time. To emphasize one aspect of the lesson over the other implies that it is more important or meaningful. Preserve the integrity of both the locating and the sharing by maintaining balance between them.

▶ Encourage Student Participation

During the first few days of this program, some students will spend their time reading to locate information and will not have time to write anything. Their papers should be dated and filed with the notation, "Reading— no writing." The teacher should give them credit for the reading part of the module and make a comment orally such as, "Maybe soon you'll not only read, but also have time to write something on your paper before it is filed."

Quantity of writing is not the purpose of this module. The purpose is to teach students how to use a variety of resources to locate information related to a topic, read about the topic, write key information and organize and share that information.

As the year progresses and students become more familiar with this study process, they will locate the suggested information faster and write more than at the beginning of the year. It will take several weeks for some students to start becoming proficient in the Research module. Because of its extreme importance, this module should not be dropped from the program, even though the first days are rather hectic, and some of the students do not "produce" a large quantity of work. Some students may have difficulty getting started for several days. As they begin to realize their papers are to be filed and to adjust to the time limit, they will move into the lesson with less hesitation. Learning to budget study time is a key element in the program.

▶ Helping Students Become Researchers

Students need praise for finding any information that they can associate, directly or indirectly, with the topic and for anything they can defend as associated with the topic.

Instruction and assistance is given on an individual basis. If students are having difficulty locating information, the teacher must help them look through the material until information is found that can be associated with the topic. Through conversation they can be helped to make a connection between what they are reading and the research topic. Later, during each conversation the student is asked to locate something in print and to explain it in relation to the topic. Frequently, students will consult other students during this time before the teacher can get to them for an individual conference. If the student has already located information, the teacher listens to the associations he or she is making before moving on to help another student.

Because students are using different materials, they will not all locate identical information and will become frustrated if instructed to do so. Teachers who teach this module are amazed at the kinds of information their students find and at their abilities to make connections and associations to the things they already know or to new knowledge. Even during the first days, the Research module can be a delight to teach if each student is not required to locate a particular item. Teachers need to relax and enjoy teaching this module! It will take time, but it's worth it.

▶ Resources for Research

What if the resources listed in the Lessons aren't readily available? No topic in the Research module should be avoided because "there are no materials on that topic in the classroom." Teachers are conditioned to be natural collectors. Reading future lessons provides a head start for collecting the suggested materials, or for changing the topic to fit the material on hand.

Instead of ordering workbooks, stencils, kits, SUCCESS teachers simply redirect funds to purchase newspaper and magazine subscriptions and paperback books. Notes to businesses, parents, and civic clubs may produce donations of forms, magazines, and other materials. State and federal agencies (departments of transportation and human resources, the forest service, and wildlife commissions, for example) are great resources for materials. Public libraries and professional offices will gladly donate magazines and other print materials that would otherwise be discarded.

Teachers find many creative ways to get the materials they need. In some cases, students can bring in the resources needed for lessons. Other materials may turn up in book storage closets. Teachers working together sometimes pool and share certain resources such as state or local maps, food labels, or telephone books. Addresses for free materials and class sets of information are often shared. Partnerships with local businesses provide not only print materials, such as classroom library sets, but mentors, volunteers, and guest experts as well.

The Research module requires a variety of materials on different levels. A concern among many teachers is that the reading level of their science, social studies, health, mathematics, or other textbooks will be too high for the students. As the students use these academic materials during the Research module, they will become more familiar and more comfortable with them. They will cease to look at the science textbook merely as the "time-for-science" book, and recognize it as a resource for learning in general. When texts of different levels are available to students, the less able readers will not hesitate to attempt the assignment. Even the smallest successes will add significantly to their knowledge and their confidence as learners. In SUCCESS students can choose to learn from any level of material, be it their own grade level, below, or beyond. The teacher does not assign a level of text or other resource based on his or her perception of a student's ability. The student's ability to locate and gain information is the primary focus, not the designated level of any text.

Many of the lessons provide options for students working in small groups; this is especially useful when materials are limited in quantity. In most lessons, students and groups will be using such a variety of materials that multiple copies of a resource will not be needed.

As the teacher becomes a teacher/researcher, he or she will develop an awareness of many things as potential resources: the menu or paper place-mat at the pizza parlor, the magazine on the airline, the travel brochures at the welcome center, and the job application form at a fast food restaurant can all be used in Research module lessons. Before they know it, teachers have more materials than they ever thought possible.

Ella Lumpkins

▶ Adapting the Lessons to the Students

The enthusiasm a teacher conveys to the students about learning new information invites them to explore new topics. Teachers lead them to read and write and become researchers by instilling the idea that learning in and of itself is interesting and rewarding. This excitement begins when teachers are invested in what they are teaching. How does this happen?

Teachers should never underestimate themselves or their students. They have the ability to be the skillful guides students will need to develop competence and confidence as researchers. Students are naturally curious and want to learn. The teacher must provide the opportunities and direct their progress. In the Research module, the questions students ask as a result of a lesson, a national event on the front page of the newspaper, or a local issue become learning opportunities; seize the moment.

When research projects can be connected to real-life problems and concerns, the resulting knowledge and presentations will be the most effective learning experiences for the students. Teachers will find student-initiated topics and school problems arising throughout the year that may become a base for study in the Research module.

For example, in 1989, teachers in South Carolina, when faced with the widespread devastation of Hurricane Hugo, used SUCCESS lessons to help students cope with the tragedy. In a community threatened with a nuclear waste disposal site, teachers and students try to understand and respond to the issue through teacher-designed Research lessons. These real life events provide opportunities for designing and implementing a survey, writing a letter to the newspapers, forming debate teams to look at both sides of the issue, and inviting experts to speak to the class. Teachable moments are recognized and honored. Students come to realize that their learning is connected to real life situations.

In another case, students noticed how frightened the younger students were in a school tornado drill, and discussed ways to help. Groups listed possible ways to share information and made a plan as a Research Project. First, they collected information about tornadoes, how they form and the dangers they present. Then they made charts and pictures to explain what a tornado was to the youngsters. They wrote and acted out short skits about how to seek a safe place during a tornado drill at home, outside, and at school. Students practiced and evaluated each other on their effectiveness as teachers sharing the seriousness of a tornado but not frightening the students. Groups then went to kindergarten and first-grade classrooms to present their information in a clear and simple format. The presentations were so successful that the fourth-graders were invited to every class to prepare the students for tornado drills.

Just as a teacher's expertise makes a difference in the classroom, the involvement of students with an issue can make a difference. They will recognize the importance of this involvement when they are encouraged to learn about an issue and make an informed decision. In order for this to occur, the teacher must be willing to choose and plan lessons that allow students to explore any issue that could be dealt with during a Research lesson. An issue need not be as dramatic as Hurricane Hugo: perhaps a social studies lesson on longitude and latitude needs to be extended because students are having difficulty with these concepts. By changing topics in the lessons to correlate with content-area topics or current events, the teacher makes the research process more relevant. The students become lifelong learners! Their teachers join them, as the SUCCESS classroom becomes a community of learners!

▶ Research Approaches

DIRECT AND INDIRECT ASSOCIATIONS

In the Research module, students are given opportunities to make both direct and indirect association. In this module reading is not restricted to direct association. Divergent thinking is valued and encouraged. Students often relate information to a specific research topic through an indirect thinking process.

For example, if the module topic is animals, it is conceivable that a student would find a word, a description, or a picture of carrots and associate carrots with rabbits. When a student responds with such an indirect association (carrots), the teacher should ask the student how he or she arrived at that answer.

Indirect association represents a higher thinking level than direct association. Both kinds of associations and thinking are important. Telling how he or she arrived at an association makes the student responsible for the thinking process, and learning takes on greater personal relevance and importance.

Making direct and indirect associations is an extremely important research skill and should be introduced as early as possible in the academic year. One of the most striking features of this approach is the relief it brings to teachers who no longer have to delay a topic until they have done the physical work of assembling directly related information. Instead, the students are involved in the process of making associations with a topic using any available materials.

▶ Integrate the Research Module

The Research module can be integrated with other modules and with content areas. What does *integration* mean in the context of SUCCESS?

First, it means that there are four five- to ten-day lesson sequences in which all four modules are related to the same topic. These sequences are indicated in the Lesson pages. In the first of these, Lessons 11 through 15, all four modules focus on machines as the topic. Students locate words in a variety of resources during Word Study that they can associate with machines. In the Writing module, students compare machines and write stories about imaginary machines. Books are suggested for read-aloud time that have machines as a theme. The teacher and students will think of myriad ways to expand what is presented in the lessons to extend and enrich this unit on machines.

There are also seven six- to ten-day Research Projects focusing on one topic and culminating in a report/presentation. While these are not totally integrated throughout all four modules, the teacher could decide to do so. Some of these six- to ten-day Research Projects may be integrated with one or more other modules. For example, Lessons 91-96 suggest a six-day Research Project on musicians. Each read-aloud book is about music or musicians. In Lessons 141-146 when students are doing a Research Project on a favorite author, the Writing module focus is wordless books, and a new wordless book is introduced each day in the read-aloud time. This allows students and teachers to examine different types of books and learn about many different authors though the discussions and sharing that will take place.

Second, integration means correlating the Lessons with content areas in the curriculum. For example, a Writing lesson that correlates with a science unit is integrating the curriculum. Introducing social studies vocabulary as the Word Study list is integrating the curriculum. Throughout the year there will be opportunities to introduce the vocabulary of a science, social studies, or health chapter during Word Study, to follow with a Writing lesson related to the topic, to locate information on the topic during Research and to follow with a Recreational Reading lesson that allows students to continue to focus on the topic. The Research lessons are not meant to replace content-area lessons but rather to enrich, extend, and supplement science, social studies, health, or mathematics. Some teachers coordinate Research lessons with music, art, current events, or local issues. When students make connections from content-area subjects to Word Study, Writing, Research, and Recreational Reading they begin to find many ways to examine and understand a subject.

▶ Assess and Grade

Some schools using SUCCESS have developed report cards that include a Research grade. The assessment of progress is based on the behaviors observed and the mastery of research skills. This does not mean that every daily activity or research project presentation is given a letter or numerical grade. If a research grade is to be given, teachers might consider task commitment, cooperative group interaction, ability to locate and organize information, and written and oral presentation skills as important factors for this evaluation.

When there is no research grade, how is the assessment of progress reported? Many SUCCESS teachers use the Research module for reading, writing, and spelling grades. Final Research Projects are sources for these grades. Students should be informed of the specific skills being assessed. For example, students completing posters for an environmental issues project should be told beforehand that spelling is important. If a written report is the form for a final Research Project, students should know that paragraph structure will be important. Assessment is ongoing. Teachers

Kendrick Waters

observe and take note of strengths and needs. This continual assessment yields important information for making decisions about all grades and about the student as a learner.

When content-area topics are the focus for Research Projects, assessments may be recorded for these subjects. For example, presentations on the topic of countries might be included as part of a social studies grade.

Teachers will find ways to incorporate assessment into the Research module, but they will observe many behaviors that have meaning and significance beyond a mere grade.

▶ Decisions

TEACHER CHOICES

Each day during the Research module, the teacher makes several choices, deciding whether to

1. use the topic and focus suggested in the Lesson plans or change it, based on student interest, other content areas being studied or the occurence of an important event;

2. use the resource suggested or change it;

3. keep or change the grouping suggested in the lesson, allowing for variety in learning styles and abilities;

4. keep or change the report-making sequence to fit the skills and needs of the students, sometimes allowing more time to collect data or materials;

5. use the writing mode suggested or change it;

6. keep or change the way the information will be shared with others.

STUDENT CHOICES

During the Research module, students may make several choices, asking themselves

1. Which resource will be best to use?

2. What information relating to my topic do I choose to write?

3. How will I record the information?

4. With whom will I work on the Research Project?

5. How will my group organize and present information to the class?

▶ Community of Learners

Teachers function as models during the Research module. They must establish themselves as researchers and learners as they share with students how to locate, record, and interpret information to plan classroom activities. The students are allowed to observe that the teacher does not know all the answers, but follows the same steps to learn as they do and joins them in the process. If he or she models the use of a variety of resources for locating information, and demonstrates how any and all kinds of questions might be answered, the students will catch on more quickly.

It is essential to be willing to change and to allow students to make their own choices and decisions about the types of topics and materials they will use to answer their questions. *All students have a natural curiosity for learning and will be able to become researchers, if the teacher expects and believes that they will.*

Ongoing evaluation should be established as part of the Research module. The class can discuss what works and what changes can be made in strategies to help in the learning process. Introducing a wide range of research methods and reporting techniques throughout the year will add variety to the module and accommodate the different abilities and talents of the students. Researchers may be invited to the class to talk about their work and the techniques they use to gather, organize, and present information. Students must be helped to recognize the value of supportive groups, in which every member is important in working toward a common goal. Finally, teachers should accept and encourage divergent thinking by stressing that there are many right answers.

▶ In Summary

Working with others, locating and organizing information, and applying the knowledge to solve problems are important skills for students to develop. The Research module lays the foundation for these skills. If we think in terms of outcomes, we want all students to be able to read, write, and think critically. We want them to have values and respect for others. We want them to solve problems and address social issues. In short, we expect that after years of education they will be ready to face the world as productive citizens. To accomplish this goal they must become lifelong learners.

Researchers decide what questions to ask and how to find the answer. They explore the world of information. They organize and share their information with others. These lifelong learning skills are the basic elements of the Research module.

Chapter 3 The Recreational Reading Module

Children in most homes are distracted from spending extended time reading books by an amazing variety of activities. Doing chores, playing with friends, watching television, talking on the telephone, and pursuing hobbies are only a few of them. There is little indication that this situation will change unless there is a concerted and deliberate effort to take action. The daily Recreational Reading module provides thirty minutes for students to explore books of their choice with few interruptions.

▶ The Rationale

Students must have the opportunity to read books at least thirty minutes a day during school time. This module can bring about one of the most significant changes in today's education, with far-reaching positive implications for the future. Indirectly, in this module, students learn science, history, geography, character analysis, value judgments, and much more while reading hundreds of books. They also develop the habit of reading. This habit of reading complete novels and other books filled with information will more likely develop when time for unassigned, sustained reading of library books for pleasure is included regularly in the instructional program.

In some elementary classrooms, students go to the library where each checks out at least one book. When the students return to the classroom, the teacher is likely to say, "Put your library book in your desk and take out your spelling book for a spelling lesson." Any interest the student had in reading the library book is immediately lost.

There are reports of secondary students and adults who have never read a novel. Because many homes do not provide a model of regular extensive reading, the school must make provisions to fill that void. Even if students have a reading model at home, they can increase their knowledge along with their competence through in-school silent reading for enjoyment.

When children begin school, their inborn eagerness to learn can either be enhanced or stifled. How do we enhance rather than stifle this natural desire to learn to read and to become a reader?

▶ Becoming Readers

Some basic principles guide what happens in the Recreational Reading module. Stated simply, students should read for thirty minutes each day, select their own books, be respected as readers, and have opportunities to share books with others. In addition they should have individual conversations with the teacher about reading.

STUDENTS READ FOR THIRTY MINUTES EACH DAY

Reading ability is the obvious foundation for school success, and nothing is more important than developing readers. If students are to *become* readers, they must *think* of themselves as readers. A reader does more than

Chapter **3**

Bethany Ann Miller

simply get the words right; a reader constructs ideas and meanings from what is read. It takes time to develop as a reader. School is the natural place for this to happen.

STUDENTS ARE FREE TO SELECT THE BOOKS THEY READ

When students are given the chance to select the books they will read each day, the teacher conveys the message, "I trust you to make good decisions." Students who have the freedom to make choices become more responsible for what they read. Removing restrictions allows them to become more spontaneous and genuine in these choices. They soon learn that the teacher is not going to tell them which story, what book, or how many pages to read.

STUDENTS ARE RESPECTED AS READERS

Teachers are often pressured to label students according to a reading level, to assign them to ability groups, and to provide them with "canned" group instruction. The SUCCESS program in contrast supports the theory that the successful reading of any and all materials the student needs and/or wishes to read is more conducive to fostering reading skills development and good reading habits.

Studies reveal that students assigned to the "low" group seldom have the positive feelings about reading that they need to improve their ability. In the SUCCESS Recreational Reading plan, no student is labeled and all students are equal, even though a wide range of reading abilities and disabilities may be present in the classroom.

The SUCCESS teacher is a skilled technician and a consummate artist. The SUCCESS approach, because it is organic and fluid, because it utilizes at the instructional level what is most sacred to children—their joy and creativity, their own thoughts—offers teachers an effective approach to teaching skills as well as plain and simple fun. And in doing what we love and what is fun, we do our best.

J. Philip Booth,
principal

STUDENTS HAVE CONVERSATIONS WITH TEACHERS

The time spent in a conversation about reading is a meaningful experience for both the teacher and the student. This one-on-one interaction gives teachers the opportunity to learn about their students in an intensely personal way. The focus on the student's reading interests, strengths, and needs provides a wealth of information for future instruction.

STUDENTS SHARE READING EXPERIENCES

Talking about books is fun, and time to share should not be denied students. Adults talk about books they have read or are reading and discuss why they are enjoying a book. Helping students discover this same pleasure in sharing books is important for producing lifelong readers.

▶ Preparing for the Recreational Reading Module

By the time they reach fourth grade, many students are "turned off to reading" because they have not succeeded as readers. The teacher must send a message to students on the first day of school that reading is enjoyable and not threatening. What can teachers do to convey this message? First, the classroom must invite students to read. Second, teachers must prepare themselves and their students to become a sharing, joyful community of readers.

CREATING THE ENVIRONMENT

Teachers must create an environment that says reading is OK in this room. Students learn in the other modules that anything in print may be read. It should be known that during this uninterrupted reading time any book may be read. The room must be "print rich."

Spaces must be provided that are inviting to the reader. A variety of such spaces will honor different learning styles and preferences. For example, many students prefer reading on the floor under a table or even under their desks. Some teachers have managed to provide sofas, pillows, or rocking chairs, which are arranged in a special reading corner for students to use during this time. Students prefer different levels of lighting when they read. The teacher can observe where students choose to read and allow their choices as long as they are involved with their books.

MATERIALS

Organizing materials so that they are easily accessible and manageable invites reading. Students should be given responsibilities for assisting with this task.

For this module, each student should have two file folders. One folder is kept in the student's desk and the second is stored in a permanent file drawer or box somewhere in the classroom. A Reading Log form is duplicated and stapled inside the file folder at their desk. (See Figure 3–1.)

To add to the classroom library, the teacher should make arrangements with the media specialist/librarian to check out two library books per student every three to four weeks (or more often if needed). This is in addition

Figure 3-1

READING LOG

```
READING LOG FOR _____


                                        Started·      Ended on
DATE            TITLE OF BOOK           on page       page
_____
_____
_____
_____
_____
_____
_____
_____
```

to the students' regularly scheduled visit to the library. The library will welcome suggestions for books to be ordered. For the classroom the teacher can order collections of paperbacks, including multiple copies of titles. (A list of books suggested for reading aloud is found on pages 41–42.)

THE TEACHER'S INVITATION TO BECOME A READER

Teachers should let students see them read and should share books with them. Teachers must model being readers and the joy that comes with reading. The teacher must believe and expect that all students will become readers. One of the most important factors in student achievement is teacher expectations. Unfortunately test scores or other assessments of the students' abilities often limit the goals they might set for their students and for their level of instruction.

BECOMING A CONNOISSEUR OF BOOKS

Collecting and becoming familiar with children's books is a necessity for the SUCCESS teacher. He or she can learn about authors and begin an authors file with the students, consulting them about the best books to read. The expertise and knowledge of the media specialists/librarians will be a valuable asset for the teacher who shares knowledge, interests, and needs with them.

Many special activities exist such as Reading Is Fundamental, book fairs, reading contests, business-sponsored programs, and public library reading programs. The teacher can broaden students' experience by arranging for them to participate or by providing the information they will need to become involved.

PARENTAL INVOLVEMENT

Parents, business persons, community leaders, authors, and others will enjoy being guest readers or doing "book talks." When parents volunteer time in the class, they can listen to students read and have conversations with students about the books they are reading. Teachers should communicate with parents about new books and prepare a list of favorite books for possible Christmas and birthday gifts.

Parents need to be aware of the reading expectations for homework. Some SUCCESS teachers ask students to read for fifteen to thirty minutes per night. Parents and their children are asked to keep records of both the time spent reading and the titles of books that are read. Parents should be encouraged to read aloud to their child as often as possible.

CREATING A COMMUNITY OF READERS

Students should be allowed to experience books and to discover the joy of sharing a favorite book. SUCCESS teachers encourage discussion, comparison, and questions about books. Many choose to close the Recreational Reading module each day by having a few students volunteer to tell the class about the books they are reading.

▶ Making the Reading Module Happen

The basic elements essential for making the Recreational Reading module happen are the established daily reading periods, the free choice of fiction and nonfiction books to read, and the teacher as a model. Teachers frequently ask, "How will I know I am covering all the skills? What resources am I going to use? How will the parents react? How will I report progress?" These concerns usually give way to the delightful experience teachers share with their students after they begin the Recreational Reading module. Most teachers report that they know more about their students and their reading abilities, strengths, and weaknesses, than they ever did before.

ESTABLISHED DAILY READING TIME

At the beginning of the year, the teacher is primarily concerned with creating an atmosphere conducive to pleasurable uninterrupted reading. Because they are not used to sitting still and reading, some students will need time to select a book and settle down. They may choose three or four books and flip through them only looking at pictures for a week before they finally begin to feel comfortable with books. Others will know what they want to read, select their books, and not move for the thirty-minute period. Often they will not want to put their book away when the reading time is over.

THE TEACHER'S ACTIVITIES

Nothing is more important to share than a genuine enthusiasm for reading and books. The teacher should share with students why he or she selected a particular book to read, what is best about the book, and something about the thoughts he or she has while reading the book. This is contagious, and students will soon be emulating their teacher's excitement about books. All of a sudden it will be "cool" to read!

▶ The Student-Teacher Conversations

The student-teacher conversations should begin as soon as the teacher has established the model of the quiet reading of self-selected fiction and non-fiction, and the class realizes this thirty minutes is a time to avoid all interruptions.

A suggested guide for focusing conversations is provided for this module in each lesson. The focus is repeated for several days to give the teacher time for a conference with each student in the class about that focus. He or she should adjust the number of days needed for a particular conversation focus, depending on the number of students in the class. Encouraging readers, especially remedial and reluctant ones, should be a part of conversations.

PURPOSES

Each conversation has two major purposes. The first is to provide time for talking with students individually about reading interests and dislikes. Discovering the students' reading interests early in the year is important. The teacher writes notes as he or she talks with the students about what they are reading and why they selected a certain book. Once teachers know the reading interest of their students, they can follow up by locating and suggesting materials a specific student may enjoy. This attention to their reading interests lets students know that they are important. It also sends the message that this module is based on an individual approach rather than the more usual group approach.

This does not mean that teachers become librarians searching for materials; however, when an individual student needs a little extra attention to get involved in reading, this effort may bring large rewards. When the teacher is able to say, "I've found several interesting books about basketball that you might like. I know you enjoy basketball and thought you might want first chance at these," the student usually responds with interest and appreciation.

The second purpose of the conversations is to provide time for the teacher to assess and teach word analysis and reading comprehension with individual students, using their selected fiction or nonfiction books.

SUGGESTED QUESTIONS

The following are some general questions to use in the first few conversations to supplement the specific conversation focus given in the Recreational Reading lessons:

1. What do you like to read about?

2. What is the best book you've read since our last conference? Why was it a good book?

3. What is the saddest book you've ever read? Why was it sad?

4. What is the most exciting book you've ever read? What parts were exciting?

5. What kind of characters do you like best?

6. What kind of books have you never read?

7. What books would you recommend to a friend to read? Why?

8. Do you have any favorite authors? Have you ever read another book by this author?

9. Why do you think the character behaved as he or she did? Have you ever known anyone like this character? What would you do if you were this character?

10. Why did you choose this book? Do you think you will complete it?

11. Have you gained any new ideas or feelings as you've read this book?

12. How much time did you spend reading at home in the last day or two? When do you read at home?

Some attention and questions will more directly focus on word attack skills and strategies, oral reading fluency, mechanics, writing techniques, and comprehension skills:

1. Summarize the main plot of your book so far.

2. Compare this character to another character.

3. Choose a passage to read to me. What is the main idea of this section?

4. Why do you think the author chose to change paragraphs at this point?

5. Have you found any words that were hard to pronounce, or ones whose meaning you didn't know? How do you try to figure out a word you don't know?

6. What is the most important part, or climax, of this story?

7. Describe what is happening at this point in your book. What do you think will happen next?

8. Describe the setting of the story. How is it important to the plot?

9. What is the theme of the book? What do you think is the author's main message or purpose in this book?

10. Who is telling the story? How might it be different if it were told from a different point of view?

11. Tell me about this illustration. What is happening? How do the illustrations add to this story?

Zerric Baskett

The conversation time should always remain a positive time of sharing between the student and teacher, and the teachers of SUCCESS classes have often found it a time to really get to know a student. Some SUCCESS teachers report that the minutes spent with a student one-to-one have much more meaning than a longer time in the group reading situation. Teachers also report that they are much better able to determine reading deficiencies through the conference approach rather than through testing.

The students do not write during the conversations; however, the teacher records notes at this time. A section on clipboard notes later in this chapter will explain more fully the kinds of notes teachers find helpful.

CONVERSATION PRINCIPLES

Teachers may choose to use the conversation focus suggested in each day's lesson plan or write in one of their own.

During conversation time the teacher should talk with as many students as possible. This focused conversation between two people who love books is powerful. The teacher is letting the students know that they are valued as individuals. It is important to maintain the integrity of this time by sincerely listening to each student and interrupting their reading time as little as possible. There are some basic requirements for maintaining the integrity of conference time. First, the teacher should have a purpose, but guard against turning the time into a testing period. Simply trying to check off skills during this period weakens the conversation. Second, the teacher should sincerely listen and respond to students about their reading. Third, reading time should be interrupted as little as possible. Fourth, a conference with one student should not go on and on at another student's expense. Every student needs and deserves the teacher's undivided attention, and every student needs time to read without being interrupted.

FOUR CONVERSATION MODELS

Conversations will vary in length and style. Four different models are suggested below. Each provides a time for having conversations with students about their reading. Recording observations of a student's reading interests, habits, understanding of written language, and the content of their reading material is an important part of each model.

Teacher-student conversations are the motivational strategy for improved reading competence and love of reading. The model may be changed when necessary to accomplish these objectives.

Model One The teacher moves among the students having as many two to three minute conversations as possible. If appropriate, the suggested focus for the lesson is discussed. (See Lessons 6–8 for examples.)

This model is especially helpful for finding out the reading interests and general comprehension level of the students. For example, the teacher might ask them to tell why they have selected a particular book or what they like best about the book or if they would recommend the book to a classmate. The observation notes will record these bits of information about the student's reading interests and habits. This information is helpful in locating books to add to the classroom collections or making suggestions about other books the student may want to read.

The main purpose of this type of conversation is to give attention and show immediate interest in the students and their reading. These short interactions will allow teachers to identify students who are struggling with comprehension or having difficultly selecting books, and to give them suggestions of titles or individual help decoding a difficult word. This model is used for three consecutive days with the same focus.

Model Two   The teacher holds seven to ten minute conversations with three or four students individually. If appropriate, the suggested content or language structure focus is discussed. For example, suppose in Writing the students have been composing dialogue. The teacher may focus on finding out if students can recognize the symbols for identifying dialogue in printed materials. The teacher might ask the student to identify a place in his or her book that has dialogue and read it together. If the student cannot identify dialogue, the teacher will give quick instruction and make note of needed follow-up if necessary. The conversation time might then proceed to other points related to plot development, character descriptions and actions, or associations between reading experiences and the life of the student. This model is used for seven days to allow more time for in-depth conversations with each student. (See Lessons 9–15.)

Jason Bradbury

Model Three   For approximately twenty minutes, everyone, including the teacher, reads for pleasure. This is a time for modeling the pleasures of reading. The teacher should use this model to reaffirm that reading time is important and valued by him or her. The teacher may use part of this time to observe the reading habits of students, to "kid watch," and to record any observed habits that may inhibit or promote the development of reading proficiency. (See the material on clipboard notes.) During the last ten to fifteen minutes, three to five students are invited to come together for an oral reading session. Students should be invited at the beginning of the module time so that they will have an opportunity to select the book from which they will read. (See Lessons 28–30.)

Model Four   During the first fifteen minutes of this model, students are reading and the teacher is having conferences as needed. During the last ten minutes, the teacher may decide to have Book Share when students are given the opportunity to share something interesting with the class about the book they are reading. There may be times when small groups discuss books/stories group members have read. Groups may be organized by book title, topic, or author. These groups can be designated by the teacher or chosen by the students. The teacher should move from group to group monitoring discussions and taking note of the information being shared. When appropriate, the teacher should share his or her own reactions to books being discussed. Two out of every twenty-three days there will be an opportunity for this conversation model. (See Lessons 41–42.)

▶ Record Keeping and Assessment

Recreational Reading is designed to be both enjoyable and instructional. It is not always easy to create the environment, monitor the progress of students, and focus on the teacher's role. One of the most important things he or she will do is to keep accurate, ongoing records of student responses during conversations and of general observations about the students' reading interests and behaviors. Students will be responsible for keeping a reading record. These records may be reviewed and discussed during the conversations between the teacher and student.

CONVERSATION NOTES

Conversation notes are taken during in-depth individual conversations. A teacher might write the student's responses to comprehension questions, opinions about books, or examples of reading strengths and needs. Some teachers develop forms for recording convenience. The following is an example.

Figure 3-2

CLASS CONFERENCE NOTE FORM

date	student	conference focus/comments	needs

Another example shows a separate form for each student.

Figure 3-3

INDIVIDUAL CONFERENCE NOTE FORM

STUDENT'S NAME_____

DATE	FOCUS/COMMENTS	STRENGTHS/NEEDS

Teachers decide how much to write using either a form such as the examples above or separate reading conversation folders kept at the desk. These records are important for assessment of student progress and instruction because they document the individual strengths and needs of each student. This documentation then becomes the basis for parent conferences and reporting student reading growth; it is also invaluable as a planning guide for further instruction.

Conversations with students are never scripted, and are not predictable, even with suggested questions and skills foci.

> **Teacher:** I've noticed that you've read several Chris Van Allsburg books. Which one is your favorite?
>
> **Student:** *Jumanji.*
>
> **Teacher:** Why do you like this book?
>
> **Student:** I like the mystery and excitement and the pictures.
>
> **Teacher:** Do you know that Mr. Van Allsburg won an award called the Caldecott Medal for his illustrations in this book? The Caldecott Medal is given each year to the most outstanding American picture book for children.
>
> **Student:** I think all his books should have an award! He's one of my favorite authors.
>
> **Teacher:** Have you read *The Polar Express*? It too won the Caldecott.
>
> **Student:** I'm thinking about how I can make the illustrations for my book as good as Chris Van Allsburg's.
>
> **Teacher:** Great! I'm sure you'll be able to use your illustrations to help make your story come to life.

The conversation continues with a discussion of boredom and what happens when you get bored. Student and teacher also identify words that denote mystery and excitement.

In this conversation the student shares something about her reading interest and, by mentioning the illustrations as one of the reasons she likes the book, gives the teacher an opportunity to tell her about a special award for children's books. Having the student locate words that indicate mystery and excitement is helpful as the teacher assesses her ability to interpret literary material. This conversation could develop into one about higher-level thinking skills such as making inferences and literary techniques.

The path taken during a reading conversation depends on many things, and taking notes on conversations also differs greatly from teacher to teacher. The main point is that teachers take the opportunity to document any ability or need a student reveals.

CLIPBOARD NOTES

Clipboard notes taken during conversations are very specific. Other clipboard notes, in contrast, are more general, focus on both individual students and the whole class, and may be recorded at any time during the day. Consistent records of observations reveal learning patterns and other information that help the teacher tailor instruction to meet the needs of the students. These notes may also call attention to behavioral patterns that create barriers to learning. The teacher, as a reflective practitioner, is always watching the students, assessing what is happening, and making decisions based on these observations. The clipboard notes suggested in the Recreational Reading module are suggestions only. They may guide observations for that day, but the teacher will be recording other behaviors as well. Sometimes these notes may simply remind the teacher of changes that need to be made to create a better learning environment.

Here is a sample of some clipboard notes:

"Jonathan—playing under the table."

"Angelia—forgot her books again."

"Mary and Sue took their books to lunch. Sat together and read."

A suggested focus for clipboard notes is included in each daily Lesson. The following is a list of some of these suggestions—things to look for while your students are reading (without interrupting them).

Who reads with whom	Who moves lips or hands
Titles being read	to guide reading
Where students choose to read	Who is searching for meaning
Which students read aloud	Who re-reads the same books
Who is reading the same	Who compares books by author,
book for more than one day	topic, etc.
Which students stay seated	Who reads books read or
Who looks up or daydreams	introduced by teacher
Who prefers which authors	Who loses or forgets book
Who talks eagerly about books	Who reads books by students
Who learns from the pictures	Who recommends books to others
Who tries new books	Who seeks recommendations

Some teachers find it useful to have copies of the class roll with space beside each name for clipboard notes. Blank spaces beside students' names remind the teacher to focus on those students. A sample form used by some teachers to record clipboard notes is shown below. The same form can be used for taking notes when teachers have two to three minute conversations at the students' desks.

STUDENT READING LOGS AND JOURNALS

This is a daily record kept by each student of his or her reading. Each day students record the book title and the number of the first page read that day on a sheet of paper or a printed form stapled to their Recreational Reading folder. (See Figure 3–1.) At the end of the reading time the stu-

Figure 3-4

FORM FOR CLIPBOARD NOTES

NAME	OBSERVATIONS

dent completes the record sheet by writing the number of the last page read. The current Reading Log is kept in the folder at the student's desk. When the log is completed, students file it in a folder kept in a box labeled Recreational Reading.

In some classrooms, students use a spiral notebook to keep a record of books being read. This notebook can also be used as a reading journal. Students can record thoughts about reading at the end of the daily Recreational Reading module. The Reading Journal can replace the Reading Log and should be filed in the box when filled. The Reading Log and/or Reading Journal become part of the permanent reading record.

▶ Read-Aloud Books

In 1985, the Commission On Reading issued a report, *Becoming a Nation of Readers,* which stated the following: "The single most important activity for building the knowledge required for eventual success in reading is reading aloud to children."[1] Read-aloud books are suggested every day in the Recreational Reading module. Teachers may read the books suggested or select others. This shared reading experience for the whole class is a non-negotiable part of the daily schedule, not an extra "if-you're-good" or "if-we-have-time" bonus. This ten to fifteen minutes should be scheduled at a time the teacher feels is best. Some teachers find that read-aloud is a great lead-in to the Recreational Reading module. Others like to end the module with sharing and reading aloud.

Below is a list of the books included in the lessons as read-aloud titles. These books are suggestions, and teachers are invited to replace them with personal favorites of students, colleagues, and friends.

> *Tales of a Fourth Grade Nothing,* Judy Blume (Dutton, 1972)
> *The Enormous Egg,* Oliver Butterworth (Little, 1956)
> *Get Ready for Robots!* Patricia Lauber (HarperCollins, 1987)
> *Home Price,* Robert McCloskey (Viking, 1943)
> *People,* Peter Spier (Doubleday, 1980)
> *Emily Upham's Revenge,* Avi (Doubleday, 1978)
> *How to Eat Fried Worms,* Thomas Rockwell (Dell, 1973)
> *Awfully Short for the Fourth Grade,* Elvira Woodruff (Dell, 1989)
> *Onion John,* Joseph Krumgold (Scholastic, 1959)
> *Sideways Stories from Wayside School,* Louis Sacher (Avon Books, 1989)
> *Jumanji,* Chris Van Allsburg (Houghton Mifflin, 1981)
> *A House for Hermit Crab,* Eric Carle (Scholastic, 1987)
> *Animals, Animals,* Eric Carle (Philomel Books, 1989)
> *The Velveteen Rabbit,* Margery Williams (Doubleday, 1922)
> *Baseball Fever,* Johanna Hurwitz (Morrow, 1981)
> *The Keeping Quilt,* Patricia Polacco (Simon and Schuster, 1988)
> *Mufaro's Beautiful Daughters,* John Steptoe (Lothrop, Lee and Shepard, 1987)
> *Invincible Louisa,* Cornelia Meigs (Little, 1968; first published in 1933)

---

[1] R. C. Anderson et al., *Becoming a Nation of Readers* (Champaign, IL: University of Illinois, Center for the Study of Reading, 1985), p. 23.

*A*s a teacher of exceptional children, I must work with children spanning a multitude of grade levels and ability levels. SUCCESS allows all students to achieve success through whole-group versus multiple small-group instruction. The student is an active participant. Textbooks and ditto sheets are not necessary.

Gloria Hathaway, teacher

M. C. Higgins, the Great, Virginia Hamilton (Macmillan, 1974)

Socks, Beverly Cleary (Dell, 1973)

Rascal, Sterling North (Dutton, 1963)

Just So Stories, Rudyard Kipling (Weathervane, 1978)

The Stranger, Chris Van Allsburg (Hougton Mifflin, 1986)

Sounder, William Armstrong (Harper, 1969)

Ramona the Pest, Beverly Cleary (Morrow, 1968)

Song and Dance Man, Karen Ackerman (Scholastic, 1988)

The Philharmonic Gets Dressed, Marc Simont (Harper & Row, 1982)

The Cricket in Times Square, George Selden (Farrar, 1960)

Wayside School Is Falling Down, Louis Sachar (Avon Books, 1989)

The Man Who Tried to Save Time, Phyllis Krasilovsky (Doubleday, 1979)

Shapes, Shapes, Shapes, Tana Hoban (Greenwillow, 1986)

How Much Is a Million? David Schwartz (Scholastic, 1985)

Roosevelt Grady, Louisa Shotwell (World, 1963)

How Many Snails, Paul Giganti (Greenwillow, 1988)

Sideways Arithmetic from Wayside School, Louis Sachar (Scholastic, 1989)

Laura Ingalls Wilder, Gwenda Blair (Putnam, 1981)

Did You Carry the Flag Today, Charley? Rebecca Caudill (Holt, 1966)

The Talking Eggs, Robert D. San Souci (Scholastic, 1989)

Sleeping Ugly, Jane Yolen (Coward-McCann, 1981)

The Magic School Bus Inside the Human Body, Joanna Cole (Scholastic, 1989)

The Giving Tree, Shel Silverstein (Harper, 1964)

The Magic School Bus at the Waterworks, Joanna Cole (Scholastic, 1986)

Owl Moon, Jane Yolen (Scholastic, 1987)

Bird Watch, Jane Yolen (Philomel, 1990)

The Cay, Theodore Taylor (Doubleday, 1969)

Whoppers, Tall Tales and Other Lies Collected from American Folklore, Alvin Schwartz (Harper, 1975)

The Iron Giant, Ted Hughes (Harper, 1985)

Good Dog Carl, Alexandra Day (Green Tiger Press, 1985)

Good Dog Carl Goes Shopping, Alexandra Day (Farrar Straus, 1989)

Will's Mammoth, Rafe Martin (G. P. Putnam's Sons, 1989)

A Boy, A Dog, A Frog, and a Friend, Mercer Mayer (Dial, 1971)

Peter Spier's Rain, Peter Spier (Doubleday, 1982)

Sebastian and the Mushroom, Fernando Krahn (Delacorte, 1976)

Roll of Thunder, Hear My Cry, Mildred Taylor (Bantam, 1976)

The Lost Garden, Laurence Yep (Silver Burdett, 1991)

Be a Perfect Person in Just Three Days, Stephen Manes (Bantam, 1984)

Babe: The Gallant Pig, Dick King-Smith (Crown, 1983)

The Fairy Rebel, Lynne Reid Banks (Doubleday, 1985)

Heidi, Johanna Spyri (Ariel Books, 1984; first published in 1946)

Sign of the Beaver, Elizabeth George Speare (Dell, 1984)

Dear Mr. Henshaw, Beverly Cleary (Dell, 1984)

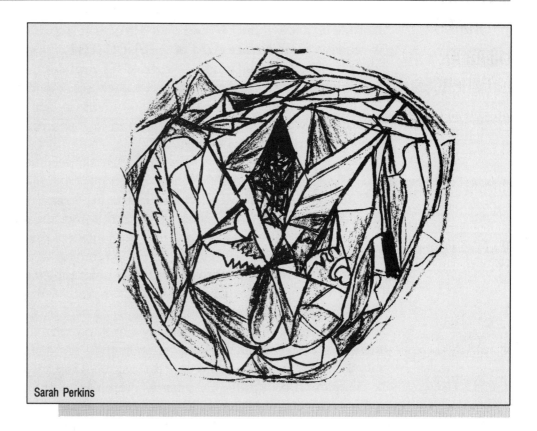

Sarah Perkins

▶ Integrate Reading Throughout the Day

The most obvious connection is the reading and writing connection. In conferences with students, the teacher is learning about the books they read. He or she will also discover excellent examples in their books that can be used to illustrate what is being taught during the Writing, Word Study, and Research modules. The conversations about books often call attention to outstanding examples of language usage and writing skills. Many students start to look at books differently—as writers—and to consider how a writer uses words.

Library books and read-aloud books are often suggested as the resource in Word Study. Students begin to see the connections between vocabulary growth and reading.

In the Research module, students might choose to base their presentations on a literature model such as a question-and-answer format. A theme or unit of study can provide opportunities for integrating the lessons in all four modules. For example, Lessons 106 through 110 develop the theme of mathematics throughout the four modules. In Word Study students select words related to mathematics for the chart. They choose activities related to this theme in Writing such as writing about math talents or anxieties; they might also write about connections between geometry and nature. A Research lesson uses mathematics for identifying geometric shapes in architecture. In the Recreational Reading module, the read-aloud books suggested are about mathematics. Literature can be the central focus of lessons in all the modules. Books are presented to students as the source of many kinds of learning.

▶ Shared Reading Experiences

If students always choose their own books, is it possible for the whole class to read the same novel as part of the SUCCESS Recreational Reading module? Of course. Shared reading experiences, oral discussions of novels, and reading and writing activities about a book are important parts of a reading plan. Teachers will want to help students select books for and work together in whole-class novel studies and in "book clubs," smaller groups choosing to read the same book.

WHOLE-CLASS NOVEL STUDY

Some teachers initiate a whole class shared reading experience by introducing some novels to the students in the first few minutes of the reading time, or during read-aloud time. Students are given time to examine the books and make a selection for class reading. A class set of copies of the book is then purchased so each student has a copy for individual reading.

Many teachers enjoy beginning a class novel study by reading aloud at the beginning of the period, discussing some aspect of what was read, and then allowing students to continue reading individually or in pairs. Reading along with the teacher or a partner gives some students the opportunity to read books they could not read alone. Many students are motivated to complete a book after they have "gotten into" the plot.

Some teachers include whole-class reading experiences in their classroom once or twice a semester and often correlate the book choice to a theme of study. While studying space in science and Research, one fourth-grade class chose a book from this group to read together: *A Wrinkle in Time, The End of the World, The Fallen Space Man,* and biographies of astronauts.

Whole-class book reading is fun. It provides limitless opportunities to develop oral discussion abilities, appreciate an author's style, laugh out loud, and even shed tears.

Scott Johanningsmeier

BOOK CLUBS

Many classes enjoy reading books in smaller groups sometimes called book clubs. Teachers allow students to choose a book from several sets of books, such as Beverly Cleary books, fantasy or science fiction books, mysteries, multiple copies of the same book, or stories from story collections. Students choose which "book club" they will join and which book they will read during Recreational Reading. Students will read individually; they might also have "partner days" for reading together. Book clubs may meet for sharing discussions at the close of the reading time or give "book talks" about their selections. These clubs are based on student choice and interest, not on books preselected by the teacher and assigned to match reading levels. Shared interests build bonds between readers. Books make friends.

▶ Spreading the Word about Books

SHARING TIME

Like adult readers, students enjoy and profit from talking about books with their friends. Sharing books is important in producing life-long readers. Sharing can be done at the end of the Recreational Reading module. Students are given a few minutes to find a partner and share what they have been reading.

When a student is particularly excited about a book, he or she should be allowed to share the excitement with the rest of the class. If a reluctant reader suddenly discovers that reading can be fun, the student may be immediately asked to share what he or she is enjoying. The teacher should always be watchful and sensitive to the perfect moment when sharing can bring personal pleasure and can motivate others.

BOOK TALK SESSIONS

Even though students learn to enjoy the Recreational Reading module, the familiar complaint may still be heard in the classroom: "I can't find any good books." Often this stems from the student's lack of a reading habit, rather than book selection itself. However, it might pay a teacher to "advertise" some books.

Book Talks for Small Groups Many teachers choose to boost interest by inviting a small group of students to a corner of the classroom for a short book talk. He or she briefly introduces several books from the library, students' homes, a personal collection, or the classroom library, making the selection as varied and as interesting as possible. Somehow, these "special" books end up being quickly chosen, even by reluctant readers. The teacher may wish to invite students, parents, or other school personnel to present a book talk. If the book talk takes place at the beginning of Recreational Reading time, it should be presented quietly, taking no more than five to ten minutes. At the end the teacher should return to the regular conference schedule.

Whole-Class Book Talks   Sometimes the teacher or a student might choose to introduce a selection of books to the entire class. The books might be new to the class or relate to the topic or theme of another module. For example, when students are writing poetry, the teacher might read some favorite poems from poetry collections available for students to choose during Recreational Reading.

In Lessons 141–145 when the read-aloud selections are wordless books and the students are to write their interpretations of a wordless book, they might also be invited to share their favorite one during the Book Share days (Lessons 141–142). students are thus exposed to many more books from which to choose one for interpretation.

Nonfiction books related to Research topics give students the opportunity to read for information as well as for pleasure. In addition, before introducing a new unit in science, social studies, or health, the teacher should ask the librarian to pull books related to the topic and share with the students one of the collection during their library time. The books can then be taken to the classroom for the students to read.

Only a few minutes are used for book talks. Often the book talks are done during the regular read-aloud period, and the teacher or student might read short passages from the books. Book talks suggested in the lessons in the Recreational Reading module are optional.

▶ Reading Levels

It is often the case with fiction and nonfiction books for adults that some are more difficult to read then others. Adult books are not classified according to their reading level. In contrast, attempts have often been made to place numerical reading levels on chidren's books; this practice could deprive students of opportunities to read some books because they are "above" or "below" a certain reading level. Students may automatically disregard books someone has deemed too hard and be ashamed to read books someone else has called too easy. Some students like to reread old favorites even though they know they are capable of reading much harder material. The content of the book is more important than any predetermined "reading level." When discussions and assessments of progress are based on what a student is reading or has read, rather than on what magic "reading level" the student has attained, real progress will become evident, expectations of students will be higher, and students will think of themselves as true readers and not occupants of some level.

Teachers are often pressured by schools and parents to identify students' reading levels. If it is necessary to assign reading levels, short, informal diagnostic reading tools of a common-sense nature, coupled with conversation notes and observations by the teacher, are recommended. These tools should be used within the framework of the Recreational Reading module, not on a group basis, and should always emphasize the individual's reading abilities and interests.

▶ Reading Interests

Reading interests will change within a day, week, month, and year when students are given opportunities to expand them. Some students' reading interests are temporary and highly subject to change. Other students may read books by only one author until they have read them all, or they may want to concentrate on books about only one topic.

Introducing new topics and kinds of literature will expand the reading interests of students. The teacher is the key to opening a door for many students when he or she helps them explore the exciting and real world of books and literature. Teachers can remove the barriers present in many schools that prevent students from reading beyond predetermined, restricted confines.

In some schools where basal readers are required, the students are not allowed to take the basal reader home because they might read the next story, or they might read a story before the teacher has introduced the new words or properly motivated the students to read it.

In schools where students may check out only one library book per week (a maximum of 36 books per academic year), a starvation diet is under way. In schools where the "Great Books" are carefully preserved until the students are old enough, it is certain that fourth-graders will not encounter any Shakespeare or Tennyson.

As long as numerical reading levels command what students will or can read, students will be at a disadvantage and will continue to not read.

▶ Non-Readers and Reluctant Readers

Through observations and conversations teachers can quickly identify the students who are reluctant or nonreaders. These students will require some special attention as the teacher establishes a community of readers. They must not be ignored. Teachers may want to consider the following suggestions for developing a plan to help these students become readers and enjoy reading, remembering that the most important factor for motivating the reluctant reader is the teacher's expectation that every student will be a reader.

CLASSROOM LIBRARIES AND BOOK CHOICES

Just as students in one classroom will have a wide range of reading interests and abilities, so the book selections available for the Recreational Reading module must offer a wide range of topics and reading difficulty. Every level of reading from wordless books to adult-level reading may be included. Indeed, some wordless books will be quite sophisticated and yet allow students who have not yet mastered word-attack strategies to successfully complete a book.

Picture books are an important part of the classroom collection and are often suggested for read-aloud selections or as models in the Writing module. If the teacher gives these books the respect they deserve, students who may be overwhelmed by long pictureless chapters, thick books, or even a page full of text will not be embarrassed to choose them. Collections of poems or riddles also provide less threatening text, as well as clues of rhythm and rhyme.

STUDENTS HELPING STUDENTS

Students who are poor readers need more attention and encouragement to develop reading strategies and positive feelings about books. Yet, the teacher will not be able to read with these students every day during the thirty minutes of Recreational Reading. Many teachers are discovering that students are a great resource for helping each other. When readers read together, they practice new strategies for analyzing words and using context clues. Through their discussions of the reading, they increase comprehension skills. Teachers should carefully plan "student-helping-student" situations. The teacher may suggest a partner for a student, but both should be open to the arrangement. The first approach might be to identify an interest that the pair have in common, collect books on that topic, and ask them to select a book to read together. The teacher will have a conference with the students to discuss working together.

RECORDED BOOKS

Tape recorded books may be another strategy for increasing a student's reading abilities. Many students benefit from the sound of the language pattern in books when they listen to them as they look at the words in print. Repeated exposure through recorded books increases their sight vocabulary. The student should know the goal of the taped reading time will be independent reading and discussion of the story. When the student has listened enough, he or she will read the story to the teacher.

▶ Evaluate and Grade

The assessment and evaluation of students as readers is a very complex task. Teachers will consider observations, conversations, and records kept by themselves and the students for determining student progress and needs. Assessment should reflect what a student can do. Evaluation is ongoing and supports instruction.

When deciding grades or preparing for student and/or parent conferences, teachers should consider the clipboard notes that document each student's reading abilities, difficulties, and progress during a specific time period. This documentation is cumulative, and growth can be charted. Plans for instruction should grow from this documentation. Taping students reading during a conversation session is another way to document growth and progress.

At the beginning of the year the teacher should let parents know that they will be partners in the assessment of their child's reading progress. They should be encouraged to read with their child as often as possible and to have their own conversations with him or her about reading.

The more teachers listen to and observe students reading the more confident and competent they will become as evaluators of their strengths and weaknesses. A grade should not be the most important consideration. The development of the students as readers should always take priority.

▶ Decisions

TEACHER CHOICES

Every day during the Recreational Reading module the teacher will decide

1. whether to use the Conversation focus suggested in the Lesson plan or change it;

2. whether to use the Conversation model suggested or change it;

3. with which students to have conversations;

4. what they will record as clipboard notes and what to write about each student;

5. what basic behavioral rules will be in effect;

6. when to do book talks;

7. when students will read together;

8. which content-area topics to integrate;

9. how and when to allow students to share.

STUDENT CHOICES

Students make the following choices each day in Recreational Reading:

1. what book(s) to read;

2. where to read;

3. with whom to read if partner reading is suggested;

4. which book to discuss in conversations with the teacher;

5. how to share their reading experiences with other students;

6. whether to finish a book or exchange it for another one.

▶ In Summary

Recreational Reading is the backbone of the SUCCESS program. Students who become readers through it discover that reading is a source of pleasure, information, ideas, and shared experiences. This module recognizes the dignity of all learners regardless of their reading abilities. It builds on the assumption that every student can and will become a reader.

Chapter 4   The Writing Module

Her book was completed, published, and she was reading it to the class. This student had a story to tell and had been given the opportunity to deal with a very sad event in her life through her writing. (See page 51 for an illustration of this book.)

▶ The Rationale

Why write? Once students personally experience the power of writing, as Joy Berry did, the answer to this question becomes obvious. When given the opportunity, students can respect and appreciate each other's writing. They will discover that writing can make others laugh, cry, think, and question. They learn to clarify their thoughts and become better able to communicate their feelings, their hopes, fears, and fantasies.

The Writing module is designed to create the environment for this discovery. For thirty minutes each day, students are thinking, composing, and sharing their thoughts. The emphasis in the SUCCESS Writing module is where it should be—on helping students experience the rewards and pleasures of written expression while encouraging accuracy in the mechanics of writing. Each lesson has a proofreading focus that allows the teacher to incorporate the mechanics of writing, but only in the context of the students' writing and not as isolated skills.

▶ Becoming Writers

In the last decade much research and writing has been done on the writing process. The basic components of the SUCCESS Writing module reflect what this research documents: Through consistent effort and daily practice students can become writers. The following elements produce an environment that supports writing growth.

STUDENTS HAVE DAILY OPPORTUNITIES TO WRITE

Writers improve their writing by writing. They learn to do what they have the opportunity to do. Writing is an important, valuable skill that is validated through the daily emphasis. Each SUCCESS module offers an opportunity for writing; at least thirty minutes each day is devoted to the Writing module. The ability to write is not developed without consistent effort and time to plan, think, and compose. When students know they will be involved in some stage of the writing process every day, they think ahead about topics and begin the first step of composing—thinking about how to say what they want to say.

STUDENTS ARE GIVEN CHOICES

Writers are more motivated to write about the things they know best; they are more comfortable writing about the things they know best. When students are given choices about topics to write about, they see themselves

While browsing around tables at the Daniel Boone Yard Sale, my brother and I spotted the calico feline. She was in a cage with a $5.00 price tag. We ran to get Mom.

"Mom, Mom, we've got to have the yard sale cat!" we begged.

Happy came to our home looking for love.

Todd and I gave her all the love she needed.

Mom and Dad loved her too.

Dad gently buried her between two evergreen trees. We planted a flower near her grave.

Mom and I painted a rock to mark the grave.

It read, "Happy, the yard sale cat".

Joy Berry

as writers and become more motivated and vested in their writing. Students will also be making decisions about who will proofread their papers, what they will publish, and how it will be published.

STUDENTS LEARN THE WRITING PROCESS

Writing, sharing, revising, and editing are necessary steps for developing a final work. In the Writing module, students are given many opportunities to develop their writing skills and become comfortable and competent writers. They begin to feel at ease with writing.

STUDENTS WRITE FOR VARIED AUDIENCES

Writers must have a focus and purpose for their writing. When students are given opportunities to write for varied audiences, they have a greater understanding of the value and power of writing. This means that the teacher is a coach and facilitator of writing and not the main audience.

STUDENTS SHARE THEIR WRITING EVERY DAY

Each lesson includes time for peer sharing. Some days this will be one-on-one. Other days the student will be sharing with a small group or the entire class. Sharing is designed to offer support for the development of the student as a writer. This sharing allows students to receive help, give help, and appreciate each other as writers.

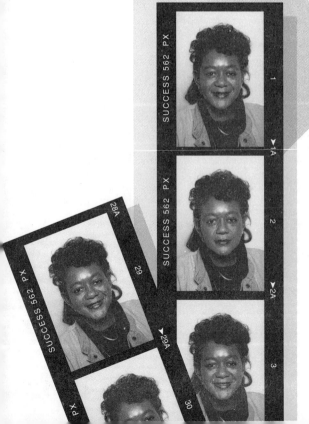

I feel good knowing that the children I teach develop good self-esteem. It is a joy seeing there is happiness in the eyes of the child who succeeds.

*Delores J. Porter,
teacher*

STUDENTS HAVE OPPORTUNITIES FOR PUBLICATION

Students will have regular opportunities to write for publication. The Lessons are designed to lead them through this process. In addition to classroom presentations, revised student publications are shared with others in a variety of formats including books, filmstrips, plays, and articles. Through publishing, students are recognized and validated as authors. They take great pride in this recognition.

Writing lessons are designed to incorporate the elements described above. Each day the Writing module begins with prewriting activities. Students write; students share; students proofread. In SUCCESS lessons, learning the process of written expression receives priority over learning the details of grammar and mechanics. This does not mean that standard English is not introduced and reinforced. It means that the students learn the elements of standard English in the most effective way—within the context of their own writing. With SUCCESS, students learn to write clearly and coherently, to feel comfortable expressing themselves, and to enjoy writing as they learn the form of written language.

▶ Prepare for the Writing Module

Two things should happen before teachers begin the Writing module. First, they should create a writing environment for their students. Second, they must prepare themselves to be teachers of writing.

CREATING AN ENVIRONMENT

When children are learning to speak, their auditory environment supports their development as effective communicators. Coaching, modeling, and constant positive feedback from others are necessary to reinforce this newly developing communication skill. Children who experience the positive responses of others to their language development feel comfortable and motivated. When parents clap and make a big fuss over new words in the child's vocabulary or call grandparents on the phone to share the latest word learned, the child learns that speaking is a rewarding activity. When children do not receive positive feedback or reinforcement for learning to speak, they often become reluctant and unwilling to risk failure; therefore, their oral language development is thwarted.

The oral language development model shows that learning to write requires coaching, modeling, and positive response to student efforts. A supportive environment that allows students to experience the rewards of oral and written communication helps them feel comfortable and willing to take risks as developing writers.

The physical environment of the classroom must also support writers. Materials are easy to obtain and should be in place before the module begins. Each student needs two file folders. One is kept in the student's desk, and the second is stored in a permanent file drawer or box somewhere in the classroom. Extra pencils and paper should be easily accessible for students who may have forgotten or can't provide them for themselves. Dictionaries and thesauruses should be available.

Teachers need to arrange desks to facilitate composing and sharing. This might mean designating some places as quiet areas and others for peer conferencing. Teachers should

- create a language-rich environment by reading aloud daily from books that contain interesting words and descriptions;
- call attention to the richness of language;
- share details about writers and how they came to be authors;
- show obvious pleasure in the written word.

TEACHERS AS WRITERS AND TEACHERS OF WRITING

Most teachers are not Judy Blume or Ernest Hemingway! Very few people are accomplished first-draft writers. Most probably go through the process of writing, deleting, adding, and marking through words as they try to express their thoughts in the most meaningful ways. Even when composing a thank-you note, writers may put down their thoughts on scrap paper before actually writing the words on stationery. A letter recapping an entire year for friends and family usually goes through several revisions before being stuffed inside the Christmas card. Teachers write letters to parents, memos to colleagues, notes to students, and comments on report cards. Each of these writing activities requires careful thinking about what should be said and how best to say it. Teachers are, in fact, writers.

Practice the Process   Teachers of writing must understand the process of writing. Practicing this difficult process leads to understanding through experience. Teachers who learn to write by writing are better able to relate to the problems and joys students will encounter as developing writers.

Know the Literature   Another way to develop as a teacher of writing is to know the literature. Much has been written describing the writing process and the experiences of teachers, students, and researchers in their quest for what works. Teachers should expand their knowledge by learning what these people have discovered. A personal philosophy for teaching writing is important if teachers are to believe in what they are doing.

Develop Resources   Developing resources is part of becoming an effective teacher of writing. Often teachers will use examples of writing to model author techniques and language patterns. Teachers need to establish a strong supportive relationship with the school librarians. Librarians are eager to share their knowledge and to assist the classroom teacher by introducing them to the latest books and professional collections of information. Teachers will want to find out about the services provided by their state department of public instruction. Many times consultants can provide the names of authors and others who are willing to speak to students about their experiences as writers. Universities and public libraries are other places to find resource persons.

Read Through the Lessons   It is important to read through the Lessons in the SUCCESS book and be familiar with suggestions for the topics and for proofreading. Teachers may decide to change and write in their own topics or proofreading focus for some lessons. Whenever possible, many teachers also integrate lessons with content-area subjects such as science, health, and social studies. Teachers will need to plan ahead to incorporate books in the writing activities.

▶ How to Teach the Writing Module

The basic components of the Writing module are Mini-lesson, Composing, and Sharing.

MINI-LESSON (5 MINUTES)

During the Mini-lesson the teacher introduces a writing topic and the proofreading focus. The main purpose of this time is to help students start thinking about and discussing the chosen topic or focus. This prewriting time should create the energy and excitement that will motivate the students to write. Teachers should not dominate this time with their own "stories to tell," but share just enough to get the students thinking about their experiences and eager to write about them. Rather than extending this time, teachers find that less is better. As teacher and students become more comfortable with the structure of the Writing module, they will want to get started on their writing. The Mini-lessons vary from discussions on a topic to write about, to specific writing suggestions such as "a monster came to school today," to editing and revision techniques.

The proofreading focus is meant to turn student attention to mechanics, such as punctuation, or to content, such as adding detail or using descriptive language.

It is useful to write the proofreading focus suggested for the lesson in a box on the chalkboard and give one or two examples of it. The teacher should not hold all students back for a lengthy discussion of the proofreading focus. Additional explanations can be made to individual students at their desks with specific references to something they are writing (or could write). Reviews and other reinforcements can occur on other days. In fact, each focus will be repeated in other lessons throughout the year. Students should not be forced to include the proofreading focus in their writing, but rather reminded of the correct way to use the focus if it occurs naturally. The main reason for the Writing module is to provide time for students to write. They expect to write, and their eagerness will force the teacher to limit "instruction" so that they can get on with the task.

COMPOSING (20 MINUTES)

Most students will begin writing immediately. A few will need extended "think time," but will get started on their own. Still others will sit and stare out the window not knowing where to begin. The teacher will probably want to move to these students first and have a conversation with them about the topic to help them see that they do have something they would like

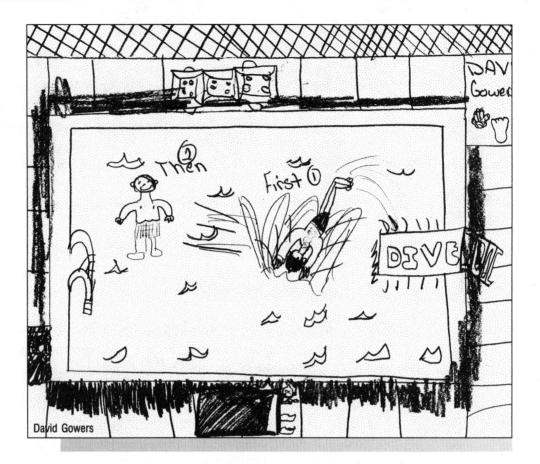

David Gowers

to write about. This may or may not be directly related to the topic you have just introduced and discussed. Students with a new sibling or puppy may be so excited about this addition to the household that they can't write about anything else until they have an opportunity to deal with the immediate in their life.

Allowing students to write what they want and need to write is to be encouraged, and the teacher should never force students to write about the same topic. What is important is that each student writes.

A few minutes before writing time is to end, the teacher may ask students to read over their papers silently and place a check mark over any example of the proofreading focus which appears in their writing. As the students are reading their papers, they may spontaneously make changes such as adding punctuation, correcting spelling, or substituting more interesting words. Students should know that they are the first and foremost proofreaders of their writing.

SHARING (5 MINUTES)

During the last five to ten minutes of the Writing module students will have a conversation about their writing with another student or students. Each one will take a turn reading his or her paper to another student or to the group and answer any questions from peers concerning the content of the writing. During this discussion the listeners may assist the author by suggesting ways to make the writing more effective.

Before this session ends, students should exchange papers and check for correct use of the proofreading focus, if there are examples of it in the writing.

Some teachers ask students to call attention to examples of incorrect uses of the proofreading focus and to check (✓) examples of correct usage. After the proofreading, students should date and file their papers in their writing folders located in their desks or stored in a box in the classroom.

In the beginning, the teacher might need to monitor carefully the time allotted to each section of the Writing module. Once students are familiar with the structure of the module, they will learn how to pace themselves in order to accomplish these tasks.

A REVIEW OF THE STEPS

What happens during this thirty-minute Writing module? Every day the basic procedures are the same. The following outlines these lesson procedures.

1. The teacher begins with the Mini-lesson: topic and proofreading focus;
2. students write;
3. the teacher moves from student to student having conversations about writing;
4. students share, proofread, and make additions and corrections to their writing;
5. students date and file papers.

▶ Respond to Students

The most important role for the teacher during the Writing module is responding daily to the students' writing. The teacher should move among the students, engaging in conversations about their writing. The three main purposes for these mini-conferences are to give positive feedback, to identify areas of need, and to document progress.

GIVING POSITIVE FEEDBACK

As discussed earlier in reference to oral communication development, nothing works like praise and recognition for motivating students to continue writing. This feedback about their writing needs to be specific and sincere.

> "When you used the words *old* and *twisted* to describe the tree, I could really see it."
> "I can see you understand how to use quotation marks."

This is the applause. This short response should leave the student with affirmation of a skill or thought that gives value to his or her efforts. For many students, this response will motivate them to continue writing.

IDENTIFYING AREAS OF NEED

The teacher should note needs that can be responded to by immediate instruction or will require additional follow-up instruction.

The teacher might begin a conversation about needs by asking, "Tell me about your writing." It is important that the teacher not ask the student to read the entire composition. He or she should assist the student in identifying one thing that could be changed or added to make the composition even better, and leave the student with a positive comment.

Teacher: What exciting time did you choose to write about, Catherine?

Catherine: I'm writing about a family trip.

Teacher: Tell me the exciting part.

Catherine: Right now, I'm writing about the night before when I couldn't sleep and my stomach was all fluttery.

Teacher: Is most of this piece about the night before your trip?

Catherine: Yes.

Teacher: I don't know where you are going. Did you put it in your paper?

Catherine: No, I'm saving it for the end . . . when we get to Texas to see my grandparents.

Teacher: I think you are right. It really works at the end.

When the teacher questioned Catherine about an important detail in her composition, she realized there was indeed a well thought-out plan.

Another conference might go this way.

Teacher: Aaron, would you read the beginning of your paper.

Student: I'm telling about when I got hit by a car. "We were playing basketball and Jerod missed his shot. I seen the ball bounce high in the air. When I ran for it, I suddenly heard the tires squeal."

Teacher: I know this must have been a frightening time for you and I'm glad to see that you want to describe and share this experience. Read your second sentence to yourself and look at the verb *seen*. Does this sound correct to you?

Student: Oh, I remember! Should it be *saw?*

Teacher: Yes, *saw* would be correct. When you use the verb *seen*, it must always be with a helping word such as *have, had,* or *has.* Now, read your sentence again using *saw* instead of *seen*. Sound correct?

Student: Yeah, that sounds better.

Teacher: You are off to a good start. I can't wait to read the rest of your story.

During this conference, the teacher has responded to the student's sharing of his experience, helped him identify an area of need, provided instruction, and given him an opportunity to correct his writing. The teacher leaves with a positive comment. These short student/teacher interactions are the backbone of the skills instruction for the SUCCESS program. The skills are taught and learned within the context of the students' own writing.

DOCUMENTING STUDENT PROGRESS

Teachers are encouraged to keep daily records of observations they make about each student's writing so that they can monitor student progress and document competencies and needs for further instruction or practice. Some teachers use a clipboard or composition notebook daily to record the skills being learned and those needing further instruction. The teacher may also decide to change a proofreading focus for a few days after observing that many students are having trouble with a particular skill.

Figure 4–1 is an example of a filled-in form that can be used to record what the teacher is finding out about students through conferences. The teacher who filled in this form also observed that several students had misused verbs and decided to do a Mini-lesson on verb tense the next day. It is important to note mastery of skills as well as to identify areas for additional instruction. Some teachers will make brief, coded notes and others will write more detailed statements.

▶ The Teacher as Model

WRITING

One of the most important ways teachers can convey to students the joys and struggles of writing is to write and share their writing. This modeling includes thinking through how to best express thoughts, writing, rewriting, changing directions, and searching for the best word or words. It establishes that the teacher is a person who, having experienced the process, understands students' frustrations and pleasures as they emerge as writers. Teachers should be sincere, legitimate, and honest with their writing. They shouldn't intentionally set up examples. Sometimes sharing this writing is necessary to introduce a concept, to teach a technique, or to show how to make editing symbols. This can be done on the overhead projector or on chart paper.

Teachers might want to consider the following suggestions for modeling:
On the first day, model writing the entire time the students are writing.
On the second, write only for a few minutes.

Figure 4-1

STUDENT SKILLS ASSESSMENT AND OBSERVATION FORM

DATE: _____

NAMES OF STUDENTS	OBSERVATIONS
1. Aaron	"I seen." Corrected with teacher's help.
2. Julie	Used quotation marks correctly.
3. Lonnie	Not focused, had trouble getting started.

By the third day, students will begin to need your response to their writing.

In order to preserve your image as a writer, return to the modeling whenever you have a need to write. Let your students see you write.

It would be nice if the teacher could spend every day writing, sharing, and discussing his or her writing as a member of the class writing community. This is not possible. The teacher must guide the students as they become writers.

REVISION AND EDITING

The students have written for several days and have had peer conferences to discuss content and to proofread. Some have made notes and have returned to pieces of writing they want to complete and revise. One effective way to introduce the editing process is to model it, with the teacher as editor.

The teacher can present a sample written during a writing period using a piece of chart paper or the overhead projector. It should be an honest, unplanned, and imperfect first draft, one that may be messy or awkward, but free of faked errors for students to correct. During the time for composing, the teacher has modeled the process of creating and has written quickly to get thoughts on paper, sometimes striking through false starts and using carets to insert new words or phrases. After the teacher finishes writing, he or she should read silently over the paper to make any obvious corrections. This is the piece to be shared with the class to demonstrate the editing process.

Jennifer Perkins

The teacher reads the writing aloud and asks the students to focus on the writing and make suggestions for improvements. Some questions to prompt them might be:

"Do you have any questions about this piece of writing? Is there any part you don't understand?"

"Do I need to tell more?"

"Did the opening bring you right into my story, or does it need some changes?"

"Are there any words that don't seem to fit in, or that you're not sure what they mean?"

As students ask questions and suggest changes, the teacher discusses them aloud, and adds to the paper those changes he or she feels are needed. It is important that the writer make the final decisions about what will be changed. The teacher should demonstrate the use of carets to insert material, use margins to note words being considered for replacements, and mark through unwanted words and phrases. The students should see that their suggestions are welcomed and cause the writer to rethink the writing, producing a better piece. When the teacher is satisfied, he or she should read the piece aloud to hear the finished result.

The teacher may want to ask for title suggestions. Maybe students will suggest a more suitable title and so he or she makes the decision to change it. The writer is always the owner of the writing, and the revision and editing process, whether with a partner, teacher, or group, should maintain this point.

As soon as the editing of the writing is complete, the teacher should lead students into their own editing conferences with partners. Revision and editing will develop over time and will need to be modeled over and over as the teacher moves among writers who are conferring with each other in sharing sessions. Establish the idea that authors are willing to listen, ask questions, make suggestions, and work together to help each other grow as writers.

The teacher may decide to demonstrate revising and editing at the end of a Writing lesson. If this modeling exercise is done with the whole class after writing time, there will be no time for student revision conferencing that day. The next day students should choose a piece of their writing to share with a partner or small group for help in editing and revision, following the basic steps used in the whole-class activity.

▶ How Often Do Students Revise?

Many teachers will start the year using the writing process cycles outlined in the Writing module. In the Lessons there are two models or cycles for introducing students to the writing process and helping them feel comfortable with it. One is a shorter cycle during which the students write on days one, two, and three; revise one selection on day four; and share their final draft on day five. The other cycle lasts for about ten days. Every eight to ten days students are given the opportunity to select one of their compositions for revision and editing. The ninth and tenth days are spent rewriting and sharing compositions selected by each student.

Even though this process is outlined in the Lessons, the frequency of revision and publishing is determined by the teacher and the students. Some students will choose to revise and rewrite papers on their own and should be encouraged to do so. These steps are repeated often to give students the experience necessary to feel comfortable with the revision process and to use it for developing their best works. Later, revision and editing may occur whenever a student decides that a piece needs them. Teachers might set definite deadlines for certain pieces, but many times the student will initiate the revision process. A minimum number (established by the teacher and the students) of revised and edited final drafts are the basis for evaluation of growth in writing.

▶ Students Helping Students

For decades, teachers have collected student papers, taken them home, spent hours reading and marking them, and returned the papers. Some students glanced at the marks, and that was about it. The teacher did the proofreading and checking; few students benefited because they did not go through the process and internalize the "pseudo-instruction." If students are to develop as writers, they must have daily and immediate feedback about their work and an audience besides the teacher that is responsive to their writing.

Current research and literature about writing suggests that students helping students is a realistic and effective method for providing daily responses to writing. These daily conversations between students lead to greater clarity in written work and cause each author to question, justify, and reexamine how his or her thoughts have been expressed.

In each Writing lesson, a method for sharing is suggested. Teacher and students must decide if this is appropriate for their particular situation. For example, the lesson may suggest that students meet one-on-one to share their writing. The teacher may decide that several students should meet in a group, others one-on-one, and still others in different arrangements. On some days whole-class sharing is suggested (Share Day). This day is usually suggested after students select a paper, revise, and edit it. This can always be changed should the teacher decide it is not appropriate.

PREPARING STUDENTS TO HELP EACH OTHER

Before students can help other students, they must know how to go about it. They tend to be excited about the simple idea of getting together to talk, and talk they will. A few straightforward directions from the teacher will start them on the right track. The teacher might say, "Your most important job is to listen to your partner's paper. Don't be looking around or working on your own paper. Listen, then ask any questions you have about the writing, or just tell what you understand about it. You are not trying to grade the paper."

After giving instructions, teachers may see some students more interested in being on the floor or under a table than in conferring, others chatting endlessly, and some papers returned with big *A*s or teacherlike comments from peer partners. It will take time for students to learn how to respond to writing. One way to help them is to model the correct procedure each time a student reads to the class. For this reason, the teacher may want to choose whole-class sharing at the beginning of the year. After a student reads work aloud, the teacher follows up with a few simple comments or questions about it. The respect given to the writer when the teacher listens carefully and responds specifically to the words will set the desired tone for the students' conversations about writing. They will catch on. Still, it will take time.

PEER CONFERENCES

The point of sharing is not just show-and-tell for an audience, but to let writers know if they have succeeded in communicating their ideas, and to help them solve problems.

One student, when asked to share her poem with the whole group, replied, "I'll read it, but one line is stupid."

Her poem about her rabbit ended with these lines:
    Funny Bunny eats like a pig,
    But he doesn't wear a wig.

The student said, "I just couldn't think of anything to rhyme with *pig* that I liked."

The teacher empathized with the problem of sometimes getting stuck in a poem that rhymes. Then she turned to the class to ask them how they would deal with this problem. Some suggestions were

"Well, all poems don't have to rhyme, so you could just forget about rhyming, and write your ideas."

"I start listing all the rhyming words I can think of in the margins or at the bottom of my paper. Sometimes I ask someone to help me think of them. Usually, I can come up with one I like."

"When that happens to me, I just skip that next line and go on with other ideas. Sometimes I don't even need it, or I find a way to rearrange it."

Without being asked for suggestions, some students quickly offered,

"What about *big*, or *dig*?"

"Is Funny Bunny fat? Is that what you mean?"

"Maybe he eats all day, or just use the words *eats* and *eats* for your rhyme."

These comments were made in response to one student's writing problem. It only took a few minutes for the other students to come up with suggestions to help her.

*O*pportunities are given to teach every child to succeed and feel that he or she has accomplished some success daily.

Ida W. Whitehead, teacher

Do Peer Conferences Help?   After students have had some experience in whole-group sharing and responding sessions, the teacher might need to ask them what they are doing that is helpful to them as writers. A Writing Mini-lesson could be used for them to tell how conferring is useful or what kinds of responses make them think about ways to be a better writer. Specifically, the teacher needs to know what works and what does not. Such a Mini-lesson will give students an opportunity to talk about how some of their partners ask silly or unimportant questions or just say, "I think it's O.K." Helping writers is not easy, nor is it easy to teach. Yet, when students realize they can develop some strategies to prod another's thinking, they often will use the same strategies when they are thinking and writing. If students ask for more details in the description of a character upon hearing a peer's story, they will be more likely to include details in their own character descriptions.

What About Peer Sharing Groups?   Adding variety to the peer sharing will enable students to continue developing as helpers of others. This might mean changing partners regularly or forming larger groups of students to listen and respond to each other's writing. Writing groups of three or four students may be especially useful when they are engaged in longer writing projects, like books or stories, and need consistent response to help them as their writing develops. It is always up to the teacher considering the individual makeup of the class to decide how to establish groups, and when and if changes will be made. Meeting in groups, each student should read and talk with others about his or her paper; any necessary attention to proofreading should be handled quickly. Content is the main focus of the conferring time. Only when time comes for the final draft will helpers turn their main attention to checking spelling and the mechanics of writing.

▶ The Reading-Writing Connection

One of the most effective ways to improve students' writing skills and style is to let them learn from the best. When teachers use literature examples in the Writing Mini-lesson, they present models and patterns that students might use as guides for their own writing.

When the focus for the Writing Mini-lesson is point of view, the teacher might quickly read a few paragraphs from a book, such as *I, Houdini,* (told by a hamster) by Lynne Reid Banks, to introduce the lesson, and ask students to suggest a point of view they might like to take in a composition.

When beginning a Writing lesson with poetry, the teacher might ask students to identify elements of poetry after listening to some of Jack Prelutsky's poems. Hearing examples of rhythm, rhyme, and alliteration generates more interest and response than listening to definitions of those terms. Students who have difficulty getting started may be prompted by another writer's style or ideas on the way to developing their own.

When teachers discuss writing styles and techniques in the books students are reading in Recreational Reading conversations, they are calling attention to writing strategies in context. When asked to describe the setting of a book in a reading conversation, students begin to notice how authors introduce and describe settings in stories. A Writing lesson about describing settings is connected with an example from the student's reading experience.

Patterns for class writing projects might be suggested by an unusual format or title. One class chose to write and illustrate an ABC book titled *Athens to Zeus* during a research project on ancient Greece, after discovering the book *Ashanti to Zulu: African Traditions* by Margaret Musgrove.

Teachers may introduce books during Recreational Reading that are related to a topic in another module. When students are writing poetry in the Writing module, the teacher may introduce several poetry books by reading from them during read-aloud time. Suddenly poetry books become popular during the Recreational Reading time. The continual exposure to quality writing in books helps students recognize, appreciate, and apply effective writing skills.

▶ Integrate the Writing Module

OTHER MODULES

SUCCESS Lessons are designed to allow teachers to include any topic in any module to produce a natural integration of ideas and skills. Some Lessons use the same general theme in all four modules for several days, such as Reading and Literacy in Lessons 60–64. In these lessons the students are designing an interview and recording their findings about others' ideas and feelings about reading during the Research module. They are learning unfamiliar words from their Recreational Reading books during Word Study. They are reacting to what they read in Writing, and they are discussing author's purpose, point of view, and tone during conversation time in the Recreational Reading module.

Leslee Pugh

CONTENT AREAS

Topics included in the Lessons often occur in fourth-grade curriculum content areas; examples are machines, environmental issues, mathematics, and musicians. When these topics are included in the modules, they reinforce and extend the social studies, science, or health unit being studied. Many Writing module lessons correlate with these content-area topics. Students might write essays, letters, or editorials about an environmental issue, write about topics related to math, or write diary entries of reactions to what is read during Recreational Reading. In such Writing lessons students have a chance to express clearly what they know and think about these topics rather than completing an unrelated language activity.

▶ Evaluate and Assess

Since teachers are held accountable for the progress and growth of their students, a question often asked is, "Where do the grades come from?" They have not put grades on daily student writings, nor administered language arts textbook tests. They have not graded duplicated skills worksheets. The grade book looks empty. What do they have for grades? A lot!

Teachers have a Writing folder of daily compositions for each student, daily observation notes, selected (edited and revised) final writings for grades, students' evaluations of their own writing progress, and their writings from other modules. Writing folders provide powerful documentation of a student's writing progress. This longitudinal record becomes the basis for evaluating their progress.

PROCEDURES

At the beginning of each grading period the teacher should tell students that their writing is being evaluated with the emphasis on the skills covered during this time. During the first six weeks of school, he or she might be observing whether they are using capital letters to begin sentences, ending sentences with correct punctuation, writing properly developed paragraphs, using more descriptive language and so forth, depending on the lessons introduced.

The observation notes made during this grading period will be helpful as the teacher determines the progress made by each individual. For example, if Aaron was having trouble with verb tense at the beginning of the grading period, is he still making verb tense errors? Is he making them less frequently, or has he learned to use tenses properly?

Every two to three weeks the teacher asks the students to select a writing that they will revise and hand in for a grade. Before they begin the revision process, the teacher should tell them what he or she will be looking for to determine their grade. The teacher might say, "We have been studying subject and verb agreement and how to write clear, concise sentences with correct punctuation. For this grade, I'll be noting whether or not you have used these writing skills correctly." After this paper has been graded, the teacher will want to hold a brief conference with each student

Figure 4-2

SELF-ASSESSMENT COVER PAGE

```
MY WRITING FROM _____ TO _____
                     (date)              (date)

 *   Things we have been working on
     _____

 *   I'm improving on
     _____

 *   I need to work on
     _____

 *   My progress as a writer is
     _____
```

to answer any questions they may have about their grades. Students then file these papers in their Writing folders.

All revised writings, publications, reports, and completed presentations from other modules are potential sources for grades.

SELF-ASSESSMENT

At certain intervals, teachers will want to ask students to do a self-assessment of their writing progress. One way to introduce the procedure to determine their language or writing grade is to ask students to look over their writing for a period of two to three weeks and see if they think their writing is improving. They should be specific and give examples of ways their writing has improved. If students are keeping their daily writing in a folder in their desks, when they transfer these writings to the permanent Writing file folder, they should go through these steps of self-assessment.

1. Arrange papers in order by date. Never discard a writing.

2. Staple or clip the papers together.

3. Include a cover page that is duplicated and given to each student to put with their papers. See Figure 4–2 for an example of such a form. Through this process, the students grow more aware of their development as writers and begin to accept responsibility for continually assessing their progress.

▶ Decisions

TEACHER CHOICES

Each day during the Writing module, the teacher decides whether to

1. use the topic suggested as part of the Mini-lesson or change it, based on student interest, other content areas of current interest, or individual student choices;

2. use the day's Proofreading focus or replace it with a skill or concept identified as more appropriate for the students;

3. have revision and editing at intervals suited to students' needs or revise and edit when suggested in the Lessons;

4. allow self-selection of partners for peer sharing or assign partners when necessary;

5. restructure and/or change writing response groups;

6. use the writing mode suggested in the lesson or change to another.

STUDENT CHOICES

During the Writing module, the students may decide the following:

1. Whether to write about the topic presented in the lesson or select another;

2. Whether to compose using the mode suggested in the Mini-lesson or try a different mode of writing;

3. Who to choose as a partner for peer sharing. (Occasionally, the teacher will need to assign partners for a specific reason);

4. Whether to continue a previous day's writing, revise a writing, or start a new one;

5. What papers to revise and publish, and hand in for evaluation.

SUCCESS has helped my teaching to be more personal and individualized. I know my students better. They know me better, and I spend more time with them. We are all happier and more interested in what we're doing. I expect more from the students, and they give more. It has truly freed me to become a professional.

Patty B. Smith,
teacher

▶ In
Summary

Writing is challenging. Learning to write is not easy. It takes practice, guidance, and time. Through the Writing module teachers and students learn to appreciate the writing process. They develop a respect for the difficult work of an author. Students begin to understand that writing is a way to communicate their thoughts, dreams, and fears to others. They learn the power of words.

Chapter 5 The Word Study Module

During the Word Study module, students explore the world of words. They read in a variety of materials to locate words related to a topic and/or a spelling pattern. Discussions are focused on the associations and connections the students make between the words they locate and the topic. Each day a class chart is developed from the words the students volunteer. This word list becomes the springboard for individual writing and partner spelling activities. From beginning to end, the students are actively involved in discovering the meanings of words, and how they are formed and used. Word Study is a fast-paced, exciting thirty minutes.

▶ The Rationale

This module is designed to allow students the freedom to discover words, use them in writing and conversations, and enjoy the benefits of a growing vocabulary. Students learn words when they attach meaning to them. Through repeated exposure and usage, words become tools for communication. The variety and excitement of the materials used and the choices students are given become powerful motivators. Lively discussion, creative and critical thinking, and exploration of word meanings are the key features of the Word Study module that keep students involved with words. Students want to use and write words that are important to them. This is the reason many children learn to write and spell such "difficult words" as *Dustin, Blake,* and *Katherine*–their own names–even before they begin school.

Traditionally, teachers have taught spelling by identifying a phonetic rule and producing lists of words that demonstrate the rule. Rarely do these lists provide examples of exceptions to the rule. These lists also control and limit the vocabulary development of students. Students concentrate only on words "appropriate" to their grade level, regardless of the word knowledge they have previously acquired.

For years American school children have been taking a spelling test each Friday for thirty-six weeks of the school year. Every lesson in the spelling book is supplemented with exercises, sentence writing, word copying, puzzles, and other mimeographed work sheets as practice for learning the twenty words in each week's lesson. Parents expect the spelling book to come home almost every night so that they can diligently call out the words and make certain their child knows them for the test. Students may complete all these activities and may spell all words correctly on the weekly spelling test, and then ironically show a lack of transfer when they use the same words in their compositions the following week. Should teachers continue to use what has been demonstrated to be a flawed pattern of learning?

Teachers' excitement and enthusiasm for helping their students explore new words and their meanings will be one of the most important elements

Chapter 5

Katie Robertson

in establishing an inviting setting for Word Study. When the teacher first announces, "This year we will be reading many different materials and resources to explore and learn about words: what they mean, how they are used, and how they are spelled," he or she is setting the stage for students to become active learners. After the first few lessons, students discover that they are making decisions and are in control of their learning. They quickly discover that the lists on the charts are more interesting and provide more opportunities for real word study than traditional spelling books and exercises.

▶ Becoming a Master of Words

What is learned during the Word Study module? Students learn to recognize spelling patterns and word structure. They increase their vocabularies as they discuss word meanings and associations. They become creative and critical thinkers. Word selection for writing, handwriting, and dictionary skills are also studied during the Word Study module. The parts of the module address the different ways in which students learn.

SPELLING PATTERNS AND WORD STRUCTURE

Each lesson contains criteria for the selection of words for that day. At the fourth-grade level, students need exposure to many different words so they can apply their knowledge of letter sounds as they encounter new words. Combinations of letters are guides to pronunciation and word recognition.

The sounds of letters in words are not always as simple as phonics rules might suggest. Sounds made by some letters may be changed by the letters that surround them, and by their position in a word. Repeated exposure to words in print builds visual word recognition and spelling skills.

The Lessons contain Spelling Emphases that ask students to focus on certain letter combinations as they choose words for the day. The combination may occur anywhere in the word, allowing students to recognize the similarities and differences both in sounds and positions within words. When students discover spelling relationships in words that have meaning for them, retention is more likely to take place.

The spelling emphasis in the fourth grade is always a single letter or a two- or three-letter combination. These letter combinations may be found in any word in print. Exceptions to phonic rules are easily recognized when students are not limited to a predetermined list of words using a certain letter combination.

VOCABULARY DEVELOPMENT

Another criterion for word selection in the lessons is called the Other Emphasis: it is usually a topic such as plants, entertainment, or politics. These are presented as a springboard for discussion and generation of words the students associate with the topic.

Because there is no controlled list of words and students are at different stages in their vocabulary development, the Word Study module allows them to learn from each other. They are exposed to a greater number and diversity of words. In the context of their reading to find words that pertain to a topic, students will select words that are familiar to them. A word that is familiar to one student may be unfamiliar to another. When students explain the connections of the words they find to the chart topic, other students have the benefit of listening, adding to the discussion, and questioning. This interaction provides meaningful reinforcement to help students remember what may be an unfamiliar word. In this module, learning a new word can happen at any time. It can happen through a discussion; it can happen through an association, or just because a student is intrigued with the length of a word. The chart in Figure 5–1 was developed for Lesson 33 by students using food labels to locate words related to the senses and/or words with a *tr* letter combination. This chart demonstrates the variety of words that can appear on a chart. The students located some words with a *tr* letter combination that were familiar to them. Other words were not as familiar and prompted brief discussions about their meanings. The words students related to their senses were individual associations based on their own experiences.

CREATIVE AND CRITICAL THINKING

When students are locating words related to the chart topic, they must think about the meaning of the word and how it relates to the topic.

"I found the word *sweet,* like 'It tastes sweet.' Taste is a sense."

Figure 5-1

A CHART FOR LESSON 33

October 17	*tr*	senses
nutritious		flavor
distributed		sweet
instructions		delicious
try		light
citric		soft
controlling		good
attract		taste
travel		call
trial		thin
NutraSweet		vision
mononitrate		hot

Their experiences allow them to make many different associations and connections. They are challenged to expand their thinking by justifying the connection.

"My word is *call*."

"How do you relate *call* to senses?"

"When I say the word *call,* I think of the sense of hearing because my Mom says I'm deaf when she calls me."

This sharing of one's knowledge in unique ways is, for many, the most exciting feature of the module. It reveals to students that there is not always "just one right answer" but often many—depending on their own experiences and creativity. Students begin to enjoy the challenges and complexities of thinking. Thinking becomes fun.

USING CHART WORDS IN WRITING

Understanding words in the context of one's own thoughts and writing promotes confident spellers and builds students' vocabularies. When they use and spell words correctly in their writing, students are not simply learning letter arrangements but are incorporating words as concepts into their own thinking. The importance of the writing time is that it lets students focus on the words and their meanings, not on repeated drills such as using each word in a sentence, copying the complete chart, or writing words over and over. During writing time in this module, the students should be encouraged to develop their imaginative and creative thinking processes. The key words are *think* and *write,* not *copy.*

I teach LD/SC class, and SUCCESS is very helpful in providing a variety of learning experiences and ideas to teach Language Arts skills. It also allows me to incorporate other subject areas. My students get a broader range of vocabulary words and words that are meaningful to them.

Nan E. Carter,
teacher

HANDWRITING

Some teachers choose to emphasize handwriting during the Word Study module. As they write the spelling emphasis on the chart each day, they call attention to the letter formations and ask the students to practice making these letters correctly. Handwriting can be integrated into each lesson and takes the place of separate, unconnected, and repetitious drills.

DICTIONARY SKILLS

Dictionaries are resources to be used during this module. At any given point in the lesson, a student may quickly look up a word to check a spelling or meaning before the teacher writes the word on the chart. Dictionaries are used when they are needed. Through this incidental, functional use of dictionaries, students develop an appreciation of this resource. They choose to use it; it becomes a learning tool for them.

▶ Prepare for the Word Study Module

Before beginning to teach this module, the teacher will need to do two things; gather the materials and review the lessons.

GATHERING THE MATERIALS

The following is a list of steps for gathering materials prior to the Word Study module.

1. Provide a file folder for each student labeled Word Study, which is stored in a permanent box in the classroom.

2. Make several dictionaries and thesauruses available and easily accessible.

3. Gather supplies such as chart paper (at least one sheet for each day), masking tape, and magic markers.

4. Have students bring or make a Word Study notebook. This can be a spiral notebook or five sheets stapled together weekly.

A variety of real-life print materials are suggested as resources in each lesson. The following list is a guide for assisting teachers with their preplanning. These materials are suggested in the Lessons over the course of the year.

newspapers	brochures and pamphlets
magazines	advertisements
textbooks	maps and globes
reference books	school handbooks and guides
catalogues	library books

Teachers who do not have the resources suggested should ask students to bring newspapers and magazines from home. Businesses and other organizations are often glad to contribute some of the suggested resources. Parents and volunteers can be enlisted to assist with the collection of these materials. It should be noted that teachers always have the choice to change a resource they lack to one that is available. Many have discovered that

Lori Walls

sharing and recycling materials with other teachers gives them greater access to a variety of resources.

REVIEWING THE LESSONS

In the Word Study module the basics are the same throughout the year. Even with this consistency, every lesson involves making decisions. Each lesson suggests a Spelling Emphasis, Other Emphasis, and a Resource. Even though these are listed in the lesson, a blank is provided for substituting a different letter combination, topic, or resource. Choices about the emphases and resource should be made before beginning the lesson.

▶ How to Teach the Word Study Module

The basic components of the Word Study module are Chart Development, Writing, Spelling, and Homework. Following is a description of each of these components.

CHART DEVELOPMENT (12–15 MINUTES)

Step One: Introducing the Emphases and the Resource   The Word Study module begins with the introduction of the letter or letters for the Spelling Emphasis, the topic for the Other Emphasis, and the Resource. The Emphases are written on a piece of chart paper attached to the chalkboard with masking tape. Students write these along with the date in their Word Study notebooks. If teachers are reviewing handwriting skills, the students should practice the letter combinations for that day.

Step Two: Students Read to Locate Words   After the introduction, students read in the designated resource to locate words they can associate with the emphases. Some teachers introduce the Spelling Emphasis and the Other Emphasis at the same time.

> "Today we will be locating words which have the letters *ie,* or relate to the topic, *subjects.* You might find some words that relate to *subjects* that have an *ie* in them. You will be using textbooks as today's resource."

Figure 5-2

CLASS CHART

September 10   *ie*   <u>subjects</u>
sc<u>ie</u>nce   bod<u>ie</u>s   trans<u>ie</u>nt
mathematics   tests   index
glossary   social stud<u>ie</u>s   colon<u>ie</u>s
language   spelling   questions
libra<u>rie</u>s   reading   introductions
review

Students can choose to look for one or both.

Other teachers decide to introduce one emphasis and give students time to locate words before introducing the next. This allows the students to concentrate on each emphasis equally. When this method is used, it is important to allow only three to five minutes for each emphasis. Some teachers use a timer, and students soon learn to switch from one emphasis to the other when the timer signals the change.

In some SUCCESS classrooms, students circle the words in the newspapers or magazines as they find them. In others, students write the words in their Word Study notebooks. When nonexpendable resources are used, the students should obviously write the words on a separate piece of paper or in the notebooks.

Step Three: Students Volunteer Words for the Chart   After approximately five to ten minutes, students volunteer words for the chart, explaining why they selected the words. As quickly as possible, the teacher writes the words volunteered by the students on the chart. Some students will not be able to pronounce the words they have located. They should be encouraged to attempt to pronounce each word and spell it aloud as the teacher writes it on the chart. Pronouncing the word and discussing its meaning will involve other students.

As students volunteer words for the Other Emphasis, they explain the associations they make between the word and the emphasis. Sometimes the associations will be direct and easily understood by all class members. Other times, the associations may be indirect. Any valid association explained by the student should be accepted. This acceptance of the student's thoughts is a powerful builder of self-esteem.

Words containing the Spelling Emphasis are written on the chart. Most teachers underline the letters of the Spelling Emphasis and briefly call attention to any similarities and differences in the sounds of the letters that may appear in the words.

The following is an example of how the Chart Development for Lesson 7 might unfold. The letters *ie* are the Spelling Emphasis and *subjects* is the Other Emphasis. The following words could appear: *science, review, colonies, social studies, libraries,* and *transient.* When the teacher introduces *ie* and *subjects* using textbooks as the material, students volunteer these words because they make an association or connection between the word and subjects they will study this year. For example, one boy gives the word *transient,* which he located in the social studies textbook. Another student gives the word *social studies.* A third student locates the word *review* in a math textbook. Each student has found a word containing an *ie* and/or relating to *subjects.* By making such connections, students find relevance in learning to spell any or all of these words. This list also illustrates the diversity of student responses.

The words on this chart also demonstrate the similarities and differences of the *ie* sound in words. Students begin to recognize that the position of the letters in words often dictates how the word is pronounced. These discoveries come from examples of words from their speaking, reading, and thinking vocabulary. Students begin to formulate their own strategies for spelling the words relevant to their learning.

The class has now a completed chart with lots of words and excited students. Their enthusiasm and eagerness about real word study leads to an invitation to write.

WRITING (5–10 MINUTES)

Each lesson provides an opportunity for a written response to the chart focus. Students decide what they will write. They may decide to add words from their reading that were not included on the chart; they may decide

Figure 5-3

WORD STUDY RECORD SHEET

DATE	SCORE WORDS/LETTERS	REVIEW WORDS
October 5	2/16	space

to write about the Other Emphasis making the associations and connections they choose to make; they may respond by writing sentences with some of the words; they may write a paragraph or a poem using one word from the chart as the focus of thought. These responses reflect the associations and connections the students make to the words on the chart or to other words. With such an open-ended writing assignment, students have opportunities for creative and critical thinking as they write. They may decide to do this writing in their Word Study notebooks or on a separate sheet of paper which will be filed in their Word Study folders.

The consistency of the steps in each day's lesson helps students develop time-management skills. During the first week, while the students are getting comfortable with the procedures, their written responses may not be extensive. As they become familiar with the structure, they will be able to move more easily through the steps of the module and will be ready to respond in many different ways.

While students are writing, the teacher is moving among the students having one- to two-minute conversations about their writing. The teacher seizes every opportunity to teach myriad skills, from phonics and spelling patterns to cursive handwriting skills or word meanings and clearly expressed thoughts. This one-on-one attention is the teacher's best opportunity to deal with individual student needs in the context of their language development.

SPELLING (5 MINUTES)

With the daily spelling activity students challenge and expand their spelling vocabularies. Growth is based on the words students select to spell. The selected words are spelled with a partner, may be used in writing, become a spelling resource list, and are reviewed as a homework assignment.

Selecting the Words   Students select words from the chart that they want to learn to spell and write them in their Word Study notebooks. There is no set number of words for each student to spell. Sometimes teachers encourage students to challenge themselves with their word selection and the number of words they select. Because of time constraints, teachers may suggest to some students that they should be more realistic in the number of words they select to spell. Students can include more words on their homework list. After a short time, students will find a reasonable range for both the difficulty and the number of words they select to spell. They are becoming responsible decision makers.

After the students have selected their words to spell, they find a partner, exchange notebooks, and team test. Partners check each other for correct spelling.

Scoring the Team Tests   The student receives one point for each letter in every word that is spelled correctly; however, if the student misses any part of a word, no points are given.

As soon as students become aware that the longer the word, the more points they receive, most want to spell longer words. The following are examples of scoring on the spelling test:

1. gravity (*gravity spelled correctly*)   = 7 points
2. spaice (*space spelled incorrectly*)   = 0 points
3. astronaut (*astronaut spelled correctly*)   = 9 points

TOTAL = 16 POINTS

Students score both the number of words spelled correctly and the number of letters in the words spelled correctly. From the example above, the student would record the data on the Word Study Record Sheet (Figure 5–3).

This Word Study Record Sheet is stapled to the inside of the Word Study folder. Each day the student records the number of words spelled correctly and the number of letters in the correct words. Misspelled words are listed in the Review Words column.

Some teachers prefer an oral test to the daily written test. Students find partners, exchange notebooks, and spell their selected words orally. As one student spells a word orally, the partner makes a small check above each letter said in the proper sequence. This checking is done in the Word Study notebook.

HOMEWORK

The minimum nightly homework assignment is for students to team test the spelling words selected for that lesson. Students should be encouraged to study the words in their review list column. When students design their own homework assignments, they gain a greater sense of control over their learning activities. Some students will accept responsibility for challenging themselves with words not on the chart completed in class. Others will only want to spell the words they selected to spell in class. Still other students, who spelled the chart words correctly, should be encouraged to select new words from their reading, other chart words, or words that the teacher might suggest. To trust in a student's competence as a decision maker helps motivate him or her in the strongest way possible.

Beyond the nightly spelling test, there are suggested homework extension activities in many of the Lessons. These activities offer a variety of ways to involve students and their parents/partners in Word Study. Teachers may decide to change, elaborate, replace, or omit these extended homework activities. Homework can be individualized to meet the needs of students and to address their ability to study independently. Homework assignments are meant to be not only concise and easy to check, but meaningful.

Remember, homework is more than just spelling words correctly. Homework assignments should include the use of a variety of materials easily accessible to children at home, such as cereal boxes or bread containers, magazines, newspapers, and books. An example of expanding an activity could be asking students to list the names of plants found in their house, classroom or yard when the topic is plants.

Each night students complete the assignment in their Word Study notebooks. These notebooks should be signed by their study partner. A study partner may be a parent, another relative, or any significant adult in their lives. Not only does this person take an active role in the student's learning experiences, but he or she also is able to observe each day's work as it is recorded in the notebook and to monitor the child's progress. Parents/partners become familiar with what is expected and appreciate the suggestions for assisting with the student's learning. Whether they give a short oral test of that day's word list or only sign the child's homework, parents/partners are positively reinforcing the child's learning. (See Chapter 6 for a fuller discussion of homework and the selection of partners.)

Some teachers ask students to take out their notebooks opened to the previous night's homework the first thing each day, and they quickly walk around to check it. After a few weeks this will become routine; because students know what to expect, the responsibility for being prepared becomes theirs.

A REVIEW OF THE STEPS

What happens during this thirty-minute module? Every day the basic procedures are the same. The following outlines these lesson procedures.

1. The Spelling and the Other Emphases are presented.
2. The reading material to be used in the lesson is distributed.
3. Students read to locate words they can associate with the focus.
4. Students volunteer words and teacher writes them on a chart. Class discusses words.
5. Students practice handwriting.
6. Students respond in writing.
7. Students select words to spell.
8. Students team test.
9. Students score, record test results, and file papers in folders.
10. Homework is assigned.

▶ Other Things to Consider

WORD STUDY NOTEBOOK

A spiral notebook for each student is suggested. Each day students will use a new sheet to list the selected test words and do the writing assignment. If the test is taken orally, the checked words are in the notebook with the classwork; if the test is written on a separate sheet of paper, the checked test paper is filed each day in a folder designated for Word Study. The classwork and homework assignments remain in the notebook until the notebook is completely filled, at which time it may be stored in the student's file in a box labeled Word Study module. After a notebook has been filled, the student begins a new one.

INAPPROPRIATE WORDS

What about inappropriate words? If a student suggests a word that he or she cannot relate to the Other Emphasis or one that does not have the Spelling Emphasis, what happens? Often, teachers write the word on the chalkboard beside the chart and explain why this word is not appropriate. Through discussion, students will understand the reasons for not putting the word on the chart. Teachers should quickly move on with the chart development and follow the same procedure for unacceptable language or profanity. Here is an example from Lesson 33.

"*Cholesterol* is my word."

"Tell me what you know about this word, *cholesterol*."

"It is bad for you and can cause heart attacks."

"That is correct. Now, can you relate the word to senses?"

"Not really."

"Then let's write your word here on the board beside the chart."

PACE AND TIME MANAGEMENT

Chart making is fun; teachers and students both enjoy this part of the lesson. Experienced SUCCESS teachers acknowledge that it is tempting to continue a lively lesson, and yet, they caution teachers to remember the schedule and try not to spend extra time on the chart. There are other modules and other subjects to be taught during the school day. Spending more than thirty to thirty-five minutes on any one module will be at the expense of others. Those wonderful "teachable moments" will arise often. Students frequently have more words to volunteer than time permits for writing on the chart. Encourage the students to put these words on their spelling lists to study or include them in their writing.

Tiffany Weber

ENCOURAGING STUDENT PARTICIPATION

If some students are not volunteering words, the teacher needs to encourage (not threaten) them privately: "Find a word today. I'd like to call on you to help make the chart."

Perhaps he or she might suggest, "Tomorrow, I hope you will find a word for the chart. Let me know if you do, so I'll be sure and call on you." For students having more difficulty, the teacher may need to move to their desks and quietly assist them in locating words for a few days until they develop the confidence to do this on their own.

TEACHER'S WORDS

Some teachers choose to add "teacher's words" to the chart. This can be an excellent way to correlate content-area vocabulary or topics of interest. For example, if the day's science lesson is about planets and includes learning about planetariums and Jupiter, the teacher might decide to add either or both to the chart as required words for all students to try to spell on that day. The "teacher's words" do not have to relate to either the Spelling or Other Emphases. Infrequent use of this option gives these words special meaning while maintaining student ownership of the chart.

CHART REVIEW TEST

An option in the Word Study module is the Chart Review Test suggested every fifth day. The teacher may suggest a particular focus for the Review Test, asking students to select the words they think are most important for the review or those they did not select previously as test words. The lists are almost always individual tests with each student selecting his or her words; the teacher may select some of the words occasionally. The number of words spelled for the Review Test varies from student to student.

After the words for the list have been identified, the students should be given the opportunity to study the words either as partners or in small groups. If the test will be for grades, the teacher may decide to let the students study the words at home before giving the test. The Review Tests can be checked by either the teacher or by student partners following the same procedure as for daily spelling test. These Chart Review Tests can be used as a measurement tool for grades since the students have selected their own lists and have had exposure to them.

The Chart Review Test is optional and is used at the teacher's discretion. The frequency of the test is also up to the teacher. It is included in the SUCCESS program as a built-in review of the words being introduced to the students.

WHAT TO DO WITH THE CHARTS

The charts generated each day should be displayed for a minimum of five days as individual charts, each one visible for students to use. After five days the charts may be stapled together to form a week of charts. These in turn may be stapled together as a month of charts and displayed permanently for students to refer to when they need to spell a word on a previous chart. Some teachers have space to hang more than five charts. Others find unique ways to display more charts, such as stringing wire or clothesline across the room and using clothespins to hang the charts. The more visible and accessible the charts are for the students, the more useful they become. "We live in a dictionary," declared a student in a SUCCESS classroom. The charts become part of the print-rich environment and are an additional resource for the students to use in all other classwork.

The charts also become prized possessions. Some teachers wait until the end of the year to give the charts to students. Others give them out at the end of a grading period. Some teachers write the name of a student on each daily chart and later present it to the student.

▶ Adapting Word Study to the Needs of the Students

Because the students are reading from a variety of materials to find words, the charts represent a broader range of words than would be found in a spelling book. The range in difficulty meets the needs of both the most academically gifted students and most reluctant learners without limiting any student.

MAKING CHANGES

SUCCESS teachers are encouraged to be decision makers who trust their abilities and professional knowledge to direct student learning. This means that on any given day the lesson presented in the SUCCESS manual may be freely adapted to students' needs. The teacher is the decision maker and, within that context, the professional willing to justify what is right for the students.

How does this work? The teacher has been using SUCCESS for several weeks and is feeling comfortable with the basic, nonnegotiable structure of the lessons. The class is beginning a science unit on space. Word Study, Lesson 38, gives *aviation* as the Other Emphasis and *br* as the Spelling Emphasis. The teacher decides instead of the Other Emphasis to introduce the vocabulary words for the science unit on space, while keeping the Spelling Emphasis suggested in the Lesson. The material for this first day might be the science textbook. Students would read to find the vocabulary words the teacher writes on the chart; or he or she may ask the students to read pages in the textbook to locate words they think are important in this unit. After the chart is completed, the teacher decides which words are basic for understanding the subject of space and words the students will be expected to know. The teacher might identify these words as important and suggest that each student include some of them in his or her writing and spelling activity. The teacher has made decisions that help students direct their learning without taking away their ownership of the words they will learn. During the writing part of the lesson, the teacher might suggest that students write the meanings for each word they do not know and write a sentence demonstrating their understanding of the words they do know.

Because of the importance or number of words to be learned, on the second day of this sequence of lessons, the teacher decides to continue using

space as the Other Emphasis. He or she might add the Spelling Emphasis *ph* to introduce words relating to space study, such as *atmosphere, troposphere, exosphere,* and *hemisphere.* The selection of *ph* is a deliberate decision because the teacher has noticed many words in the unit with *ph.* He or she wants to introduce the *ph* as a unique letter combination with a sound different from the separate letters. The base word *sphere* was also clearly important to understanding the content in this science unit.

BENEFITS

In other lessons, the Other Emphasis suggested might include words related to the oral reading selection, words about an important news event, words that relate to a suggested writing topic, or words from another content-area subject. This integration of vocabulary from other modules and subjects offers opportunities for students to make connections and for the teacher to tailor each lesson to students' needs. Teachers decide what is immediate, relevant, and useful for their classes.

What does this integration with other subjects or modules accomplish? Students become more aware of the importance of vocabulary development. They begin to see the words on the chart as something more than just a list of words to spell. Students are provided with opportunities to use these words in both their oral and written communication. Students begin to feel ownership of their vocabulary and a sense of control and security from their increased understanding. Once they feel at ease with their vocabulary, the applications and connections they will make are endless. These student applications and connections signal real learning.

▶ Evaluate and Assess

By far, the most important measure of a student's learning is observed in all written work throughout the day and, indeed, throughout the year. Daily spelling tests filed in the folders and the writing in Word Study notebooks are sources for grades. These sources reveal a student's ability to learn to spell words and use them properly. Students should know that the teacher is assessing word usage in their daily writings. Some teachers write the following messages:

> "I am looking for the difficulty of the words you select to spell. Don't always select the easiest words. Challenge yourself."
>
> "I am looking to see how you use these words in other assignments."
>
> "I will be determining whether or not you can recognize misspelled words in your compositions and make corrections when you revise and edit."

Revised and edited compositions and reports should also be considered as sources for spelling grades. Students again need to understand that spelling in the context of one's own writing is something that counts. The importance of spelling is not a test list on Friday. In and of itself the mechanical skill of spelling is totally useless if students cannot think and make connections from the word to ideas and concepts.

Adrian Jackson

▶ Decisions

TEACHER CHOICES

On any given day, the teacher makes the following choices:

1. to use the Spelling Emphasis suggested or change it to meet other identified needs of the class;

2. to use the Other Emphasis suggested or change it to correlate with a content area or any topic of interest;

3. to let the students have an open response or make specific suggestions for written responses;

4. to add words to the chart for the students to spell or not;

5. to have students take written or oral tests;

6. to use the suggested resource or change it;

7. to assign partners for spelling tests or let the students select their own;

8. to give additional homework assignments or not;

9. to have whole-class chart review tests/assessments or individual chart review tests/assessments;

10. to allow students to include words not on the chart or not.

STUDENT CHOICES

In the course of each daily Word Study lesson, the students decide

1. which words to volunteer for the chart;

2. the associations and connections they will make to the Other Emphasis;

3. which words to spell and how many words to spell;

4. how they will respond to the chart in the writing activity;

5. their partner for the spelling test;

6. to take an oral or a written test;

7. their homework lists for team testing.

▶ In
Summary

The main focus of this module is, as the title indicates, Word Study. The value of this module is expanding vocabularies, building new concepts, and encouraging creative thinking, not simply putting every letter in every word in its proper place. Of course, phonics will be learned through the Spelling Emphases and oral pronunciation and discussion, but phonics is not the primary focus. The SUCCESS program is building thinking communicators, not just spellers.

Chapter 6 Evaluation, Communication, and Materials

SUCCESS teachers are upbeat, high energy, always searching and looking for better ways to do things. When they get together, they share what works for them and are anxious to know more about the latest research and how to improve as professionals.

SUCCESS teachers enjoy the challenges of each lesson because they are always learning. They have new stories to share in the teachers' lounge about their discoveries. The tone of their discussions about lessons and their students reflects positive experiences and excitement. They are involved in developing curriculum and in understanding how kids learn.

A collegial and cooperative spirit permeates any SUCCESS gathering. Teachers are sharing their latest "best children's book" discovery. They share writing topics that generated excitement and interest with their students. They discuss how Research topics led to integrated lessons in all modules. These teachers are becoming reflective practitioners, and their professional spirit is contagious.

This chapter is all about what happens as teachers move from the basics of how to teach the modules to making SUCCESS their own. Some of the topics and issues most frequently discussed when SUCCESS teachers get together for conferences, workshops, and teaching seminars are presented.

▶ Assess and Evaluate

One of the most frequently asked questions is "Where do I get the grades?" The record-keeping emphasis in this program is on performance, evidence of progress, and positive self-concept on the part of students who realize they are enjoying learning.

Ideally, assessment begins with allowing students to demonstrate their strengths and weaknesses through their reading and writing. Teachers then facilitate learning opportunities that allow students to build on their strengths and to improve areas of weakness through consistent feedback. More simply stated, on the first day of school a teacher looks at a class and asks, "What do these students know? What do they need to know? What do they want to know? How will I help them learn?"

Through consistent observation and documentation of demonstrated applied knowledge, the teacher is able to determine a student's needs and progress more accurately. After a few days in a SUCCESS classroom, the teacher has several pieces of writing, observation notes, and conversations with students that are clues to what students already know, to what they need help to learn, and to how they learn.

SUCCESS teachers address these needs through the lessons provided or they change the lessons. Each interaction with a student offers an opportunity for individual instruction in response to his or her needs. With this approach to instruction, assessment and reporting are backed up with concrete evidence of student performance. The student folders from each

Amber Powell

module, records of books read, research presentations, and published writings are all sources for evaluating student progress. Combined with teacher observations and notes, these provide more information about each student's reading and writing abilities and progress than any standardized, criterion-reference, or fill-in-the-blank tests.

In Chapters 2 through 4 are specific suggestions for evaluating student progress. (See Evaluate and Assess sections in Chapters 2–4.) Teachers will choose what is important for evaluation and develop their own system for dealing with grading requirements. SUCCESS recognizes the importance of the teacher's professional judgment. Teachers new to SUCCESS may feel

Figure 6-1

LETTER TO PARENTS

Dear Parents,

As we begin our school year, I would like to say that I am delighted to have your child as a fourth-grade student. This year your child will be involved in an innovative and creative program for teaching language arts—SUCCESS in Reading and Writing. Working together and as individuals, students will participate each day in two hours of language arts instruction, during which they will read a variety of materials and produce their own writing. The program consists of four modules:

1. Research helps students become familiar with all types of printed materials, including magazines, newspapers, encyclopedias, and textbooks. Students learn how to look for information and make use of it.
2. Recreational Reading allows students to read a variety of printed materials on an individual basis. These include readers, textbooks, library and paperback books, and newspapers. The teacher conducts individual and group conferences to check and work on skills.
3. Writing involves students in listening, speaking, reading, and writing.
4. Work Study teaches students word attack skills, spelling, sentence structure, vocabulary development, and handwriting.

Supplies—In addition to personal supplies, your child will need three separate spiral notebooks for the SUCCESS program. These will help your child become more organized and provide you with a record of activities.
Other Materials—Magazines (Time, Life, Good Housekeeping, Reader's Digest, etc.), catalogues, newspapers, and recipes are essential in our SUCCESS program. We will accept any that you would like to contribute.
Homework—Daily assignments will vary. At the least, your child will spell words with a study partner (you or another adult) and share his or her writing. The partner will sign the child's Word Study notebook nightly. I strongly encourage your child to read a book of his or her choice for at least fifteen minutes per night.

Soon we will be planning a special evening for you to come to school and see the SUCCESS program in action. If you have any questions, please feel free to call me.

Sincerely,

Matthew Mason

uncomfortable and unsure about this aspect of the assessment process. With experience and constant interaction with students, teachers will find themselves looking more closely at students and their work and less at artificial numbers in a grade book. They will come to trust themselves.

▶ Talking to Parents

SUCCESS, in all likelihood, is different from the way most parents were taught to read and write and from how their child may have been taught in the past. It is important that parents know and understand the *SUCCESS in Reading and Writing* approach to helping their child grow as a reader, writer, and thinker. Communication between parents and teacher should be consistent and ongoing throughout the school year.

On the first day of the school year, most SUCCESS teachers send a letter to parents such as Figure 6–1. In the letter they explain the SUCCESS philosophy and briefly describe what will be happening in each of the module lessons.

Some SUCCESS teachers invite parents to a Parents' Night at the school. There, the teacher explains the four SUCCESS modules, gives a brief demonstration in which the parents play the roles of students, and lets parents examine their child's work. The teacher responds to questions and comments.

A weekly class newsletter that includes examples of student writing, the research topics, and lists of books being read is another way SUCCESS teachers and their students keep parents informed about what is happening. Suggestions to parents on how they can reinforce classroom activities may be included, also. Figure 6–2 is an example of such a newsletter.

During parent-teacher conferences, the teacher will be using the folders of student's writing and other work to help parents understand the progress and needs of their child. This is the clearest, most important reporting that takes place. Most parents find more meaning in a conversation about their child's work with the teacher than looking at grades on a report card.

Teachers need to show parents their notes, checklists, and other records. Teachers must communicate to parents the extensive knowledge they have about their children. Videotaping SUCCESS lessons is an excellent way to help parents and others understand what happens in a SUCCESS classroom. Some schools have produced school or school district videos with parents as participants.

There are many opportunities to involve parents directly with SUCCESS and the daily activities in the classroom. Parents can help secure materials and resources. They can listen to students read. They can assist with book publishing. The invitation to participate is often all that parents need to become involved with and supportive of what is happening in the classroom.

Parents appreciate being informed of what is happening in the daily school life of their child, but more important, they appreciate a happy, motivated learner. A teacher's best communication to parents comes through their child.

Nikki Thomas

Figure 6-2

NEWSLETTER

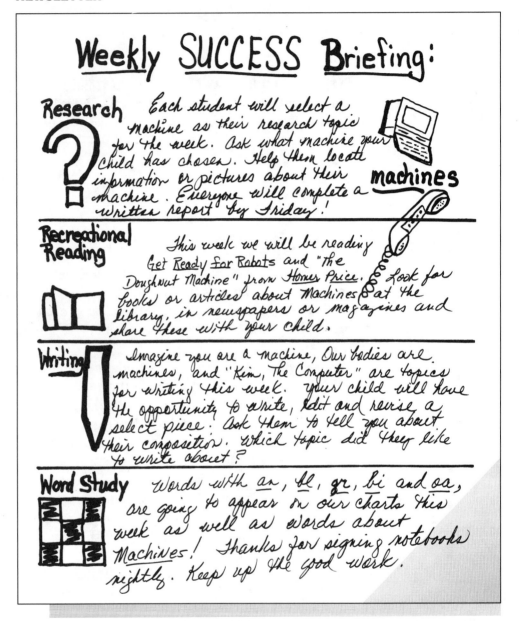

Weekly SUCCESS Briefing:

Research Each student will select a machine as their research topic for the week. Ask what machine your child has chosen. Help them locate information or pictures about their machine. Everyone will complete a written report by Friday!

Recreational Reading This week we will be reading _Get Ready for Robots_ and "The Doughnut Machine" from _Homer Price_. Look for books or articles about Machines at the library, in newspapers or magazines and share these with your child.

Writing Imagine you are a machine, Our bodies are machines, and "Kim, The Computer" are topics for writing this week. Your child will have the opportunity to write, edit and revise a select piece. Ask them to tell you about their composition. Which topic did they like to write about?

Word Study Words with _an_, _tl_, _gr_, _bi_ and _oa_, are going to appear on our charts this week as well as words about _Machines!_ Thanks for signing notebooks nightly. Keep up the good work.

▶ Homework

SUCCESS homework is intended to be HOMEFUN! It emphasizes vocabulary development and the rich, exciting world of language usage. A sense of familiarity and comfort with words only develops through usage—oral, written, and visual. Homework assignments are designed to be concise, simple to check, and most important, meaningful. The SUCCESS program supports the concept of homework each night of the school week (or at least Monday through Thursday nights). For this reason, the Word Study module in each lesson suggests that students share their writing and spell words with a partner. They are to have their Word Study notebooks signed nightly.

Beyond sharing writing and spelling words in Word Study, teachers and students may design homework extension activities in other modules. Teachers may add homework assignments in any module as needed.

It is important to encourage parents/partners to read with students and to have conversations about what they read. Discussing the meanings of words and doing activities like word games that facilitate language development are also suggested. Parents and students sharing a pleasant learning time is the most important goal.

It is necessary to understand the students' home situations and to suggest appropriate times and places for homework study as well as suitable partners. When parents are not available to be active partners in their child's learning experiences, substitutes might include older brothers or sisters; after-school care-givers or baby-sitters; business people or community volunteers; volunteer retirees.

Including the parent or other adult is very significant, since not only will they take an active role in the student's learning, but they also will observe each day's work and monitor the child's progress. SUCCESS teachers may wish to explain the important role of parents/partners during parent-teacher conferences or in a letter sent to each one at the beginning of the year. The actual time required of the parent/partner need not be lengthy because the homework is designed to be short, with clear directions, and easily shared with others.

Letting students design their own homework gives them ownership of their learning activities. When students are doing research projects, they may want to make models and posters or develop other extensions of their reports as homework in addition to their group project. Students should be encouraged to read material of their own choice each night. For many students, this trust in their competence as decision makers is a greater motivation than grades.

▶ Building a Community of Learners

In SUCCESS, working together as a class or in nonthreatening and noncompetitive teams and groups (cooperative learning) is a basic instructional strategy. It is integral to each SUCCESS lesson, not a frill or a reward. SUCCESS provides numerous opportunities for students to interact with each other in helpful, meaningful, and supportive ways. The emphasis is on students developing an understanding of what is required for people to work together.

Current research suggests that cooperative learning allows for the following:

- Greater mastery and retention of material (Cooperative discussion of reading passages increases retention of reading content.)
- Positive attitudes toward the experience (Cooperative groups produce more and better ideas than do individuals working alone or competitively.)

- Improved intergroup relation: "People who cooperate learn to like and appreciate each other." (Cooperative discussion improves problem solving behavior. People enjoy working together.)
- Increased self-esteem
- Greater acceptance of mainstreamed students

"One for all and all for one" becomes an understood motto for such classrooms. In the Word Study module, developing the chart and team testing spelling lists is a time for students to learn from and help each other. The proofreading and sharing in the Writing module also involves reciprocal learning. The many different kinds of team and group work in Research and the book talks and sharing in the Recreational Reading module are all examples of times when the classroom becomes a community of learners.

▶ SUCCESS and Technology

Many teachers already incorporate computers into the daily SUCCESS plan. There is a wide range of software and technology available for creative teaching. However, the final gain will be determined by *how* the student and teacher *interact* and utilize the technology.

WORD PROCESSING AND DESKTOP PUBLISHING SOFTWARE

Word processing programs would seem to be a natural way to develop the reading/writing connection in the SUCCESS classroom. Virtually any Writing lesson can be completed at a computer, and both teachers and students are usually excited about the possibilities. Many programs address the obvious advantages of editing on the computer and producing more legible first drafts, as well as elevated self-esteem and pride in the final publication. With regular computer use and well-designed software, elementary students can use word processing effectively, especially in the revising and editing stages. The students need the writing time to think, to formulate their ideas, and to share their experiences in their own words. Teachers will still need to move among the students at the computers to respond to their writing and to help them clarify their thoughts.

Desktop publishing programs extend word processing capabilities. Teachers find it useful to have students use these programs to create books, magazines, newspapers, posters, and pamphlets, complete with mastheads, headlines, columns, and graphic designs. The computer does the time-consuming work of layouts and column structure. Some SUCCESS teachers might very well find that students can produce their articles in the Writing lessons and then use the desktop publishing program to type the final drafts for a professional-looking publication, ready to be copied, displayed, and distributed. Student-written newspapers are great for communicating with parents and administrators.

ENCYCLOPEDIA/RESEARCH SOFTWARE

The increasing availability of technology products has opened new doors for student researchers. Extensive video libraries and computer software

I have only been using SUCCESS for one month and have already experienced a tremendous amount of positive learning in my self-contained emotionally handicapped class. They have seen more smiles and heard higher levels of learning than I ever thought possible. I love it and will never go to another method of teaching!

Jennifer Freeman, teacher

on nonfiction topics are a part of many media centers today. Complete encyclopedias are computerized, and laser videodiscs offer a multimedia approach to a wide range of topics for Research lessons. Student presentations may be enhanced by Hypermedia programs that can compile and integrate video, text, graphics, and sound into exciting final products. Interactive software allows students to create time lines, graphs, crossword puzzles, word finds, and charts to present information they have collected. The combination of the motivational appeal of computers for students and the up-to-date information available in quality software programs adds an extra dimension to research resources. SUCCESS teachers have discovered the power of the electronic page as partners work at computers during the Research module.

Chris Held, a SUCCESS teacher in Bellevue, Washington, assisted students in creating a database of books read by the class in Recreational Reading (*SUCCESS Stories,* Spring, 1988). Students decided what information they wanted to enter, including their name, the title of the book, author, number of pages, and their evaluation of the book. Students created scales for rating the book and its readability. Students would then use the database to help them select a book. (Five hundred eighty-seven books were entered!)

Libby Pollett and Debbie Head, SUCCESS teachers from Shelbyville, Kentucky, have had enthusiastic responses from their class when using the computer monitor as an electronic Word Study Chart, typing the words students volunteer and then printing copies for writing and spelling activities.

LANGUAGE AND READING SOFTWARE

SUCCESS teachers might find some language and reading skills programs useful for diagnostic purposes, for lesson design, and as a management tool. A teacher could identify and insert proofreading skills into the Writing Mini-lessons based on the results of student performance on language usage programs. Such performance might also help determine areas on which to focus in Recreational Reading conversations.

However, because most of these programs isolate language and reading skills from the natural speaking and writing of the student, they seldom reflect a student's true understanding. When a student uses the skill successfully in his or her own writing and speaking, then mastery is demonstrated. Such mastery will be best observed by the teacher throughout the day in the students' progress in writing, spelling, and reading of real-life printed matter and books. Computer reading programs rarely involve the reader with an exciting plot, and unforgettable character, stir the emotions, or promote spontaneous conversations with a friend.

Computers motivate students when they do not simply present repetitive worksheets of segmented skills on a screen. Even computers will fail to enthrall students when the programs are slower than the user, below his or her competency level, or devoid of interesting content.

Specific computer applications for special needs students as well as for regular students can be integrated into every classroom. The creative use of technology can be a part of any instructional program, and student-generated products connecting stories and research reports from the word processor, computer graphics, and videotaping and/or slide shows are realistic products that blend well with the SUCCESS philosophy.

▶ Materials and Resources

There are some basic materials needed to begin using *SUCCESS in Reading and Writing*. A detailed description of what is needed is also given in each module chapter. Here are the basics:

- a minimum of four manila folders per student for storing their work;
- chart paper, magic markers, masking tape;
- one spiral notebook per student for use in the Word Study module;
- writing materials available to students at all times—paper and pencils;
- project and special presentation materials—poster board, glue, scissors, colored pencils, and markers;
- two copies of *SUCCESS in Reading and Writing* for the teacher—one for home and sharing, and one for use as the daily lesson guide;
- storage boxes for folders.

Ginny Jenkins

Resources must come from all facets of real life. They should be varied in both reading difficulty and content. The purpose is to teach students to read any material they encounter and need or want to read.

CLASSROOM RESOURCES

The following is a list of the resources found in most SUCCESS classrooms:

- one adult dictionary for each student;
- various mathematics, science, social studies, health, and music textbooks—grade levels two through six;
- at least two to three subscriptions to a newspaper per school day, August through May;
- magazines and journals on various subjects and topics;
- one set of encyclopedias per classroom;
- thesauruses;
- maps, catalogues, telephone books, forms, "survival" reading materials such as contracts, leases, and applications;
- a minimum of fifty library books every three weeks should be checked out in the name of the class;
- multi-media resources such as videos, computer software, and filmstrips.

Some teachers will have resources available that other teachers will not have. Not all schools or classrooms are equally funded. The teachers of some SUCCESS classes ask friends, parents of students in their classes, and others to save and donate newspapers, magazines, telephone books, maps, encyclopedias, and other needed resources for their classes. With the current trend for businesses to become more directly involved with education, a source for resources might be local or regional companies.

Teachers should never omit a lesson or a module because of a lack of resources. It is better to substitute what is available or borrow from and share with colleagues. Looking ahead and planning for future lessons is a big help.

FILING AND STORING STUDENT WORK

The use of file folders is a convenient method for keeping up with students' work in each of the four modules. Some teachers have students use spiral notebooks instead of file folders for organizing work.

In some SUCCESS classrooms the students keep the folders in their desks for daily filing and then move their work to boxes of folders at the end of the week or the end of a grading period. In other classrooms, the students file their papers after each lesson in boxes where their folders are kept. The number of boxes provided per module is a teacher decision. Here are some helpful tips from veteran SUCCESS teachers:

- Divide the boxes alphabetically so that the traffic flow around each box is not so hectic.
- Place the storage boxes in different areas of the room to control traffic flow.
- Use colored file folders to separate the modules or groups.
- Designate (and rotate) student representatives to file papers for an entire group.

The most important thing is for teachers to design a method that is workable for them and their students and allows for efficient filing.

▶ Extensions

The creativity of SUCCESS teachers is forever abundant. Once they grasp the basics of SUCCESS, they are off and running with ways to expand and enrich the reading and writing experiences of their students. The ideas that follow are examples of such extensions of SUCCESS.

WORD OF THE WEEK

A student's vocabulary is always growing. Vocabulary development evolves naturally when students are exposed to words and a print-rich environment. With SUCCESS, vocabulary development takes place in each of the modules. Many teachers can create additional opportunities for vocabulary expansion by introducing new words daily or weekly and giving a brief two- to three-minute Word Talk on the Word of the Week. As the students learn this technique for introducing words to the class, they can be encouraged to give the Word Talks. Words such as *capitalism, rendezvous,* and *tempestuous* are examples of Words of the Week from different SUCCESS classrooms. The teacher or student explains why the particular word was selected, what the word means, and gives an example of the use of the word in context with other words. Students are encouraged to introduce the word to their families each time there is a Word Talk.

Some teachers set aside special bulletin board areas to display these words. After the words are presented, they are displayed for students to use in their writing and speaking. Some students also choose to include them in their spelling list. If tag board, sentence strips, and markers are available, some students might make a word card to take home with them.

SUCCESS WRITERS' CONFERENCES

Students need a purpose for writing, an audience, and response to their published works. A natural extension of the Writing module has been the creation of Writers' Conferences. In SUCCESS classrooms the first such conferences take place when students have completed works that are shared in groups of three to five. Students learn to appreciate the recognition and rewards of being an author. After some classroom experience, the students want to expand their audience. This may lead to sharing with other classes or a special evening for parents and other invited guests. Some school systems invite students to participate in district Writers' Conferences.

Teachers who are interested in providing experiences beyond the classroom for their students will want to plan ahead. Some guidelines for arranging Writers' Conferences include the following:

1. Practice author sharing strategies with the students. Ask *why* they chose to write on a topic, *how* they get ideas, and to *tell about* their writing techniques.

2. Form a planning committee of teachers, students, and parents.

3. Invite published authors to attend the conference and share their writing and experiences as authors with students and guests.

4. Arrange to have one adult per six to seven students to facilitate discussion. These people need to meet prior to the conference for some discussion of their roles and the goals of the conference.

5. Invite businesses to be partners in this effort. Ask them to provide such things as pencils, pens, tablets, and gifts for participants. Businesses can also provide spaces for public displays of students' work.

6. Involve newspapers, radio, and television in the publicity of the SUCCESS Writers' Conference. Students can make posters for display throughout the school community.

7. Arrange a location that is easily accessible, provides adequate spaces for small groups to read and discuss their writings, and a space for a larger group to meet.

Teachers can be creative in designing opportunities for students to share their writing. Vary the types of programs and audiences. Tailor the conferences to meet the needs of the students as developing authors.

STUDENT PUBLICATION CENTERS

Throughout the year, students will be revising and publishing writings. Anything that is edited, revised, and rewritten and then shared or displayed is considered published writing. This varies from the simplest form of publications—the student or class booklet stapled together with a cover—to the bound book complete with illustrations and hardback covers. Because making books becomes an exciting way for students to share their writing and creativity, a publication center motivates students to work toward authorship. Parent volunteers are a valuable resource for setting up this center and providing assistance when students are ready to publish. When students have a completed manuscript, parents can help them put together the hardback cover, plan page breaks and illustrations, and sew the pages. In some publication centers, typewriters and computers are available to students and parents. More detailed instructions are outlined in Figure 6–3. This is only one suggestion for binding hardback books.

NEW WAYS WITH CHARTS

"Do students get tired of making a Word Study chart each day?" Surprisingly, they do not. On the surface, the structure of the Word Study module does not change. What does change is the student response to new words, spelling patterns, and ideas.

New emphases for charts will often be suggested by students and by class events. A particularly involving read-aloud selection will prompt a chart to record characters, interesting phrases and descriptions, or an exciting sequence of events.

A class field trip to the art museum might prompt a before-and-after list of interesting sights and events on the trip. Such a list is a way to prepare students on what to expect and to find out what impressed them after the trip.

Sometimes students want to use one day's chart to list important words, phrases, or concepts from a unit of study as a review before a test. Students become involved in making their own study notes and practice spelling and using the content words before the test. Asking the students to volunteer and elaborate on important ideas learned during the unit helps the teacher evaluate comprehension and effectiveness of the learning, while making the students responsible for their own review.

Special class projects also lend themselves to chart emphases, such as a class alphabet book about space, or "our town." Teachers become comfortable with the basic idea that words used in the classroom, found in print, and suggested by the students are worth learning. It is not difficult to adapt the chart, making time for the needs and interests of the class and keeping student involvement and motivation high.

Some SUCCESS teachers use simple variations in materials for making special charts. These might include using orange and black markers at Halloween, using colored paper for charts, using shape charts, letting students occasionally illustrate words or whole charts. Teachers can be creative. If a teacher decides a variation is appropriate, is a meaningful addition to Word Study, and doesn't interfere with the basic goals of this module, he or she should add the personal touch. Sometimes students will have great ideas to extend chart making.

Figure 6-3

BOOKMAKING INSTRUCTIONS

Materials for Hardback Books

2 pieces cardboard or packing board, 6" x 9"
plastic book tape or binding tape
wallpaper or other covering paper
rubber cement glue
5-10 sheets of paper (ditto, bond, etc.)
needle and thread or dental floss

ruler
scissors
paper clips
cellophane tape, optional

Bookmaking Steps:

1. *Cover the cardboard pieces with wallpaper.*

   Line up the wallpaper with one edge of the cardboard and glue with rubber cement. Cut the corners off and glue edges to the inside of the cardboard, pulling the covers tight to make smooth edges and sharp corners. Use tape to help hold the edges in place as they dry (optional).

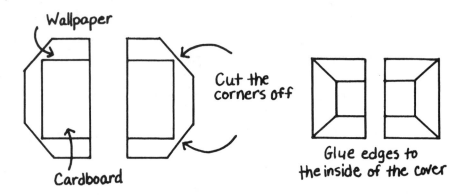

2. *Tape the covered cardboard pieces together.*

   Cut a piece of book tape about 13-14" long and tape the cover pieces together, leaving about 1/4" space between the covers for the gutter of the book. (The number of pages in the book will determine how much space is needed for the gutter. Usually about 1/4" is ample.)

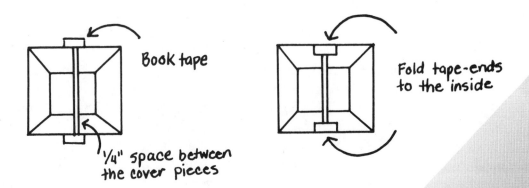

BOOKMAKING INSTRUCTIONS

3. *Sew together the pages and end pages to make a booklet.*

   Fold the sheets of paper for the pages of the book in half to form a booklet (5 1/2" x 9"). Put the pages together, one inside the other.
   Fold 2 pieces of construction paper into a 6" x 9" rectangle and put the pages inside the construction paper sheets, forming a cover for the booklet of pages.

   Open the booklet flat. Use paper clips to help hold the pages firmly so that the fold stays together as you punch holes down the centerfold about 1" apart. Use a large darning needle or other needle. The holes should go through the pages and the construction paper.

   Thread a needle with heavy thread or dental floss, about 20-30" long. Begin on the back of the construction paper side of the pages at one end. Tape the knotted end of the thread to the construction paper to keep it from pulling through as you sew. Sew to the end of the pages, and then continue sewing to return to the starting place, using an over under stitch, pulling the thread tight after each stitch. End the sewing on the back side of the booklet with a knot, and tape the knotted thread for extra strength.

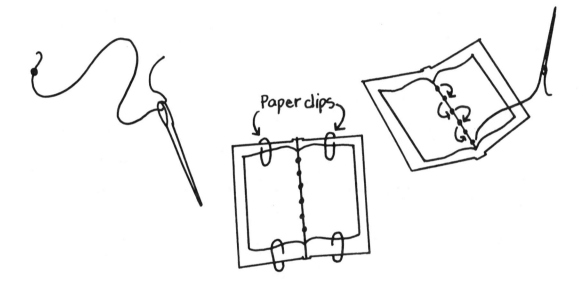

   Paper clips

4. *Glue the pages and end pages booklet to the cover.*

   Before you glue the booklet of pages into the book covers, put it into the book covers to make sure it will fit exactly. Sometimes trimming on a paper cutter will adjust any edges that are slightly long.

   Put glue on the inside of the front cover and in the tape gutter of the book. Glue the construction paper cover to the cardboard, forming the inside of the cover. (The other piece of construction forms the end pages and is not glued.)

   Press out any wrinkles, and glue the back cover in the same way. Glue completely to the edges to insure sharp edges that will last. Let dry.

▶ In
Summary

SUCCESS promotes high expectations for students and teachers. Every day students read books of their choice. They write about things they choose to write about. They develop lifelong learning skills through research projects. The student is respected as a learner, and the teacher is respected as a professional who is capable of making myriad decisions throughout the day to direct the learning of the students. These basic premises foster a joyful community of learners. This letter (Figure 6–4) received from a principal sharing the results of a year with SUCCESS in her school is confirmation of these premises. Welcome to a natural way of learning!

Figure 6-4

LETTER IN SUPPORT OF SUCCESS

Toler-Oak Hill Elementary School

Route 7, Box 311
Oxford, North Carolina 27565
Phone (919) 693-8935

Judy S. Phillips, Principal

Debbie Mertz, Lead Teacher
Lula Wagstaff, Lead Teacher

Willie V. Royster, Secretary
John Hall, Administrative Assistant

June 11, 1990

Dear Pat,

I am so pleased to share the marvelous response of our staff and students to "SUCCESS" here at Toler-Oak Hill. Our halls and classrooms are lined with student writings and drawings. Visitors to our school have been overwhelmed by the "print rich" environment they see. Even our maintenance department helped out by installing plastic clothesline so teachers could display even more work.

It has been wonderful to see individual children taking to heart their "SUCCESS" module experiences. A fourth grader eagerly explained, "I read about this in the library when I was doing research," as he participated in a science activity related to butterflies.

To sum up, our first year with SUCCESS has been a SUCCESS. We regained our recognition as a School of Merit, our county excellence program, again this year. We improved test scores significantly in reading and writing and rated high on teacher, student and parent opinion surveys.

We've had a great year and we thank you for your help and support.

Sincerely,

Judy S. Phillips
Judy S. Phillips
Principal
Toler-Oak Hill

The mission of Toler-Oak Hill School is to ensure learning for all students consistent with their needs, abilities, and interests, and to prepare them to function as responsible citizens of society.

Lessons

These lesson plans were designed as daily suggestions and starting points for each of the four modules described in the previous chapters. Teachers should use, adapt, or replace them as necessary. Blank lines indicate many opportunities for teachers to substitute different themes for the ones suggested. What should remain is the basic objective and structure of each module described below.

Research
In the Research module students practice the processes of locating, organizing, and sharing information. They learn to use a wide range of resources as they expand their knowledge.

Recreational Reading
Students read books of their choice and have conversations with the teacher and other students to share their growth as readers and their joy of reading. The Lessons suggest books for a regularly scheduled Read-Aloud time, or teachers may choose favorite books of their own.

Writing
Students write each day. Teachers and students make choices about writing topics. They practice the steps of the writing process and share published works.

Word Study
Students expand their vocabulary and thinking as they select the words they associate with a topic. They learn to recognize spelling patterns and develop spelling strategies.

Lesson 1

Research

LEAD-IN
Teacher introduces the Research Project:
Topic and Focus: People/Alphabetizing or _____
Resource: Student handbook or printed list of school personnel and a class roll sheet or _____

RESEARCH PROJECT
Read the names of school personnel and/or classmates. Select names from the lists. Write the names, then write them in alphabetical order.

SHARING
Students read their lists to each other, discuss correct pronunciation of names and titles, and check partners' papers for correct alphabetical order.
Papers are dated and filed.

Recreational Reading

For approximately 30 minutes, all students read books.

CONVERSATIONS
No conversations. Teacher models reading for pleasure.

CLIPBOARD NOTES
No clipboard notes. Teacher models reading.

READ-ALOUD BOOK
Tales of a Fourth Grade Nothing by Judy Blume or _____

Writing

MINI-LESSON
These first ten lessons introduce the writing process. Discuss writing and topics students would like to write about. You may want to share something you have written.
Proofreading: capital letters in titles

COMPOSING
Students write down all the topics they think they would like to write about; then write a sentence about the topic or a title for a story using that topic or something factual about the topic. The teacher may want to model this brainstorming process by writing a list.

SHARING
Students in teams of two to four share with each other why they are interested in writing about the topics they've listed. Partners check for the correct use of capital letter.
Papers are dated and filed.

Word Study

CHART DEVELOPMENT
Spelling Emphasis: *as* or _____
Other Emphasis: Words or phrases related to school opening, including the names of teacher, principal, school, etc., or _____
Resource: Student handbooks, lists of faculty and staff of school, or _____

WRITING
Students write response to chart focus.

SPELLING
Select words to spell, team test, complete Word Study Record Sheet.
Papers are dated and filed.

HOMEWORK
Share writing and spell words with a partner.
Notebook signed.

Lesson **2**

Research

LEAD-IN
Teacher introduces the Research Project:
Topic and Focus: People/Alphabetizing or _____
Resource: Social Studies textbook or _____

RESEARCH PROJECT
Read to locate the names of famous people and some facts about at least one person. Make a list of names and put the names in alphabetical order, and/or write some facts about one famous person.

SHARING
Students in groups of three to four share the information learned about one person.
Papers are dated and filed.

Recreational Reading

For approximately 30 minutes, all students read books.

CONVERSATIONS
No conversations. Teacher models reading.

CLIPBOARD NOTES
No clipboard notes. Teacher models reading.

READ-ALOUD BOOK
Tales of a Fourth Grade Nothing by Judy Blume or _____

Writing

MINI-LESSON
Select a topic from the previous day's list.
Proofreading: Simple sentences begin with capital letter and end with punctuation and express a complete thought.

COMPOSING
Students write about their selected topic.

SHARING
Partners respond to the information and thoughts in writing.
Check for complete sentences with proper punctuation.
Papers are dated and filed.

Word Study

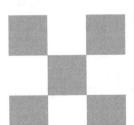

CHART DEVELOPMENT
Spelling Emphasis: *ea* or _____
Other Emphasis: Words or phrases related to expectations about the new school year, or _____
Resource: Student handbooks, news articles from newspapers, magazines related to school openings or educational issues, or _____

WRITING
Students write response to chart focus.

SPELLING
Select words to spell, team test, complete Word Study Record Sheet.
Papers are dated and filed.

HOMEWORK
Share writing and spell words with a partner.
Notebook signed.

Lesson 3

Research

LEAD-IN
Teacher introduces the Research Project:
Topic and Focus: People/Alphabetizing or _____
Resource: Newspapers or _____

RESEARCH PROJECT
Read to find headlines in the newspaper with people's names. Copy headlines; then put the words from the headlines in alphabetical order.

SHARING
Discuss the information learned from the headlines. Check to see that the alphabetical order is correct.
    Papers are dated and filed.

Recreational Reading

For approximately 30 minutes, all students read books.

CONVERSATIONS
For 20 minutes everyone, including the teacher, reads for pleasure. During the last ten minutes the teacher talks with some students about what they have read or _____.

CLIPBOARD NOTES
On a clipboard, teacher notes types of books students are reading or _____.

READ-ALOUD BOOK
Continue current selection or _____.

Writing

MINI-LESSON
Write "A monster came to school today." on the chalkboard as an example of a simple subject in a sentence. Students volunteer other sentences about monsters. Mark the subject in each sentence. Or _____.

    Proofreading: Check the simple subject in a sentence/s.

COMPOSING
Write about a monster. Or students may choose to write about previous day's topic or another topic.

SHARING
Partners share writing about monsters or _____.
    Check subject in at least one sentence.
    Papers are dated and filed.

Word Study

CHART DEVELOPMENT
Spelling Emphasis: or or _____
Other Emphasis: Words or phrases related to cafeteria or _____
Resource: Food charts and posters, menu sheets and rules for cafeteria behavior discussed orally or duplicated, or

_____

WRITING
Students write response to chart focus.

SPELLING
Select words to spell, team test, complete Word Study Record Sheet.
    Papers are dated and filed.

HOMEWORK
Share writing and spell words with a partner.
    Notebook signed.

Lesson 4

Research

LEAD-IN
Teacher introduces the Research Project:
Topic and Focus: People/Alphabetizing or _____
Resource: Magazines or _____

RESEARCH PROJECT
Read to find words about things people like to do. The words should begin with the same letter. Make a list of the words and put them in alphabetical order. Note the most interesting things people like to do.

SHARING
Partners share the information learned and check the alphabetical order list for accuracy.
 Papers are dated and filed.

Recreational Reading

For approximately 30 minutes, all students read books.

CONVERSATIONS
For 20 minutes everyone, including the teacher, reads for pleasure. During the last ten minutes the teacher talks with some students about what they have read or _____.

CLIPBOARD NOTES
On a clipboard, teacher notes types of books students are reading or _____.

READ-ALOUD BOOK
Continue current selection or _____.

Writing

MINI-LESSON
Write "Many people like sports." on the chalkboard and mark the verb. Students volunteer sentences about sports. Mark the verb in each sentence or _____.
 Proofreading: Check at least one verb in a sentence/s.

COMPOSING
Write about your favorite sport or a special sporting event. Or _____.

SHARING
Students share their knowledge, interest, and experiences about sports. Or _____.
 Check for correct verb identification.
 Papers are dated and filed.

Word Study

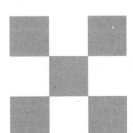

CHART DEVELOPMENT
Spelling Emphasis: us or _____
Other Emphasis: Words or phrases related to school bus or traffic safety or

_____
Resource: School bus safety manual or other safety printed materials including information in a health book, or

_____

WRITING
Students write response to chart focus.

SPELLING
Select words to spell, team test, complete Word Study Record Sheet.
 Papers are dated and filed.

HOMEWORK
Share writing and spell words with a partner.
 Notebook signed.

Lesson 5

Research

LEAD-IN
Teacher introduces the Research Project:
Topic and Focus: People/Alphabetizing or _____
Resource: Fiction or nonfiction books or _____

RESEARCH PROJECT
Read to locate words that describe people. Make a list of the words and then put them in alphabetical order.

SHARING
Students discuss their favorite words describing people. Check for accuracy with the alphabetical order.
   Papers are dated and filed.

Recreational Reading

For approximately 30 minutes, all students read books.

CONVERSATIONS
For 20 minutes everyone, including the teacher, reads for pleasure. During the last ten minutes the teacher talks with some students about what they have read or _____.

CLIPBOARD NOTES
On a clipboard, teacher notes types of books students are reading or _____.

READ-ALOUD BOOK
Continue current selection or _____.

Writing

MINI-LESSON
Write "Many people are important to me." on the chalkboard. Write sentences volunteered by students about the theme sentence, emphasize any "being" verbs. Or _____.
   Proofreading: sentences using being verbs *is/are, was/were*

COMPOSING
Students write about the theme or _____. Some sentences should contain a "being" verb.

SHARING
Students read their papers to a partner. Encourage discussions about the content of the paper.
   Check for one "being" verb used correctly.
   Papers are dated and filed.

Word Study

CHART DEVELOPMENT
Spelling Emphasis: *ar* or _____
Other Emphasis: Words or phrases related to the library or _____
Resource: Students' knowledge of library or _____

WRITING
Students write response to chart focus.

SPELLING
Select words to spell, team test, complete Word Study Record Sheet.
   Papers are dated and filed.

HOMEWORK
Share writing and spell words with a partner.
   Notebook signed.

Lesson 6

Research

LEAD-IN
Teacher introduces the Research Project:
Topic and Focus: Food/Locating information or _____
Resource: Encyclopedias or
_____

RESEARCH PROJECT
Select any food to read about in your volume of an encyclopedia. Write the guide words at the top of the page where you located the information about a food. Write facts you learned about the food.

SHARING
With your partner, share the facts you learned about your food. Tell the two guide words at the top of the pages and the purpose of these words.
Papers are dated and filed.

Recreational Reading

For approximately 30 minutes, all students read books.

CONVERSATIONS
Teacher moves among students having two to three minute conversations with as many students as possible discussing reading interests, habits, book choices and/or _____.

CLIPBOARD NOTES
Teacher makes notes about conversation discoveries or _____.

READ-ALOUD BOOK
The Enormous Egg by Oliver Butterworth or _____

Writing

MINI-LESSON
Write "I have a pet dinosaur." on the chalkboard. Mark the subject/predicate in the sentence. Students suggest other sentences and mark the subject/predicate. Or
_____.
    Proofreading: complete subject/complete predicate

COMPOSING
Students write about pet dinosaur or make-believe animals as pets. Or
_____.

SHARING
Partners exchange papers and mark the subject/predicate for two sentences and discuss the content of the papers.
    Check for capital letters and punctuation.
    Papers are dated and filed.

Word Study

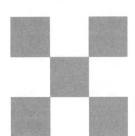

CHART DEVELOPMENT
Spelling Emphasis: *oo* or _____
Other Emphasis: Words or phrases that describe the classroom or _____
Resource: The classroom itself or
_____

WRITING
Students write response to chart focus.

SPELLING
Select words to spell, team test, complete Word Study Record Sheet.
    Papers are dated and filed.

HOMEWORK
Share writing and spell words with a partner.
    Notebook signed.

Lesson 7

Research

LEAD-IN
Teacher introduces the Research Project:
Topic and Focus: Foods/Locating information or _____
Resource: Dictionaries or _____

RESEARCH PROJECT
Skim the dictionary to find foods that begin with *t* or another letter selected by the student. Write the foods in a list. Write the guide words from the pages on which the food words were found.

SHARING
With a partner, share word lists and guide words.
  Papers are dated and filed.

Recreational Reading

For approximately 30 minutes, all students read books.

CONVERSATIONS
Teacher moves among students having two to three minute conversations with as many students as possible discussing reading interests, habits, book choices and/or _____.

CLIPBOARD NOTES
Teacher makes notes about conversation discoveries or _____.

READ-ALOUD BOOK
Continue current selection or _____.

Writing

MINI-LESSON
Discuss "My most embarrassing moment."
Write sentences volunteered by students.
Capitalize the pronoun *I*. Or _____.
  Proofreading: Use pronoun *I* in at least one sentence.

COMPOSING
Write about your most embarrassing moment. Use descriptive language that paints a picture for others. Or _____.

SHARING
With two or three other students, read your papers and react to the content.
  Check for capitalization of *I*.
  Papers are dated and filed.

Word Study

CHART DEVELOPMENT
Spelling Emphasis: *ie* or _____
Other Emphasis: Words or phrases related to school subjects studied or _____

Resource: Textbooks or _____

WRITING
Students write response to chart focus.

SPELLING
Select words to spell, team test, complete Word Study Record Sheet.
  Papers are dated and filed.

HOMEWORK
Share writing and spell words with a partner.
  Notebook signed.

Lesson 8

Research

LEAD-IN
Teacher introduces the Research Project:
Topic and Focus: Animals/Locating information or _____
Resource: Textbooks or _____

RESEARCH PROJECT
Read through the glossary and/or index and locate information about animals. Write as many facts as you can about animals and tell where you found the information.

SHARING
In a group of three or four read the most interesting information you located about animals. Did anyone else find the same information about the same animals? Different animals?
    Papers are dated and filed.

Recreational Reading

For approximately 30 minutes, all students read books.

CONVERSATIONS
Teacher moves among students having two to three minute conversations with as many students as possible discussing reading interests, habits, book choices and/or _____.

CLIPBOARD NOTES
Teacher makes notes about conversation discoveries or _____.

READ-ALOUD BOOK
Continue current selection or _____.

Writing

MINI-LESSON
The Revision Process. This process should be explained to students following the suggestions on page 62 in Chapter 4. Or _____.
    Proofreading: content clarity, read for complete, clear, interesting sentences

COMPOSING
Students make any changes as a result of conversations with partners or their own proofreading. Or _____.

SHARING
With a partner discuss papers and make suggestions for improving the writing.
    Papers are dated and filed.

Word Study

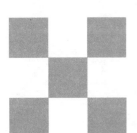

CHART DEVELOPMENT
Spelling Emphasis: *es* or _____
Other Emphasis: Words or phrases related to classroom schedules including the days of the week or _____
Resource: Calendars (one per student or pair of students) or _____

WRITING
Students write response to chart focus.

SPELLING
Select words to spell, team test, complete Word Study Record Sheet.
    Papers are dated and filed.

HOMEWORK
Share writing and spell words with a partner.
    Notebook signed.

Lesson 9

Research

LEAD-IN
Teacher introduces the Research Project:
Topic and Focus: Animals/Locating
information or _____
Resource: Magazines, newspapers,
Readers' Guide to Periodicals or Reader's
Guide to Magazines, or _____

RESEARCH PROJECT
Read to locate information about one animal in two different resource materials.
Describe the kinds of information given
in the resource materials you used.

SHARING
With a partner, share the kinds of information you located about your animal.
Discuss where to find different kinds of
information.
    Papers are dated and filed.

Recreational Reading

For approximately 30 minutes, all students read books.

CONVERSATIONS
Teacher has seven to ten minute conversations with individual students about
reading and checks for student's use of
context clues to tell meanings of unfamiliar words or _____.

CLIPBOARD NOTES
Teacher makes notes about discoveries
during conversations or _____.

READ-ALOUD BOOK
Continue current selection or _____.

Writing

MINI-LESSON
Revision and editing process outlined on
page 62 in Chapter 4. Or _____.
    Proofreading: Briefly review the
proofreading in Lessons 1–7.

COMPOSING
Students do self-editing and make corrections to their papers. After Peer Sharing,
complete rewriting of paper. Or
_____.

SHARING
With a partner read for editing misspelled words and proofreading thrusts
from Lessons 1–7.
    Papers are dated and filed.

Word Study

CHART DEVELOPMENT
Spelling Emphasis: *en* or _____
Other Emphasis: Words or phrases
related to events of the first six months
of the year, including the months, or

_____
Resource: Calendars used in previous
lesson or _____

WRITING
Students write response to chart focus.

SPELLING
Select words to spell, team test, complete
Word Study Record Sheet.
    Papers are dated and filed.

HOMEWORK
Share writing and spell words with a
partner.
    Notebook signed.

Research

LEAD-IN
Teacher introduces the Research Project:
Topic and Focus: People, Food, or
Animals/Locating information or
_____

Resource: Students select a reference
material of choice or _____

RESEARCH PROJECT
Locate information about selected topic in
the selected resource. Write down the resource used and tell why you selected it.
Write the most interesting thing you
learned about your topic.

SHARING
In groups of four or five students, share
the information you located and tell
where you located the information.
    Papers are dated and filed.

Recreational Reading

For approximately 30 minutes, all students read books.

CONVERSATIONS
Teacher has seven to ten minute conversations with individual students about
reading and checks for student's use of
context clues to tell meanings of unfamiliar words or _____.

CLIPBOARD NOTES
Teacher makes notes about discoveries
during conversations or _____.

READ-ALOUD BOOK
Continue current selection or _____.

Writing

MINI-LESSON
Sharing Day or _____

COMPOSING
Discuss listening and responding as
others share their writing. Teacher decides design of sharing time: small
groups, whole group, partners, etc. Or
_____.

SHARING
Student responses to shared writing or
_____
    Papers are dated and filed.

Word Study

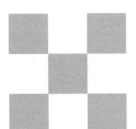

CHART DEVELOPMENT
Spelling Emphasis: *ai* or _____
Other Emphasis: Words or phrases
related to the last six months of the year
including the months or Chart Review
Test or _____
Resource: Calendars used in previous
lessons or _____

WRITING
Students write response to chart focus.

SPELLING
Select words to spell, team test, complete
Word Study Record Sheet.
    Papers are dated and filed.

HOMEWORK
Share writing and spell words with a
partner.
    Notebook signed.

Lesson 11

Research

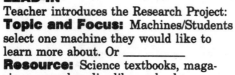

Five-day integrated lessons: Machines

LEAD-IN
Teacher introduces the Research Project:
Topic and Focus: Machines/Students select one machine they would like to learn more about. Or _____
Resource: Science textbooks, magazines, encyclopedia, library books, or _____

RESEARCH PROJECT
Read to locate information on the origin of the machine selected: who invented, where, when, why? Take notes on the information you find. Write the most important facts from your reading.

SHARING
If some students have selected the same machine, suggest they work together. If not, let them select their partners to read and comment on their writing.
Papers are dated and filed.

Recreational Reading

For approximately 30 minutes, all students read books.

CONVERSATIONS
Teacher has seven to ten minute conversations with individual students about reading and checks for student's use of context clues to tell meanings of unfamiliar words or _____.

CLIPBOARD NOTES
Teacher makes notes about discoveries during conversations or _____.

READ-ALOUD BOOK
Get Ready For Robots by Patricia Lauber or _____

Writing

MINI-LESSON
Introduce the word machine. Ask students to imagine they are a machine. Or _____.
Proofreading: Use descriptive words, adjectives in your description of the imagined machine.

COMPOSING
Imagine you are a machine. Describe your machine. Or _____.

SHARING
Partners read papers, discuss the machine descriptions, and respond to each others writing.
Proofread for adjectives.
Papers are dated and filed.

Word Study

CHART DEVELOPMENT
Spelling Emphasis: *an* or _____

Other Emphasis: Science vocabulary words from a chapter on machines or chapter selected by teacher or _____
Resource: Science textbooks or _____

WRITING
Students write response to chart focus.

SPELLING
Select words to spell, team test, complete Word Study Record Sheet.
Papers are dated and filed.

HOMEWORK
Share writing and spell words with a partner.
Notebook signed.

Lesson 12

Research

LEAD-IN
Teacher introduces the Research Project:
Topic and Focus: Machines or
_____

Resource: Student- and teacher-selected materials or _____

RESEARCH PROJECT
Read to locate information about your machine's current use. How has it changed since it was first invented? Write about the information read.

SHARING
Read and discuss information discovered with a self-selected partner.
Papers are dated and filed.

Recreational Reading

For approximately 30 minutes, all students read books.

CONVERSATIONS
Teacher has seven to ten minute conversations with individual students about reading and checks for student's use of context clues to tell meanings of unfamiliar words or _____.

CLIPBOARD NOTES
Teacher makes notes about discoveries during conversations or _____.

READ-ALOUD BOOK
Continue current selection or _____.

Writing

MINI-LESSON
Machines: "Our bodies are machines." Or _____.
Proofreading: subject/verb agreement.

COMPOSING
Students write to compare the body to a machine (body to car). Or _____.

SHARING
Students read, respond to, and proofread partner's paper.
Papers are dated and filed.

Word Study

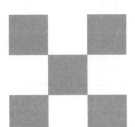

CHART DEVELOPMENT
Spelling Emphasis: *bl* or _____
Other Emphasis: Machines or _____

Resource: Science textbook, encyclopedias, dictionaries, or _____

WRITING
Students write response to chart focus.

SPELLING
Select words to spell, team test, complete Word Study Record Sheet.
Papers are dated and filed.

HOMEWORK
Share writing and spell words with a partner.
Notebook signed.

Lesson **13**

Research

LEAD-IN
Teacher introduces the Research Project:
Topic and Focus: Machines or
_____

Resource: Student- and teacher-
selected materials or _____

RESEARCH PROJECT
Read to locate information about how
your machine (from previous lesson) is
important to man or helps man. Write
about the information you read.

SHARING
Read and discuss the information discov-
ered with a self-selected partner.
   Papers are dated and filed.

Recreational Reading

For approximately 30 minutes, all students read books.

CONVERSATIONS
Teacher has seven to ten minute conversations with individual students about
reading and checks for student's use of
context clues to tell meanings of unfamiliar words or _____.

CLIPBOARD NOTES
Teacher makes notes about discoveries
during conversations or _____.

READ-ALOUD BOOK
Homer Price by Robert McCloskey (The
Doughnut Machine) or _____

Writing

MINI-LESSON
Machines: "Kim, The Computer." Or
_____.
   Proofreading: Indent to show new
paragraph.

COMPOSING
Write a short story about "Kim, The
Computer." Or _____.

SHARING
Students read, respond to, and proofread
partner's paper.
   Papers are dated and filed.

Word Study

CHART DEVELOPMENT
Spelling Emphasis: *gr* or _____
Other Emphasis: Machines or
_____

Resource: Magazines, newspapers,
science textbooks, or _____

WRITING
Students write response to chart focus.

SPELLING
Select words to spell, team test, complete
Word Study Record Sheet.
   Papers are dated and filed.

HOMEWORK
Share writing and spell words with a
partner.
   Notebook signed.

Research

LEAD-IN
Teacher introduces the Research Project:
Topic and Focus: Machines/Organizing report or _____
Resource: _____

RESEARCH PROJECT
Students begin to organize the information they have discovered for their written report. The reports should have at least three paragraphs: origin of the machine, use or value to man, and how the machine has changed since it was invented.

SHARING
Read and discuss partner's paper.
  Papers are dated and filed.

Recreational Reading

For approximately 30 minutes, all students read books.

CONVERSATIONS
Teacher has seven to ten minute conversations with individual students about reading and checks for student's use of context clues to tell meanings of unfamiliar words or _____.

CLIPBOARD NOTES
Teacher makes notes about discoveries during conversations or _____.

READ-ALOUD BOOK
Continue current selection or _____.

Writing

MINI-LESSON
Student-selected paper for revision. Or _____.
  Proofreading: From the three previous papers, students select one paper to revise and rewrite.

COMPOSING
Students begin to revise, edit, and rewrite paper. Or _____.

SHARING
Students read, respond to, and proofread partner's paper.
  Papers are dated and filed.

Word Study

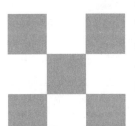

CHART DEVELOPMENT
Spelling Emphasis: *bi* or _____
Other Emphasis: Machines or

_____
Resource: Teacher- and student-selected materials or _____

WRITING
Students write response to chart focus.

SPELLING
Select words to spell, team test, complete Word Study Record Sheet.
  Papers are dated and filed.

HOMEWORK
Share writing and spell words with a partner.
  Notebook signed.

Lesson **15**

Research

LEAD-IN
Teacher introduces the Research Project:
Topic and Focus: Machines/Writing
report or _____
Resource: _____

RESEARCH PROJECT
Read draft report very carefully and edit.
Complete written report.

SHARING
Continue to share report with a partner.
Papers are dated and filed.

Recreational Reading

For approximately 30 minutes, all students read books.

CONVERSATIONS
Teacher has seven to ten minute conversations with individual students about reading and checks for student's use of context clues to tell meanings of unfamiliar words or _____.

CLIPBOARD NOTES
Teacher makes notes about discoveries during conversations or _____.

READ-ALOUD BOOK
Continue current selection or _____.

Writing

MINI-LESSON
Machines or _____

COMPOSING
Complete the revision of paper or
_____.

SHARING
In groups of three or four, share writing.
Papers are dated and filed.

Word Study

CHART DEVELOPMENT
Spelling Emphasis: *oa* or _____
Other Emphasis: Machines or

_____
Resource: Social Studies or Health or
Math textbooks or _____

WRITING
Students write response to chart focus.

SPELLING
Select words to spell, team test, complete
Word Study Record Sheet.
Papers are dated and filed.

HOMEWORK
Share writing and spell words with a
partner.
Notebook signed.

Lesson 16

Research

LEAD-IN
Teacher introduces the Research Project:
Topic and Focus: Recipes/Sequence
or _____
Resource: Labels from food packages, recipe cards/books, magazines, or
_____

RESEARCH PROJECT
Read the directions for preparing a main dish, dessert or other food. In your own words write the steps taken to prepare the dish.

SHARING
Exchange papers with a partner and tell the sequence of steps for preparing your food.
Papers are dated and filed.

Recreational Reading

For approximately 30 minutes, all students read books.

CONVERSATIONS
No conversations. Teacher models reading for pleasure.

CLIPBOARD NOTES
Teacher models reading.

READ-ALOUD BOOK
People by Peter Spier or _____

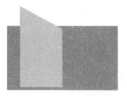

Writing

MINI-LESSON
Dreams or _____
    Proofreading: use of vivid words to "paint a picture"

COMPOSING
Write about a dream you have had, or if you do not have dreams, why you think people have dreams or something you would like to dream about. Or
_____.

SHARING
Students read, respond to, and proofread partner's paper.
Papers are dated and filed.

Word Study

CHART DEVELOPMENT
Spelling Emphasis: *pl* or _____
Other Emphasis: People or
_____

Resource: Current magazines or
_____

WRITING
Students write response to chart focus.

SPELLING
Select words to spell, team test, complete Word Study Record Sheet.
Papers are dated and filed.

HOMEWORK
Share writing and spell words with a partner.
Notebook signed.

Lesson 17

Research

LEAD-IN
Teacher introduces the Research Project:
Topic and Focus: Television/
Sequence or _____
Resource: Television viewing, TV Guide, schedules from newspapers, or _____

RESEARCH PROJECT
Read to find programs watched or recall from memory favorite programs. Make a schedule for your television viewing for one night. List the times and programs watched.

SHARING
Read and discuss your schedule with a self-selected partner.
   Papers are dated and filed.

Recreational Reading

For approximately 30 minutes, all students read books.

CONVERSATIONS
During the last ten minutes, small groups discuss books they are reading. Groups may be organized by topic, author, same book, or any other appropriate grouping. Or _____.

CLIPBOARD NOTES
Teacher notes how students listen and respond in discussions or _____.

READ-ALOUD BOOK
Emily Upham's Revenge by Avi or _____

Writing

MINI-LESSON
Discuss exotic birds or _____.
   Proofreading: Use at least one present-tense verb.

COMPOSING
Write about imaginary exotic birds or real birds you think are exotic.

SHARING
Students read, respond to, and proofread partner's paper.
   Papers are dated and filed.

Word Study

CHART DEVELOPMENT
Spelling Emphasis: *pr* or _____
Other Emphasis: People or
_____
Resource: Recreational reading books or _____

WRITING
Students write response to chart focus.

SPELLING
Select words to spell, team test, complete Word Study Record Sheet.
   Papers are dated and filed.

HOMEWORK
Share writing and spell words with a partner.
   Notebook signed.

Lesson 18

Research

LEAD-IN
Teacher introduces the Research Project:
Topic and Focus: Experiments or projects/Sequence or _____
Resource: Science textbooks or
_____

RESEARCH PROJECT
Read to locate science experiments or projects. Write the proper sequence for completing the experiment or project.

SHARING
Explain to a partner the sequence of steps to complete the experiment or project.
    Papers are dated and filed.

Recreational Reading

For approximately 30 minutes, all students read books.

CONVERSATIONS
Teacher moves from student to student having two to three minute conversations about sequence of events in the books students are reading or _____.

CLIPBOARD NOTES
Teacher makes notes about discoveries during conversations or _____.

READ-ALOUD BOOK
Continue current selection or _____

Writing

MINI-LESSON
Discuss a favorite relative or _____.
    Proofreading: Use at least one past-tense verb.

COMPOSING
Write about a favorite relative or
_____.

SHARING
Students read, respond to, and proofread partner's paper.
    Papers are dated and filed.

Word Study

CHART DEVELOPMENT
Spelling Emphasis: *gl* or _____
Other Emphasis: Sports or

_____
Resource: Newspapers or _____

WRITING
Students write response to chart focus.

SPELLING
Select words to spell, team test, complete Word Study Record Sheet.
    Papers are dated and filed.

HOMEWORK
Share writing and spell words with a partner.
    Notebook signed.

Lesson 19

Research

LEAD-IN
Teacher introduces the Research Project:
Topic and Focus: History/Sequence
or _____
Resource: Social Studies textbook or
_____

RESEARCH PROJECT
Read to locate interesting facts about
historical events. Make a list of these
events in proper sequence (use dates).

SHARING
With two partners, describe the historical
event in proper sequence.
Papers are dated and filed.

Recreational Reading

For approximately 30 minutes, all students read books.

CONVERSATIONS
Teacher moves from student to student
having two to three minute conversations
about sequence of events in the books students are reading or _____.

CLIPBOARD NOTES
Teacher makes notes about discoveries
during conversations or _____.

READ-ALOUD BOOK
Continue current selection or _____

Writing

MINI-LESSON
Special friends or _____
Proofreading: Use at least one past-
tense verb with a helping verb.

COMPOSING
Write about a special friend or
_____.

SHARING
Students read, respond to, and proofread
partner's paper.
Papers are dated and filed.

Word Study

CHART DEVELOPMENT
Spelling Emphasis: fl or _____
Other Emphasis: Nature or

_____
Resource: Newspapers or _____

WRITING
Students write response to chart focus.

SPELLING
Select words to spell, team test, complete
Word Study Record Sheet.
Papers are dated and filed.

HOMEWORK
Share writing and spell words with a
partner.
Notebook signed.

Lesson 20

Research

LEAD-IN
Teacher introduces the Research Project:
Topic and Focus: Travel/Making charts or _____
Resource: Maps or _____

RESEARCH PROJECT
Read mileage chart on a map. Make a chart to show mileage for some trips you would like to take. Example of chart headings: FROM, TO, MILES

SHARING
With a partner, tell the places you will travel and the total miles of your trip.
   Papers are dated and filed.

Recreational Reading

For approximately 30 minutes, all students read books.

CONVERSATIONS
Teacher moves from student to student having two to three minute conversations about sequence of events in the books students are reading or _____.

CLIPBOARD NOTES
Teacher makes notes about discoveries during conversations or _____.

READ-ALOUD BOOK
Continue current selection or _____.

Writing

MINI-LESSON
"The Magic Race Car" or _____
   Proofreading: correct use of verbs

COMPOSING
Write a short story about "The Magic Race Car." Or _____.

SHARING
Students read, respond to, and proofread partner's paper.
   Papers are dated and filed.

Word Study

CHART DEVELOPMENT
Spelling Emphasis: *sm* or _____

Other Emphasis: Money or _____

Resource: Magazines or _____

WRITING
Students write response to chart focus.

SPELLING
Select words to spell, team test, complete Word Study Record Sheet.
   Papers are dated and filed.

HOMEWORK
Share writing and spell words with a partner.
   Notebook signed.

123

Lesson 21

Research

LEAD-IN
Teacher introduces the Research Project:
Topic and Focus: Travel/Arranging information in a chart or _____
Resource: Travel folders, travel advertisements in magazines, or _____

RESEARCH PROJECT
Read travel information to plan a trip. Find as many items of expense as possible. Make a chart to show travel expenses. Example of chart headings: ITEM, EXPENSE

SHARING
Read and discuss your chart with a partner.
Papers are dated and filed.

Recreational Reading

For approximately 30 minutes, all students read books.

CONVERSATIONS
Teacher moves from student to student having seven to ten minute conversations about the main idea in a reading passage or _____.

CLIPBOARD NOTES
Teacher makes notes of discoveries during conversations or _____.

READ-ALOUD BOOK
Continue current selection or _____.

Writing

MINI-LESSON
"The Magic Race Car" or _____
Proofreading: Use at least one s-form of a verb.

COMPOSING
Continue the story begun in previous day's lesson or _____.

SHARING
Students read, respond to, and proofread partner's paper.
Papers are dated and filed.

Word Study

CHART DEVELOPMENT
Spelling Emphasis: *sc* or _____
Other Emphasis: Weather or

_____
Resource: Science textbooks or

_____

WRITING
Students write response to chart focus.

SPELLING
Select words to spell, team test, complete Word Study Record Sheet.
Papers are dated and filed.

HOMEWORK
Share writing and spell words with a partner.
Notebook signed.

Research

LEAD-IN
Teacher introduces the Research Project:
Topic and Focus: Transportation/
Information in charts or _____
Resource: Newspapers or _____

RESEARCH PROJECT
Read in the newspaper for words relating
to transportation. Make a list of transportation words. Make a chart to put these
words into categories.

SHARING
Read and discuss the words on your chart
with a partner. Explain why you put
words in selected categories.
   Papers are dated and filed.

Recreational Reading

For approximately 30 minutes, all students read books.

CONVERSATIONS
Teacher moves from student to student
having seven to ten minute conversations
about the main idea in a reading passage
or _____.

CLIPBOARD NOTES
Teacher makes notes of discoveries during conversations or _____.

READ-ALOUD BOOK
How to-Eat Fried Worms by Thomas
Rockwell or _____

Writing

MINI-LESSON
Discuss traits and how things are alike
and different. Or _____.
   Proofreading: Identify a plural noun in
your writing.

COMPOSING
Write about two things in your desk or
classroom. Tell how they are alike and
different. Or _____.

SHARING
Students read, respond to, and proofread
partner's paper.
   Papers are dated and filed.

Word Study

CHART DEVELOPMENT
Spelling Emphasis: *fr* or _____
Other Emphasis: Art or _____
Resource: Magazines or _____

WRITING
Students write response to chart focus.

SPELLING
Select words to spell, team test, complete
Word Study Record Sheet.
   Papers are dated and filed.

HOMEWORK
Share writing and spell words with a
partner.
   Notebook signed.

Lesson 23

Research

LEAD-IN
Teacher introduces the Research Project:
Topic and Focus: Transportation/
Information in charts or _____
Resource: Science and health books or
_____

RESEARCH PROJECT
Read to locate words associated with
transportation. Make a chart to present
information located. Example: BOOK,
PAGES, TRANSPORTATION WORDS

SHARING
With a partner, explain why you selected
the words associated with transportation.
Compare lists.
   Papers are dated and filed.

Recreational Reading

For approximately 30 minutes, all students read books.

CONVERSATIONS
Teacher moves from student to student
having seven to ten minute conversations
about the main idea in a reading passage
or _____.

CLIPBOARD NOTES
Teacher makes notes of discoveries during conversations or _____.

READ-ALOUD BOOK
Continue current selection or _____.

Writing

MINI-LESSON
Discuss traits of animals or _____.
   Proofreading: subject/verb agreement

COMPOSING
Write a comparison of two animals dis-
cussing their likenesses and differences.
Or _____.

SHARING
Students read, respond to, and proofread
partner's paper.
   Papers are dated and filed.

Word Study

CHART DEVELOPMENT
Spelling Emphasis: *sk* or _____
Other Emphasis: Travel or
_____
Resource: Recreational reading books
or _____

WRITING
Students write response to chart focus.

SPELLING
Select words to spell, team test, complete
Word Study Record Sheet.
   Papers are dated and filed.

HOMEWORK
Share writing and spell words with a
partner.
   Notebook signed.

Research

LEAD-IN
Teacher introduces the Research Project:
Topic and Focus: Transportation/
Information in charts or _____
Resource: Social Studies textbooks or
_____

RESEARCH PROJECT
Read to locate the different kinds of
transportation used throughout history.
Make a chart to show the mode of travel,
date/s in history, and people using this
mode of travel. Example: MODE,
DATE/S, WHO USED

SHARING
Read and discuss the information discov-
ered with a self-selected partner.
Papers are dated and filed.

Recreational Reading

For approximately 30 minutes, all students read books.

CONVERSATIONS
Teacher moves from student to student
having seven to ten minute conversations
about the main idea in a reading passage
or _____.

CLIPBOARD NOTES
Teacher makes notes of discoveries during conversations or _____.

READ-ALOUD BOOK
Continue current selection or _____.

Writing

MINI-LESSON
Discuss seasons or _____.
Proofreading: simple subject/simple
predicate

COMPOSING
Write a comparison of two seasons discussing their likenesses and differences.

SHARING
Students read, respond to, and proofread
partner's paper.
Papers are dated and filed.

Word Study

CHART DEVELOPMENT
Spelling Emphasis: *sp* or _____
Other Emphasis: Music or
_____

Resource: Newspapers or _____

WRITING
Students write response to chart focus.

SPELLING
Select words to spell, team test, complete
Word Study Record Sheet.
Papers are dated and filed.

HOMEWORK
Share writing and spell words with a
partner.
Notebook signed.

Lesson 25

Research

LEAD-IN
Teacher introduces the Research Project:
Topic and Focus: Transportation/
Information in charts or _____
Resource: Newspapers or _____

RESEARCH PROJECT
Read the car, truck, motorcycle, and boat advertisements to find costs of different vehicles. Make a chart to show information. Example: VEHICLE, YEAR, MAKE, COST

SHARING
With a partner, discuss the best buy in a vehicle and why.
Papers are dated and filed.

Recreational Reading

For approximately 30 minutes, all students read books.

CONVERSATIONS
Teacher moves from student to student having seven to ten minute conversations about the main idea in a reading passage or _____.

CLIPBOARD NOTES
Teacher makes notes of discoveries during conversations or _____.

READ-ALOUD BOOK
Continue current selection or _____.

Writing

MINI-LESSON
Discuss the sun and the moon or _____.
Proofreading: complete subject/complete predicate

COMPOSING
Write a comparison of the sun and the moon. Discuss their likenesses and differences. Or _____.

SHARING
Students read, respond to, and proofread partner's paper.
Papers are dated and filed.

Word Study

CHART DEVELOPMENT
Spelling Emphasis: *st* or _____
Other Emphasis: Accidents or _____

Resource: Newspapers or _____

WRITING
Students write response to chart focus.

SPELLING
Select words to spell, team test, complete Word Study Record Sheet.
Papers are dated and filed.

HOMEWORK
Share writing and spell words with a partner.
Notebook signed.

Lesson 26

Research

LEAD-IN
Teacher introduces the Research Project:
Topic and Focus: Transportation
and people/Information in charts or

Resource: Newspapers, magazines, or
_____

RESEARCH PROJECT
Read to locate information about someone
traveling. Make a chart to show who,
where, how, and when information about
the person traveling. Example of column
heads: WHO, WHERE, HOW, WHEN

SHARING
With a group of three to four share your
information. Compare charts.
Papers are dated and filed.

Recreational Reading

For approximately 30 minutes, all students read books.

CONVERSATIONS
Teacher moves from student to student
having seven to ten minute conversations
about the main idea in a reading passage
or _____.

CLIPBOARD NOTES
Teacher makes notes of discoveries during conversations or _____.

READ-ALOUD BOOK
Continue current selection or _____.

Writing

MINI-LESSON
Discuss modes of transportation or
_____.
Proofreading: run-on sentences

COMPOSING
Write a comparison about two modes of
transportation. Discuss the likenesses and
differences. Or _____.

SHARING
Students read, respond to, and proofread
partner's paper.
Papers are dated and filed.

Word Study

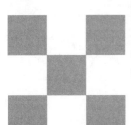

CHART DEVELOPMENT
Spelling Emphasis: _dr_ or _____
Other Emphasis: Time or _____
Resource: Math textbooks or
_____

WRITING
Students write response to chart focus.

SPELLING
Select words to spell, team test, complete
Word Study Record Sheet.
Papers are dated and filed.

HOMEWORK
Share writing and spell words with a
partner.
Notebook signed.

Lesson 27

Research

LEAD-IN
Teacher introduces the Research Project:
Topic and Focus: Occupations/
Reading pictures or _____
Resource: Magazines or _____

RESEARCH PROJECT
Read to locate pictures of people working. List the words or phrases or write sentences about the kinds of work shown in the pictures.

SHARING
With a partner/s share information discovered from pictures.
   Papers are dated and filed.

Recreational Reading

For approximately 30 minutes, all students read books.

CONVERSATIONS
Teacher moves from student to student having seven to ten minute conversations about the main idea in a reading passage or _____.

CLIPBOARD NOTES
Teacher makes notes of discoveries during conversations or _____.

READ-ALOUD BOOK
Awfully Short for the Fourth Grade by Elvira Woodruff or _____

Writing

MINI-LESSON
Discuss the proverb "All work and no play makes Jack a dull boy." Or _____.
   Proofreading: expressing thoughts clearly

COMPOSING
Write your interpretation of the proverb and give an example. Or _____.

SHARING
Students read, respond to, and proofread partner's paper.
   Papers are dated and filed.

Word Study

CHART DEVELOPMENT
Spelling Emphasis: *sw* or _____

Other Emphasis: Occupations/work or _____
Resource: Health or science textbooks or _____

WRITING
Students write response to chart focus.

SPELLING
Select words to spell, team test, complete Word Study Record Sheet.
   Papers are dated and filed.

HOMEWORK
Share writing and spell words with a partner.
   Notebook signed.

Research

LEAD-IN
Teacher introduces the Research Project:
Topic and Focus: Work/Interpreting information in pictures or _____
Resource: Encyclopedias or
_____

RESEARCH PROJECT
Locate pictures of people working and read the captions and/or locate information about one occupation. Write as many facts as you can from the pictures, captions, or articles you read.

SHARING
Read and discuss the information discovered with a self-selected partner.
Papers are dated and filed.

Recreational Reading

For approximately 30 minutes, all students read books of their choice.

CONVERSATIONS
Teacher models reading for first 20 minutes. Teacher invites four or five students at the beginning of the reading time to gather for an oral reading session during the last ten minutes. Each student chooses a selection from a book read previously or one they will read that day. Or _____.

CLIPBOARD NOTES
Teacher records observations made about oral reading fluency or _____.

READ-ALOUD BOOK
Continue current selection or _____.

Writing

MINI-LESSON
Discuss the proverb "One picture is worth a thousand words." Or _____.
Proofreading: expressing ideas clearly

COMPOSING
Write your interpretation of the proverb. Give some examples. Or _____.

SHARING
Students read, respond to, and proofread partner's paper.
Papers are dated and filed.

Word Study

CHART DEVELOPMENT
Spelling Emphasis: *ance* or
_____

Other Emphasis: Language or
_____

Resource: Newspapers or _____

WRITING
Students write response to chart focus.

SPELLING
Select words to spell, team test, complete Word Study Record Sheet.
Papers are dated and filed.

HOMEWORK
Share writing and spell words with a partner.
Notebook signed.

Lesson 29

Research

LEAD-IN
Teacher introduces the Research Project:
Topic and Focus: Technology/
Interpreting information in pictures or
_____

Resource: Magazines or _____

RESEARCH PROJECT
Read to locate pictures showing technology. Write about the technology and how it helps people do work.

SHARING
Read and discuss the information discovered with a self-selected partner.
Papers are dated and filed.

Recreational Reading

For approximately 30 minutes, all students read books.

CONVERSATIONS
Teacher models reading for first 20 minutes. Teacher invites four or five students at the beginning of the reading time to gather for an oral reading session during the last ten minutes. Each student chooses a selection from a book read previously or one they will read that day. Or _____.

CLIPBOARD NOTES
Teacher records observations made about oral reading fluency or _____.

READ-ALOUD BOOK
Continue current selection or _____.

Writing

MINI-LESSON
Discuss the proverb "The best things in life are free." Or _____.
Proofreading: expressing ideas clearly

COMPOSING
Write your interpretation of the proverb and give an example. Or _____.

SHARING
Students read, respond to, and proofread partner's paper.
Papers are dated and filed.

Word Study

CHART DEVELOPMENT
Spelling Emphasis: *dw* or
_____

Other Emphasis: Technology or
_____

Resource: Magazines or _____

WRITING
Students write response to chart focus.

SPELLING
Select words to spell, team test, complete Word Study Record Sheet.
Papers are dated and filed.

HOMEWORK
Share writing and spell words with a partner.
Notebook signed.

Research

LEAD-IN
Teacher introduces the Research Project:
Topic and Focus: Advertising/
Interpreting information in pictures or
_____

Resource: Catalogues of various kinds
or _____

RESEARCH PROJECT
Browse through a catalogue paying attention to the pictures used to invite you to
buy the products advertised. Tell which
articles you would buy and why. Was
your decision influenced by the pictures
or illustrations of the article/s?

SHARING
Compare your list of articles with a part-
ner and your reasons for buying them.
   Papers are dated and filed.

Recreational Reading

For approximately 30 minutes, all students read books.

CONVERSATIONS
Teacher models reading for first 20
minutes. Teacher invites four or five students at the beginning of the reading
time to gather for an oral reading session
during the last ten minutes. Each student
chooses a selection from a book read
previously or one they will read that day.
Or _____.

CLIPBOARD NOTES
Teacher records observations made about
oral reading fluency or _____.

READ-ALOUD BOOK
Continue current selection or _____.

Writing

MINI-LESSON
Discuss the proverb "Business before
pleasure." Or _____.
   Proofreading: Indent for new
paragraphs.

COMPOSING
Write your interpretation of the proverb
and give an example. Or _____.

SHARING
Students read, respond to, and proofread
partner's paper.
   Papers are dated and filed.

Word Study

CHART DEVELOPMENT
Spelling Emphasis: *tw* or
_____

Other Emphasis: Business or
_____

Resource: Newspapers or _____

WRITING
Students write response to chart focus.

SPELLING
Select words to spell, team test, complete
Word Study Record Sheet.
   Papers are dated and filed.

HOMEWORK
Share writing and spell words with a
partner.
   Notebook signed.

133

Lesson 31

Research

LEAD-IN
Teacher introduces the Research Project:
Topic and Focus: Space Exploration/Selecting resources or _____
Resource: A variety including encyclopedias, science textbooks, newspapers, magazines, filmstrips, fiction and nonfiction books relating to topic, maps, charts, pamphlets, photos, or _____

RESEARCH PROJECT
Teacher and students discuss the various resources available. Teacher asks questions: Which resource would you use to find _____? Students write answers. Discuss student responses as a class.

SHARING
This is a class share and discussion day.
Papers are dated and filed.

Recreational Reading

For approximately 30 minutes, all students read books.

CONVERSATIONS
Teacher moves from student to student having two to three minute conversations asking students to identify parts of speech in context of reading or _____.

CLIPBOARD NOTES
Teacher makes notes of discoveries during conversations or _____.

READ-ALOUD BOOK
Continue current selection or _____.

Writing

MINI-LESSON
Editing and revision or _____.
Proofreading: sentence structure, subject/verb agreement, punctuation, and capital letters

COMPOSING
Students will edit and revise writing of their choice. Or _____.

SHARING
Students read, respond to, and proofread partner's paper.
Papers are dated and filed.

Word Study

CHART DEVELOPMENT
Spelling Emphasis: *tw* or _____

Other Emphasis: Astronomy or _____

Resource: Science textbooks or _____

WRITING
Students write response to chart focus.

SPELLING
Select words to spell, team test, complete Word Study Record Sheet.
Papers are dated and filed.

HOMEWORK
Share writing and spell words with a partner.
Notebook signed.

Lesson **32**

Research

LEAD-IN
Teacher introduces the Research Project:
Topic and Focus: Space Explora-
tion/Selecting the correct resource or
_____

Resource: Resources vary; selected by
students. Or _____

RESEARCH PROJECT
Students read to locate information pertaining to the topic. Write the information discovered, the reference used, and
why it was selected.

SHARING
Students share information learned with
a partner.
   Papers are dated and filed.

Recreational Reading

For approximately 30 minutes, all students read books.

CONVERSATIONS
Teacher moves from student to student
having two to three minute conversations
asking students to identify parts of
speech in context of reading or
_____.

CLIPBOARD NOTES
Teacher makes notes of discoveries during conversations or _____.

READ-ALOUD BOOK
Onion John by Joseph Krumgold or
_____

Writing

MINI-LESSON
Editing and revision begun in previous
lesson continues. Or _____.
   Proofreading: same as previous lesson

COMPOSING
Students complete the editing and revision of writing.

SHARING
Students read, respond to, and proofread
partner's paper.
   Papers are dated and filed.

Word Study

CHART DEVELOPMENT
Spelling Emphasis: *cl* or _____
Other Emphasis: Energy or
_____

Resource: Any textbook or _____

WRITING
Students write response to chart focus.

SPELLING
Select words to spell, team test, complete
Word Study Record Sheet.
   Papers are dated and filed.

HOMEWORK
Share writing and spell words with a
partner.
   Notebook signed.

Lesson 33

Research

LEAD-IN
Teacher introduces the Research Project:
Topic and Focus: Solar System/
Selecting the correct reference or
_____

Resource: Varied; selected by students. Or _____

RESEARCH PROJECT
Students work in groups of three or four. Each group decides on a subtopic of Solar System (e.g., planet Pluto) and writes three to five questions they have about this planet or subtopic. They then decide in which references to look for the answers to their questions. Students read to locate answers and write the answers and reference/pages where information was found.

SHARING
Each group shares information discovered with another group.
    Papers are dated and filed.

Recreational Reading

For approximately 30 minutes, all students read books.

CONVERSATIONS
Teacher moves from student to student having two to three minute conversations asking students to identify parts of speech in context of reading or _____.

CLIPBOARD NOTES
Teacher makes notes of discoveries during conversations or _____.

READ-ALOUD BOOK
Continue current selection or _____.

Writing

MINI-LESSON
Writing dialogue: Frogs. Or _____.
    Proofreading: quotation marks

COMPOSING
Write about your encounter with a speaking frog. Write the conversation that takes place. Or _____.

SHARING
Students read, respond to, and proofread partner's paper.
    Papers are dated and filed.

Word Study

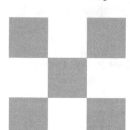

CHART DEVELOPMENT
Spelling Emphasis: tr or _____
Other Emphasis: Senses or
_____

Resource: Food labels or _____

WRITING
Students write response to chart focus.

SPELLING
Select words to spell, team test, complete Word Study Record Sheet.
    Papers are dated and filed.

HOMEWORK
Share writing and spell words with a partner.
    Notebook signed.

Research

LEAD-IN
Teacher introduces the Research Project:
Topic and Focus: Astronauts/
Selecting correct resources or _____
Resource: Varied; selected by students. Or _____

RESEARCH PROJECT
Follow the same format as Lesson 33.

SHARING
Groups share information discovered with another group.
  Papers are dated and filed.

Recreational Reading

For approximately 30 minutes, all students read books.

CONVERSATIONS
Teacher holds seven to ten minute conversations with students checking word attack skills or _____.

CLIPBOARD NOTES
Teacher makes notes about discoveries made during conversations or _____.

READ-ALOUD BOOK
Continue current selection or _____.

Writing

MINI-LESSON
Writing dialogue: being lost. Or
_____.
  Proofreading: use of comma in dialogue

COMPOSING
Write about being lost from parents or being lost on a trip with your parents. Include the conversation which may have taken place. Or _____.

SHARING
Students read, respond to, and proofread partner's paper.
  Papers are dated and filed.

Word Study

CHART DEVELOPMENT
Spelling Emphasis: *wh* or
_____

Other Emphasis: Politics or
_____

Resource: Newspapers or _____

WRITING
Students write response to chart focus.

SPELLING
Select words to spell, team test, complete Word Study Record Sheet.
  Papers are dated and filed.

HOMEWORK
Share writing and spell words with a partner.
  Notebook signed.

Lesson **35**

Research

LEAD-IN
Teacher introduces the Research Project:
Topic and Focus: Space vehicles/
Selecting the correct resource or
_____

Resource: Varied; selected by students. Or _____

RESEARCH PROJECT
Same format as Lesson 33.

SHARING
Groups share with other groups their discovered information.
  Papers are dated and filed.

Recreational Reading

For approximately 30 minutes, all students read books.

CONVERSATIONS
Teacher holds seven to ten minute conversations with students checking word attack skills or _____.

CLIPBOARD NOTES
Teacher makes notes about discoveries made during conversations or _____.

READ-ALOUD BOOK
Continue current selection or _____.

Writing

MINI-LESSON
Writing dialogue: Scary things. Or
_____.
  Proofreading: punctuation of written conversation

COMPOSING
Include conversation in writing about a real or imaginary experience with a scary thing. Or _____.

SHARING
Students read, respond to, and proofread partner's paper.
  Papers are dated and filed.

Word Study

CHART DEVELOPMENT
Spelling Emphasis: *ch* or _____
Other Emphasis: Movies or
_____

Resource: Newspapers or _____

WRITING
Students write response to chart focus.

SPELLING
Select words to spell, team test, complete Word Study Record Sheet.
  Papers are dated and filed.

HOMEWORK
Share writing and spell words with a partner.
  Notebook signed.

Research

LEAD-IN
Teacher introduces the Research Project:
Topic and Focus: Space/Selecting
resources or _____
Resource: Student-selected _____

RESEARCH PROJECT
As a class activity, student categorize on
charts the kinds of information to be
found in the various resources.

SHARING
This is a class sharing lesson.
   Papers are dated and filed.

Recreational Reading

For approximately 30 minutes, all students read books.

CONVERSATIONS
Teacher holds seven to ten minute conversations with students checking word
attack skills or _____.

CLIPBOARD NOTES
Teacher makes notes about discoveries
made during conversations or _____.

READ-ALOUD BOOK
Continue current selection or _____.

Writing

MINI-LESSON
Writing dialogue: Talking trees. Or
_____.
   Proofreading: adjectives

COMPOSING
Write the conversation you might have
with talking trees in a magic forest. Or
_____.

SHARING
Students read, respond to, and proofread
partner's paper.
   Papers are dated and filed.

Word Study

CHART DEVELOPMENT
Spelling Emphasis: *th* or _____
Other Emphasis: Theatre or
_____

Resource: Newspapers or _____

WRITING
Students write response to chart focus.

SPELLING
Select words to spell, team test, complete
Word Study Record Sheet.
   Papers are dated and filed.

HOMEWORK
Share writing and spell words with a
partner.
   Notebook signed.

Lesson **37**

Research

LEAD-IN
Teacher introduces the Research Project:
Topic and Focus: Television person-
alities/Listening skills or _____
Resource: TV Guide or _____

RESEARCH PROJECT
Teacher reads article about a television
personality. Teacher asks factual questions based on the article. Write answers
to the questions asked by teacher.

SHARING
Read and discuss information discovered
with a self-selected partner.
  Papers are dated and filed.

Recreational Reading

For approximately 30 minutes, all students read books.

CONVERSATIONS
Teacher holds seven to ten minute conversations with students checking word
attack skills or _____.

CLIPBOARD NOTES
Teacher makes notes about discoveries
made during conversations or _____.

READ-ALOUD BOOK
Sideways Stories From Wayside School by
Louis Sachar or _____

Writing

MINI-LESSON
Writing dialogue: aliens. Or _____.
  Proofreading: change of paragraph to
show change of speaker.

COMPOSING
Write what you would say in a conversation with a being from another planet. Or
_____.

SHARING
Students read, respond to, and proofread
partner's paper.
  Papers are dated and filed.

Word Study

CHART DEVELOPMENT
Spelling Emphasis: *sh* or _____
Other Emphasis: Crime or
_____

Resource: Magazines or _____

WRITING
Students write response to chart focus.

SPELLING
Select words to spell, team test, complete
Word Study Record Sheet.
  Papers are dated and filed.

HOMEWORK
Share writing and spell words with a
partner.
  Notebook signed.

Research

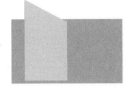

LEAD-IN
Teacher introduces the Research Project:
Topic and Focus: Famous people/
Listening skills or _____
Resource: Biographies, autobiographies, or _____

RESEARCH PROJECT
Teacher reads about a famous person.
Students write questions (with answers)
to ask a partner.

SHARING
Read and discuss information discovered
with a self-selected partner.
    Papers are dated and filed.

Recreational Reading

For approximately 30 minutes, all students read books.

CONVERSATIONS
Teacher holds seven to ten minute conversations with students checking word attack skills or _____.

CLIPBOARD NOTES
Teacher makes notes about discoveries
made during conversations or _____.

READ-ALOUD BOOK
Continue current selection or _____.

Writing

MINI-LESSON
Writing dialogue: pencils. Or _____.
    Proofreading: Indent to show change in
speakers.

COMPOSING
Imagine having a conversation with your
pencil or write a conversation your pencil
might have with a piece of paper. Or
_____.

SHARING
Students read, respond to, and proofread
partner's paper.
    Papers are dated and filed.

Word Study

CHART DEVELOPMENT
Spelling Emphasis: *br* or _____
Other Emphasis: Aviation or
_____
Resource: Newspapers or _____

WRITING
Students write response to chart focus.

SPELLING
Select words to spell, team test, complete
Word Study Record Sheet.
    Papers are dated and filed.

HOMEWORK
Share writing and spell words with a
partner.
    Notebook signed.

Lesson 39

Research

LEAD-IN
Teacher introduces the Research Project:
Topic and Focus: Current Events/
Listening skills or _____
Resource: Newspaper, news magazines, or _____

RESEARCH PROJECT
Teacher reads a current event article.
Students write questions and answers to
ask a partner.

SHARING
Read and discuss information discovered
with a self-selected partner.
Papers are dated and filed.

Recreational Reading

For approximately 30 minutes, all students read books.

CONVERSATIONS
Teacher holds seven to ten minute conversations with students checking word
attack skills or _____.

CLIPBOARD NOTES
Teacher makes notes about discoveries
made during conversations or _____.

READ-ALOUD BOOK
Continue current selection or _____.

Writing

MINI-LESSON
Writing dialogue: editing and revision. Or
_____.
Proofreading: all elements of writing
conversation

COMPOSING
For two days, students will edit and revise a previously begun writing. Or
_____.

SHARING
Students read, respond to, and proofread
partner's paper.
Papers are dated and filed.

Word Study

CHART DEVELOPMENT
Spelling Emphasis: *al* or _____
Other Emphasis: Freedom or
_____
Resource: Social Studies books or
_____

WRITING
Students write response to chart focus.

SPELLING
Select words to spell, team test, complete
Word Study Record Sheet.
Papers are dated and filed.

HOMEWORK
Share writing and spell words with a
partner.
Notebook signed.

Research

LEAD-IN
Teacher introduces the Research Project:
Topic and Focus: Short Stories/
Listening skills or _____
Resource: Basal reading books or
_____

RESEARCH PROJECT
Teacher reads a selected short story. Students answer questions asked by the teacher after story is read.

SHARING
Read and discuss information discovered with a self-selected partner.
    Papers are dated and filed.

Recreational Reading

For approximately 30 minutes, all students read books.

CONVERSATIONS
Teacher holds seven to ten minute conversations with students checking word attack skills or _____.

CLIPBOARD NOTES
Teacher makes notes about discoveries made during conversations or _____.

READ-ALOUD BOOK
Continue current selection or _____.

Writing

MINI-LESSON
Continue editing and revision. Or
_____.
    Proofreading: all elements of writing dialogue.

COMPOSING
Continue to edit and revise. Or
_____.

SHARING
Students read, respond to, and proofread partner's paper.
    Papers are dated and filed.

Word Study

CHART DEVELOPMENT
Spelling Emphasis: *cl* or _____
Other Emphasis: Taxes or
_____
Resource: Magazines, newspapers, or
_____

WRITING
Students write response to chart focus.

SPELLING
Select words to spell, team test, complete Word Study Record Sheet.
    Papers are dated and filed.

HOMEWORK
Share writing and spell words with a partner.
    Notebook signed.

Lesson 41

Research

LEAD-IN
Teacher introduces the Research Project:
Topic and Focus: Animals/
Classifying or _____
Resource: None or _____

RESEARCH PROJECT
For three minutes teacher asks students to brainstorm all the animals they can as he or she writes them on the board. Students then suggest some categories for classifying the animals. Each student writes his or her own classifications.

SHARING
Whole class shares to see the different categories used to classify the list.
Papers are dated and filed.

Recreational Reading

For approximately 30 minutes, all students read books.

CONVERSATIONS
Teacher reads for 20 minutes modeling reading. Book Share: Students volunteer to share something about the books they are reading during the last ten minutes. Or _____.

CLIPBOARD NOTES
Teacher notes who eagerly volunteers and what kinds of books they are reading and who seems interested in the book after the sharing time. Or _____.

READ-ALOUD BOOK
Continue current selection or _____.

Writing

MINI-LESSON
Writing cinquains: Spaghetti. Write a cinquain together as a class about spaghetti. Or _____.
Proofreading: Check for cinquain form.

COMPOSING
Write a cinquain poem about your favorite food or any topic you choose. Or _____.

SHARING
Students read, respond to, and proofread partner's paper.
Papers are dated and filed.

Word Study

CHART DEVELOPMENT
Spelling Emphasis: *ee* or _____
Other Emphasis: Careers or
_____
Resource: Magazines or _____

WRITING
Students write response to chart focus.

SPELLING
Select words to spell, team test, complete Word Study Record Sheet.
Papers are dated and filed.

HOMEWORK
Share writing and spell words with a partner.
Notebook signed.

Research

LEAD-IN
Teacher introduces the Research Project:
Topic and Focus: Animals/
Classifying or _____
Resource: Magazines or _____

RESEARCH PROJECT
Choose a picture with animals in it, and
cut it out. Study the picture carefully.
Classify all items in the picture according
to categories you choose. Work with a
partner.

SHARING
Read and discuss information discovered
with another team.
  Papers are dated and filed.

Recreational Reading

For approximately 30 minutes, all students read books.

CONVERSATIONS
Teacher models reading for 20 minutes.
Book Share: Students volunteer to share
something about the books they are reading during the last ten minutes. Or
_____.

CLIPBOARD NOTES
Teacher notes who eagerly volunteers and
what kinds of books they are reading and
who seems interested in the book after
the sharing time. Or _____.

READ-ALOUD BOOK
Jumanji by Chris Van Allsburg or
_____

Writing

MINI-LESSON
Writing haiku. Discuss nature. Write a
haiku poem together as a class about
something in nature. Or _____.
  Proofreading: correct haiku form

COMPOSING
Write a haiku about something in nature
or a topic of your choice. Or _____.

SHARING
Students read, respond to, and proofread
partner's paper.
  Papers are dated and filed.

Word Study

CHART DEVELOPMENT
Spelling Emphasis: *y* or _____
Other Emphasis: Music or

_____
Resource: Music textbooks, basal
readers, or _____

WRITING
Students write response to chart focus.

SPELLING
Select words to spell, team test, complete
Word Study Record Sheet.
  Papers are dated and filed.

HOMEWORK
Share writing and spell words with a
partner.
  Notebook signed.

Lesson 43

Research

LEAD-IN
Teacher introduces the Research Project:
Topic and Focus: Animals/
Classifying or _____
Resource: Reference materials and
textbooks or _____

RESEARCH PROJECT
Students working in groups of three or
four list different habitats of animals.
Read to locate names of as many animals
as possible or take previous list and classify according to habitat.

SHARING
Read and discuss information with an-
other team.
   Papers are dated and filed.

Recreational Reading

For approximately 30 minutes, all students read books.

CONVERSATIONS
Teacher moves from student to student
having two to three minute conversations
about recognizing dialogue in the book
they are reading. Or _____.

CLIPBOARD NOTES
Teacher makes notes about discoveries
during conversations or _____.

READ-ALOUD BOOK
A House for Hermit Crab by Eric Carle or
_____

Writing

MINI-LESSON
Discuss "country life" or being outdoors.
Discuss free verse: no rhyme or meter. Or
_____.
   Proofreading: Capitalize each line of
poetry.

COMPOSING
Write a poem in free verse about "country
life," outdoor adventures, or a topic of
your choice. Or _____.

SHARING
Students read, respond to, and proofread
partner's paper.
   Papers are dated and filed.

Word Study

CHART DEVELOPMENT
Spelling Emphasis: *i* or _____
Other Emphasis: Medicine or
_____
Resource: Newspapers or _____

WRITING
Students write response to chart focus.

SPELLING
Select words to spell, team test, complete
Word Study Record Sheet.
   Papers are dated and filed.

HOMEWORK
Share writing and spell words with a
partner.
   Notebook signed.

Lesson 44

Research

LEAD-IN
Teacher introduces the Research Project:
Topic and Focus: Animals/Classifying
or _____
Resource: Fiction books or _____

RESEARCH PROJECT
Students read to locate animal characters
they can classify as make-believe or real.

SHARING
Read and discuss information with a self-
selected partner.
Papers are dated and filed.

Recreational Reading

For approximately 30 minutes, all students read books.

CONVERSATIONS
Teacher moves from student to student
having two to three minute conversations-
about recognizing dialogue in the book
they are reading or _____.

CLIPBOARD NOTES
Teacher makes notes about discoveries
during conversations or _____.

READ-ALOUD BOOK
Animals, Animals by Eric Carle or
_____

Writing

MINI-LESSON
Discuss animals as a topic for limericks.
Discuss humor, nonsense, and limericks.
Or _____.
Proofreading: correct rhyme and rhythm
in limericks

COMPOSING
Write a limerick about an animal or topic
of your choice. Or _____.

SHARING
Students read, respond to, and proofread
partner's paper.
Papers are dated and filed.

Word Study

CHART DEVELOPMENT
Spelling Emphasis: *e* or _____
Other Emphasis: Comedy or

_____
Resource: Magazines or _____

WRITING
Students write response to chart focus.

SPELLING
Select words to spell, team test, complete
Word Study Record Sheet.
Papers are dated and filed.

HOMEWORK
Share writing and spell words with a
partner.
Notebook signed.

Lesson 45

Research

LEAD-IN
Teacher introduces the Research Project:
Topic and Focus: Animals/Classifying
or _____
Resource: Reference books, textbooks,
or _____

RESEARCH PROJECT
Use a previous list of animals or write a
new one to classify animals by the foods
they eat.

SHARING
Read and discuss information discovered
with a self-selected partner.
 Papers are dated and filed.

Recreational Reading

For approximately 30 minutes, all students read books.

CONVERSATIONS
Teacher moves from student to student
having two to three minute conversations
about recognizing dialogue in the book
they are reading or _____.

CLIPBOARD NOTES
Teacher makes notes about discoveries
during conversations or _____.

READ-ALOUD BOOK
The Velveteen Rabbit by Margery Wil-
liams or _____

Writing

MINI-LESSON
Introduce couplets. Discuss seasons of the
year. Write one or more couplets on board
with students. Or _____.
 Proofreading: couplet form; rhyming
words

COMPOSING
Write couplets about seasons or topic of
your choice. Or _____.

SHARING
Students read, respond to, and proofread
partner's paper.
 Papers are dated and filed.

Word Study

CHART DEVELOPMENT
Spelling Emphasis: *a* or _____
Other Emphasis: Government or

_____
Resource: Social Studies textbooks or
_____

WRITING
Students write response to chart focus.

SPELLING
Select words to spell, team test, complete
Word Study Record Sheet.
 Papers are dated and filed.

HOMEWORK
Share writing and spell words with a
partner.
 Notebook signed.

Research

LEAD-IN
Teacher introduces the Research Project:
Topic and Focus: Sports/Notetaking
or _____
Resource: Newspapers, Language text-book section on notetaking, or _____

RESEARCH PROJECT
Students select a favorite sport and locate information. Write important or interesting information in own words. Words, phrases, or sentences are acceptable.

SHARING
Tell your partner the most interesting thing you learned from reading about your selected sport using only your notes.
Papers are dated and filed.

Recreational Reading

For approximately 30 minutes, all students read books.

CONVERSATIONS
Teacher moves from student to student having seven to ten minute conversations to determine students' comprehension of reading selections or _____.

CLIPBOARD NOTES
Teacher takes notes related to comprehension skills or _____.

READ-ALOUD BOOK
Continue current selection or _____.

Writing

MINI-LESSON
Discuss "A Special Gift." Read aloud some poems to illustrate rhythm in poetry. Or
_____.
Proofreading: use of adjectives to describe emotions

COMPOSING
Write a poem of four or more lines telling of a special gift or special time. Or
_____.

SHARING
Students read, respond to, and proofread partner's paper.
Papers are dated and filed.

Word Study

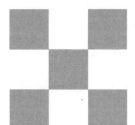

CHART DEVELOPMENT
Spelling Emphasis: *o* or _____
Other Emphasis: Health or

_____
Resource: Magazines or _____

WRITING
Students write response to chart focus.

SPELLING
Select words to spell, team test, complete Word Study Record Sheet.
Papers are dated and filed.

HOMEWORK
Share writing and spell words with a partner.
Notebook signed.

Lesson 47

Research

LEAD-IN
Teacher introduces the Research Project:
Topic and Focus: Sports/Notetaking
or _____
Resource: Autobiography or biography
about a sports celebrity. Or _____

RESEARCH PROJECT
Find out about early life and how person
got started in sports. Record dates and
key words.

SHARING
Tell your partner about the sport
celebrity's early life using only the notes:
key words or phrases you wrote.
    Papers are dated and filed.

Recreational Reading

For approximately 30 minutes, all students read books.

CONVERSATIONS
Teacher moves from student to student
having seven to ten minute conversations
to determine students' comprehension of
reading selections or _____.

CLIPBOARD NOTES
Teacher takes notes related to comprehension skills or _____.

READ-ALOUD BOOK
Baseball Fever by Johanna Hurwitz or
_____

Writing

MINI-LESSON
Discuss picture or shape poems. Share
poems whose shape or form lends to the
title or theme of the poem. (For example,
kites) Or _____.
    Proofreading: use of similes

COMPOSING
Write a poem about a topic you choose in
a certain shape or picture that helps illustrate your title or subject. Or
_____.

SHARING
Students read, respond to, and proofread
partner's paper.
    Papers are dated and filed.

Word Study

CHART DEVELOPMENT
Spelling Emphasis: *u* or _____
Other Emphasis: Food or _____
Resource: Health textbooks or
_____

WRITING
Students write response to chart focus.

SPELLING
Select words to spell, team test, complete
Word Study Record Sheet.
    Papers are dated and filed.

HOMEWORK
Share writing and spell words with a
partner.
    Notebook signed.

Research

LEAD-IN
Teacher introduces the Research Project:
Topic and Focus: Sports/Notetaking
or _____
Resource: Magazines (preferably
sports magazines) or _____

RESEARCH PROJECT
Continue to find information about the
same sport or celebrity as before, or research another. Record recent important
events with the sport or celebrity.

SHARING
Tell your partner about recent events in
the life of the celebrity or something exciting about the sport you read about.
    Papers are dated and filed.

Recreational Reading

For approximately 30 minutes, all students read books.

CONVERSATIONS
Teacher moves from student to student
having seven to ten minute conversations
to determine students' comprehension of
reading selections or _____.

CLIPBOARD NOTES
Teacher takes notes related to comprehension skills or _____.

READ-ALOUD BOOK
Continue current selection or _____.

Writing

MINI-LESSON
Discuss "a pet elephant." Read Ogden
Nash's "The Leopard," "Hippopotamus,"
"A Purple Cow," or other humorous po-
etry. Or _____.
    Proofreading: Each line is capitalized.

COMPOSING
Write a humorous poem entitled "A Pet
_____" or one about a topic of your
choice. Or _____.

SHARING
Students read, respond to, and proofread
partner's paper.
    Papers are dated and filed.

Word Study

CHART DEVELOPMENT
Spelling Emphasis: *aw* or
_____
Other Emphasis: Disease or
_____
Resource: Newspapers or _____

WRITING
Students write response to chart focus.

SPELLING
Select words to spell, team test, complete
Word Study Record Sheet.
    Papers are dated and filed.

HOMEWORK
Share writing and spell words with a
partner.
    Notebook signed.

Lesson 49

Research

LEAD-IN
Teacher introduces the Research Project:
Topic and Focus: Sports/Notetaking
or _____
Resource: Encyclopedia or _____

RESEARCH PROJECT
Locate information about how a sport is played. Write important words and phrases to help you remember how the game or sport is played.

SHARING
Tell a partner how to play the sport you read about using your notes only.
Papers are dated and filed.

Recreational Reading

For approximately 30 minutes, all students read books.

CONVERSATIONS
Teacher moves from student to student having seven to ten minute conversations to determine students' comprehension of reading selections or _____.

CLIPBOARD NOTES
Teacher takes notes related to comprehension skills or _____.

READ-ALOUD BOOK
Continue current selection or _____.

Writing

MINI-LESSON
Read all poems written. Edit any you wish. Select one to share with group. Or _____.

Proofreading: all poetry form and spelling correct

COMPOSING
Make any corrections on poems already written. Or _____.

SHARING
Students in groups of four or five share their selected poem and others respond.
Papers are dated and filed.

Word Study

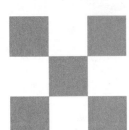

CHART DEVELOPMENT
Spelling Emphasis: *qu* or _____

Other Emphasis: Poverty or _____

Resource: Newspapers or _____

WRITING
Students write response to chart focus.

SPELLING
Select words to spell, team test, complete Word Study Record Sheet.
Papers are dated and filed.

HOMEWORK
Share writing and spell words with a partner.
Notebook signed.

Lesson 50

Research

Ten-day Research Project

LEAD-IN
Teacher introduces the Research Project:
Topic and Focus: Countries/Locating and organizing information or _____
Resource: Students will be selecting references. Or _____

RESEARCH PROJECT
Students brainstorm countries of the world they might like to learn more about. After three or four minutes, ask students to decide among ten to twelve countries the one they would like to research. Ask students to work in teams of three or four for this project. Teams decide what they want to know about the country and where they might locate the information.

SHARING
This entire lesson is a sharing lesson.
  Papers are dated and filed.

Recreational Reading

For approximately 30 minutes, all students read books.

CONVERSATIONS
Teacher moves from student to student having seven to ten minute conversations to determine students' comprehension of reading selections or _____.

CLIPBOARD NOTES
Teacher takes notes related to comprehension skills or _____.

READ-ALOUD BOOK
Continue current selection or _____.

Writing

MINI-LESSON
Selecting a poem for class poetry booklet or for a bulletin board display. Or

_____.
  Proofreading: any corrections in grammar, spelling, or form that should be made

COMPOSING
Rewrite selected poem for publication in class poetry booklet or for display on bulletin board. Or _____.

SHARING
Students read, respond to, and proofread partner's paper.
  Papers are dated and filed.

Word Study

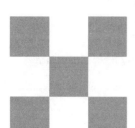

CHART DEVELOPMENT
Spelling Emphasis: er or _____
Other Emphasis: Wealth or

_____

Resource: Magazines or _____

WRITING
Students write response to chart focus.

SPELLING
Select words to spell, team test, complete Word Study Record Sheet.
  Papers are dated and filed.

HOMEWORK
Share writing and spell words with a partner.
  Notebook signed.

Lesson 51

Research

LEAD-IN
Teacher introduces the Research Project:
Topic and Focus: Countries/Organizing information or _____
Resource: Students begin to select the resources they will use. Teacher might suggest starting with encyclopedia. Or _____

RESEARCH PROJECT
Students read from encyclopedias or other selected references to locate information about their country.

SHARING
Groups meet and students share and discuss information found. Students begin to organize their information under topics such as customs, location, early history, etc.
Papers are dated and filed.

Recreational Reading

For approximately 30 minutes, all students read books.

CONVERSATIONS
Teacher moves from student to student having seven to ten minute conversations to determine students' comprehension of reading selections or _____.

CLIPBOARD NOTES
Teacher takes notes related to comprehension skills or _____.

READ-ALOUD BOOK
Continue current selection or _____.

Writing

MINI-LESSON
Letters of invitation. Or _____.
Proofreading: comma after greeting and closing

COMPOSING
Draw a name of a classmate from a box. Write an invitation to a party in letter form. Or _____.

SHARING
Students read, respond to, and proofread partner's paper.
Papers are dated and filed.

Word Study

CHART DEVELOPMENT
Spelling Emphasis: *in* or _____
Other Emphasis: Literature or _____

Resource: Magazines or _____

WRITING
Students write response to chart focus.

SPELLING
Select words to spell, team test, complete Word Study Record Sheet.
Papers are dated and filed.

HOMEWORK
Share writing and spell words with a partner.
Notebook signed.

Research

LEAD-IN
Teacher introduces the Research Project:
Topic and Focus: Countries/Organizing information or _____
Resource: Varies according to student selection. Or _____

RESEARCH PROJECT
Students continue to read from selected resources information about their country.

SHARING
Even though group members are reading and writing independently, it is important to share each day what they are discovering and to make a plan for locating additional information about the country.
  Papers are dated and filed.

Recreational Reading

For approximately 30 minutes, all students read books.

CONVERSATIONS
Teacher moves from student to student having seven to ten minute conversations to determine students' comprehension of reading selections or _____.

CLIPBOARD NOTES
Teacher takes notes related to comprehension skills or _____.

READ-ALOUD BOOK
My Place by Nadia Wheatley and Donna Rawlins or _____

Writing

MINI-LESSON
Letters of reply to invitations. Or
_____.
  Proofreading: use of commas to separate city, state, day, and year

COMPOSING
Deliver invitations written in previous lesson to classmate. Write your response to invitation received. Or _____.

SHARING
Students read, respond to, and proofread partner's paper.
  Papers are dated and filed.

Word Study

CHART DEVELOPMENT
Spelling Emphasis: *ur* or _____
Other Emphasis: Geography or _____

Resource: Atlas, maps, Social Studies books, or _____

WRITING
Students write response to chart focus.

SPELLING
Select words to spell, team test, complete Word Study Record Sheet.
  Papers are dated and filed.

HOMEWORK
Share writing and spell words with a partner.
  Notebook signed.

Lesson **53**

Research

LEAD-IN
Teacher introduces the Research Project:
Topic and Focus: Countries/Organizing information or _____
Resource: Student-selected or
_____

RESEARCH PROJECT
Students continue to read to gather information on their country.

SHARING
Groups should come together, share, and discuss information discovered. Continue to organize information by topics.
Papers are dated and filed.

Recreational Reading

For approximately 30 minutes, all students read books.

CONVERSATIONS
Teacher models reading for first 20 minutes. Teacher invites four or five students at the beginning of the reading time to gather for an oral reading session during the last ten minutes. Each student chooses a selection from a book read previously or one they will read that day. Or _____.

CLIPBOARD NOTES
Teacher records observations made about oral reading fluency or _____.

READ-ALOUD BOOK
Continue current selection or _____.

Writing

MINI-LESSON
Friendly letters to relatives. Or
_____.
Proofreading: use of periods after *Mr.,
Mrs., Dr.,* etc.

COMPOSING
Through your letter to a selected relative, share what is happening in your life as it relates to school and home. Or
_____.

SHARING
Students read, respond to, and proofread partner's paper.
Papers are dated and filed.

Word Study

CHART DEVELOPMENT
Spelling Emphasis: *ir* or _____
Other Emphasis: Love or _____
Resource: Student-selected book or
_____

WRITING
Students write response to chart focus.

SPELLING
Select words to spell, team test, complete Word Study Record Sheet.
Papers are dated and filed.

HOMEWORK
Share writing and spell words with a partner.
Notebook signed.

Research

LEAD-IN
Teacher introduces the Research Project:
Topic and Focus: Countries/Organizing information or _____
Resource: Varies according to student selection. Or _____

RESEARCH PROJECT
This is the final day for reading to locate information about the selected country. Students should complete the information collection and organizing.

SHARING
As students share the information discovered, they will be organizing by topics.
Papers are dated and filed.

Recreational Reading

For approximately 30 minutes, all students read books.

CONVERSATIONS
Teacher models reading for first 20 minutes. Teacher invites four or five students at the beginning of the reading time to gather for an oral reading session during the last ten minutes. Each student chooses a selection from a book read previously or one they will read that day. Or _____.

CLIPBOARD NOTES
Teacher records observations made about oral reading fluency or _____.

READ-ALOUD BOOK
The Keeping Quilt by Patricia Polacco or _____

Writing

MINI-LESSON
Letter expressing thanks for gifts. Or _____.
    Proofreading: punctuation in a friendly letter

COMPOSING
In a letter, write to thank someone for a gift you have received or would like to receive. Or _____.

SHARING
Students read, respond to, and proofread partner's paper.
Papers are dated and filed.

Word Study

CHART DEVELOPMENT
Spelling Emphasis: *ss* or _____
Other Emphasis: Furniture or _____

Resource: Catalogues or magazines or _____

WRITING
Students write response to chart focus.

SPELLING
Select words to spell, team test, complete Word Study Record Sheet.
Papers are dated and filed.

HOMEWORK
Share writing and spell words with a partner.
Notebook signed.

Lesson **55**

Research

LEAD-IN
Teacher introduces the Research Project:
Topic and Focus: Countries/Planning presentations or _____
Resource: Teacher, group members, and any pages from a Language Arts book giving information about how to do effective reports and presentations may be assigned for reading. Or _____.

RESEARCH PROJECT
Working together, students will develop the plan for their presentation to the class. The information they have discovered may be presented in many different ways.

SHARING
Planning and discussing how the report will be presented and which group members will be responsible for what will take most of this period.
   Papers are dated and filed.

Recreational Reading

For approximately 30 minutes, all students read books.

CONVERSATIONS
Teacher models reading for first 20 minutes. Teacher invites four or five students at the beginning of the reading time to gather for an oral reading session during the last ten minutes. Each student chooses a selection from a book read previously or one they will read that day. Or _____.

CLIPBOARD NOTES
Teacher records observations made about oral reading fluency or _____.

READ-ALOUD BOOK
Mufaro's Beautiful Daughters by John Steptoe or _____

Writing

MINI-LESSON
Sharing information about school with students in other countries. Or _____.
   Proofreading: use of contractions

COMPOSING
Begin a letter that will share with a student from another country what your school life is like. Or _____.

SHARING
Students read, respond to, and proofread partner's paper.
   Papers are dated and filed.

Word Study

CHART DEVELOPMENT
Spelling Emphasis: *ment* or _____

Other Emphasis: Seasons or _____

Resource: Science textbooks or _____

WRITING
Students write response to chart focus.

SPELLING
Select words to spell, team test, complete Word Study Record Sheet.
   Papers are dated and filed.

HOMEWORK
Share writing and spell words with a partner.
   Notebook signed.

Research

LEAD-IN
Teacher introduces the Research Project:
Topic and Focus: Countries/Planning presentations or _____
Resource: Varies according to student selection. Or _____

RESEARCH PROJECT
Students gather the materials needed to do the group presentation. Groups will be doing different tasks depending on the nature of their presentation. Encourage creative approaches and assist when appropriate. Much learning will take place through discovery of what works and what does not work.

SHARING
Groups should come together at the end of this time to assess their progress and develop plan for next day's work.
Papers are dated and filed.

Recreational Reading

For approximately 30 minutes, all students read books.

CONVERSATIONS
Teacher moves from student to student having two to three minute conversations about locating prefixes and suffixes from reading selection. Discuss word meanings. Or _____.

CLIPBOARD NOTES
Teacher makes notes about discoveries during conversations or _____.

READ-ALOUD BOOK
Invincible Louisa by Cornelia Meigs or _____

Writing

MINI-LESSON
Continue discussion from previous lesson. Or _____.
Proofreading: use of descriptive words to give best picture

COMPOSING
Continue the letter begun in previous lesson. Or _____.

SHARING
Students read, respond to, and proofread partner's paper.
Papers are dated and filed.

Word Study

CHART DEVELOPMENT
Spelling Emphasis: *milli* or _____

Other Emphasis: Mathematics or _____

Resource: Math textbooks or _____

WRITING
Students write response to chart focus.

SPELLING
Select words to spell, team test, complete Word Study Record Sheet.
Papers are dated and filed.

HOMEWORK
Share writing and spell words with a partner.
Notebook signed.

Lesson 57

Research

LEAD-IN
Teacher introduces the Research Project:
Topic and Focus: Countries/Group work or _____
Resource: _____

RESEARCH PROJECT
Groups work on reports. Each group will submit two questions to be answered in their report. These questions should be put on a chart by the teacher or students. This is a good time for teacher observation.

SHARING
Even though group members may be working independently on parts of the presentation, each day they should come together to assess progress and plan for next day.
Papers are dated and filed.

Recreational Reading

For approximately 30 minutes, all students read books.

CONVERSATIONS
Teacher moves from student to student having two to three minute conversations about locating prefixes and suffixes in reading selection. Discuss word meanings. Or _____.

CLIPBOARD NOTES
Teacher makes notes about discoveries during conversations or _____.

READ-ALOUD BOOK
Continue current selection or _____.

Writing

MINI-LESSON
Letters to the editor expressing one's view and ideas for solutions to local problems. Or _____.
Proofreading: use of *and, but,* and *or*

COMPOSING
Each student identifies a problem or situation they want to respond to in a letter to the editor of the local paper. Or _____.

SHARING
Students read, respond to, and proofread partner's paper.
Papers are dated and filed.

Word Study

CHART DEVELOPMENT
Spelling Emphasis: *ty* or _____
Other Emphasis: Entertainment or _____

Resource: TV Guide, entertainment section of newspapers, or _____

WRITING
Students write response to chart focus.

SPELLING
Select words to spell, team test, complete Word Study Record Sheet.
Papers are dated and filed.

HOMEWORK
Share writing and spell words with a partner.
Notebook signed.

Research

LEAD-IN
Teacher introduces the Research Project:
Topic and Focus: Countries/Group
work, making reports or _____
Resource: _____

RESEARCH PROJECT
Groups complete reports and begin
presentations. Presentations may take
several days depending on the time al-
loted for each report.

SHARING
As students share the information discovered through their presentations, others
listen and respond by identifying
strengths of the presentation and suggesting improvements.
   Papers are dated and filed.

Recreational Reading

For approximately 30 minutes, all students read books.

CONVERSATIONS
Teacher moves from student to student
having two to three minute conversations
about locating prefixes and suffixes in
reading selection. Discuss word meanings.
Or _____.

CLIPBOARD NOTES
Teacher makes notes about discoveries
during conversations or _____.

READ-ALOUD BOOK
Continue current selection or _____.

Writing

MINI-LESSON
Review letter writing. Or _____.
   Proofreading: forms and punctuation in
letters

COMPOSING
Choice: Edit and revise a letter written in
a previous lesson or write a new letter to
anyone about topic of your choice. Or
_____.

SHARING
Students read, respond to, and proofread
partner's paper.
   Papers are dated and filed.

Word Study

CHART DEVELOPMENT
Spelling Emphasis: *un* or
_____
Other Emphasis: Failure or
_____
Resource: Teacher-selected or
_____

WRITING
Students write response to chart focus.

SPELLING
Select words to spell, team test, complete
Word Study Record Sheet.
   Papers are dated and filed.

HOMEWORK
Share writing and spell words with a
partner.
   Notebook signed.

Lesson 59

Research

LEAD-IN
Teacher introduces the Research Project:
Topic and Focus: Countries/Making
reports or _____
Resource: _____

RESEARCH PROJECT
Reports continue as begun in previous
lesson. If an additional day was needed
for preparation, then reports begin today.
Students are listening to presentations
and responding. When reports are completed, class answers questions from the
charts.

SHARING
This entire period is a whole class sharing lesson.
    Papers are dated and filed.

Recreational Reading

For approximately 30 minutes, all students read books.

CONVERSATIONS
Teacher has seven to ten minute conversations with students to discuss author's
purpose, point of view, and tone related
to book student is reading or _____.

CLIPBOARD NOTES
Teacher takes notes about students' interpretive skills or _____.

READ-ALOUD BOOK
Continue current selection or _____.

Writing

MINI-LESSON
Continue previous day's lesson. Or
_____.
    Proofreading: forms and punctuation of
letters

COMPOSING
Continue writing, editing, and revision
begun in previous lesson. Or _____.

SHARING
Students read, respond to, and proofread
partner's paper.
    Papers are dated and filed.

Word Study

CHART DEVELOPMENT
Spelling Emphasis: *ish* or
_____

Other Emphasis: Strength or
_____

Resource: Recreational Reading book
or _____

WRITING
Students write response to chart focus.

SPELLING
Select words to spell, team test, complete
Word Study Record Sheet.
    Papers are dated and filed.

HOMEWORK
Share writing and spell words with a
partner.
    Notebook signed.

Research

Five-day integrated lessons: Reading and literacy

LEAD-IN
Teacher introduces the Research Project:
Topic and Focus: Reading and literacy/Interviews or _____
Resource: Classmates and other persons or _____

RESEARCH PROJECT
Students in small groups discuss reading and literacy: their meaning and importance. Plan the questions to be asked in interviews with classmates or other persons to determine how they feel about the importance of reading, what it means to be literate, and/or other things students want to learn about reading and literacy.

SHARING
Read and discuss information discovered with a self-selected partner.
Papers are dated and filed.

Recreational Reading

For approximately 30 minutes, all students read books.

CONVERSATIONS
Teacher has seven to ten minute conversations with students to discuss author's purpose, point of view, and tone related to book student is reading or _____.

CLIPBOARD NOTES
Teacher takes notes about students' interpretive skills or _____.

READ-ALOUD BOOK
Continue current selection or _____.

Writing

MINI-LESSON
Discuss diaries as records of one's thoughts and reactions, the use of a diary to react and respond to what you are reading during Recreational Reading. Or

_____.
  Proofreading: use of commas in series

COMPOSING
Write your thoughts and reactions to what you read yesterday or today during Recreational Reading. Or _____.

SHARING
Students read, respond to, and proofread partner's paper.
Papers are dated and filed.

Word Study

CHART DEVELOPMENT
Spelling Emphasis: *tion* or

_____

Other Emphasis: Unfamiliar words or _____
Resource: Recreational Reading book or _____

WRITING
Students write response to chart focus.

SPELLING
Select words to spell, team test, complete Word Study Record Sheet.
Papers are dated and filed.

HOMEWORK
Share writing and spell words with a partner.
Notebook signed.

Lesson **61**

Research

LEAD-IN
Teacher introduces the Research Project:
Topic and Focus: Reading and literacy/Interviews or _____
Resource: Using the interview design from previous lesson, students in pairs should interview each other. Or _____

RESEARCH PROJECT
Listening replaces reading in this series of lessons. Note key words and phrases. After the interview, use these to write the report of the information you discovered.

SHARING
Read and discuss information discovered with a self-selected partner.
Papers are dated and filed.

Recreational Reading

For approximately 30 minutes, all students read books.

CONVERSATIONS
Teacher has seven to ten minute conversations with students to discuss author's purpose, point of view, and tone related to book student is reading or _____.

CLIPBOARD NOTES
Teacher takes notes about students' interpretive skills or _____.

READ-ALOUD BOOK
M. C. Higgins, the Great by Virginia Hamilton or _____

Writing

MINI-LESSON
Discuss characters and their attributes. What is likeable or not likeable about characters in books? Or _____.
Proofreading: adjectives

COMPOSING
Write about the main character from the book you are reading or have read recently. Tell why you do or do not like him or her or continue to write in your diary your reactions or thoughts about what you are reading. Or _____.

SHARING
Students read, respond to, and proofread partner's paper.
Papers are dated and filed.

Word Study

CHART DEVELOPMENT
Spelling Emphasis: *ness* or
_____
Other Emphasis: Unfamiliar words or _____
Resource: Recreational Reading book or _____

WRITING
Students write response to chart focus.

SPELLING
Select words to spell, team test, complete Word Study Record Sheet.
Papers are dated and filed.

HOMEWORK
Share writing and spell words with a partner.
Notebook signed.

Lesson 62

Research

LEAD-IN
Teacher introduces the Research Project:
Topic and Focus: Reading and literacy/Interviews or _____
Resource: Students from another class. Arrange ahead of time to have your students paired with students from another class to continue interviews. Or _____

RESEARCH PROJECT
Listening skills are practiced. Take notes for later use when writing a summary of information discovered through the interview.

SHARING
Read and discuss information discovered with a self-selected partner.
Papers are dated and filed.

Recreational Reading

For approximately 30 minutes, all students read books.

CONVERSATIONS
Teacher has seven to ten minute conversations with students to discuss author's purpose, point of view, and tone related to book student is reading or _____.

CLIPBOARD NOTES
Teacher takes notes about students' interpretive skills or _____.

READ-ALOUD BOOK
Continue current selection or _____.

Writing

MINI-LESSON
Discuss settings. Or _____.
  Proofreading: adjectives

COMPOSING
Describe another setting that you think could replace the one in the book you are reading or continue to write in your diary your reactions and thoughts about what you are reading. Or _____.

SHARING
Students read, respond to, and proofread partner's paper.
Papers are dated and filed.

Word Study

CHART DEVELOPMENT
Spelling Emphasis: *inter* or
_____
Other Emphasis: Unfamiliar words or _____
Resource: Recreational Reading book or _____

WRITING
Students write response to chart focus.

SPELLING
Select words to spell, team test, complete Word Study Record Sheet.
Papers are dated and filed.

HOMEWORK
Share writing and spell words with a partner.
Notebook signed.

Lesson **63**

Research

LEAD-IN
Teacher introduces the Research Project:
Topic and Focus: Reading and literacy/Summarizing information or _____

Resource: Notes and writings from interviews conducted or _____

RESEARCH PROJECT
Read your notes and the writing from each of the two interviews. Begin to write

your conclusions from the interviews based on the questions you asked. If you determine you need to do additional interviews to draw conclusions, ask classmates or parents or other adults if you can interview them before writing your results.

SHARING
Read and discuss information discovered with a self-selected partner.
   Papers are dated and filed.

Recreational Reading

For approximately 30 minutes, all students read books.

CONVERSATIONS
Teacher has seven to ten minute conversations with students to discuss author's purpose, point of view, and tone related to book student is reading or _____.

CLIPBOARD NOTES
Teacher takes notes about students' interpretive skills or _____.

READ-ALOUD BOOK
Continue current selection or _____.

Writing

MINI-LESSON
Making predictions. Or _____.
   Proofreading: words that denote time

COMPOSING
Based on what you have read, what do you think will happen next in the book you are reading? Write this in your diary or continue to write your reactions and thoughts about what you are reading. Or _____.

SHARING
Students read, respond to, and proofread partner's paper.
   Papers are dated and filed.

Word Study

CHART DEVELOPMENT
Spelling Emphasis: *ly* or _____
Other Emphasis: Unfamiliar words or _____
Resource: Recreational Reading book or _____

WRITING
Students write response to chart focus.

SPELLING
Select words to spell, team test, complete Word Study Record Sheet.
   Papers are dated and filed.

HOMEWORK
Share writing and spell words with a partner.
   Notebook signed.

Research

LEAD-IN
Teacher introduces the Research Project:
Topic and Focus: Reading and literacy/Media or _____
Resource: Newspapers and magazines or _____

RESEARCH PROJECT
Find articles or quotes about reading and literacy. Explain how what you read compares with the information you discovered through your interviews.

SHARING
Have a class discussion on reading and literacy and the importance of learning to read and the pleasure of reading.
Papers are dated and filed.

Recreational Reading

For approximately 30 minutes, all students read books.

CONVERSATIONS
Teacher has seven to ten minute conversations with students to discuss author's purpose, point of view, and tone related to book student is reading or _____.

CLIPBOARD NOTES
Teacher takes notes about students' interpretive skills or _____.

READ-ALOUD BOOK
Continue current selection or _____.

Writing

MINI-LESSON
Fact and opinion. Or _____.
Proofreading: beginning sentences with words such as *if, when, after, as*

COMPOSING
In your opinion, is the book you are reading a good book? Tell why or why not. Or _____.

SHARING
Students read, respond to, and proofread partner's paper.
Papers are dated and filed.

Word Study

CHART DEVELOPMENT
Spelling Emphasis: *ing* or
_____
Other Emphasis: Unfamiliar words or _____
Resource: Recreational Reading book or _____

WRITING
Students write response to chart focus.

SPELLING
Select words to spell, team test, complete Word Study Record Sheet.
Papers are dated and filed.

HOMEWORK
Share writing and spell words with a partner.
Notebook signed.

Lesson 65

Research

Six-day Research Project

LEAD-IN
Teacher introduces the Research Project:
Topic and Focus: Students and teacher agree on topic from Science, Social Studies or Health. Example: butterflies. Or _____
Resource: Students begin to collect resources. Or _____

RESEARCH PROJECT
Read to locate interesting information about the topic. Write the important and interesting information about the topic.

SHARING
During the last ten minutes, students volunteer information from their research on the topic to put on a class chart. This chart is developed much like the word study charts.
　Papers are dated and filed.

Recreational Reading

For approximately 30 minutes, all students read books.

CONVERSATIONS
Teacher has seven to ten minute conversations with students to discuss author's purpose, point of view, and tone related to book student is reading or _____.

CLIPBOARD NOTES
Teacher takes notes about students' interpretive skills or _____.

READ-ALOUD BOOK
Continue current selection or _____.

Writing

MINI-LESSON
Writing comparisons: fruits or vegetables/musical instruments. Or _____.
　Proofreading: run-on sentences

COMPOSING
Compare a fruit or vegetable to a musical instrument. Or _____.

SHARING
Students read, respond to, and proofread partner's paper.
　Papers are dated and filed.

Word Study

CHART DEVELOPMENT
Spelling Emphasis: *pre* or

_____

Other Emphasis: Prefixes or

_____

Resource: Newspapers or _____

WRITING
Students write response to chart focus.

SPELLING
Select words to spell, team test, complete Word Study Record Sheet.
　Papers are dated and filed.

HOMEWORK
Share writing and spell words with a partner.
　Notebook signed.

Research

LEAD-IN
Teacher introduces the Research Project:
Topic and Focus: Continue with the same topic selected in previous day's lesson. Or _____
Resource: Resources vary; selected by students. Or _____

RESEARCH PROJECT
Continue to read and locate information pertaining to the topic. Write the information discovered.

SHARING
During the last ten minutes make the second class chart, recording information shared by students.
Papers are dated and filed.

Recreational Reading

For approximately 30 minutes, all students read books.

CONVERSATIONS
Students read for twenty minutes and then have Book Share for last ten minutes. Students volunteer to share something about the book they are reading. Or _____.

CLIPBOARD NOTES
Teacher notes book selections, willingness to share, and students' reading interests. Or _____.

READ-ALOUD BOOK
Socks by Beverly Cleary or _____

Writing

MINI-LESSON
Writing Comparisons: teacher/artist. Or _____.
Proofreading: singular subject/being-verb relationship

COMPOSING
Consider the likenesses and differences of a teacher and an artist. Or _____.

SHARING
Students read, respond to, and proofread partner's paper.
Papers are dated and filed.

Word Study

CHART DEVELOPMENT
Spelling Emphasis: *un* or

_____

Other Emphasis: Prefixes or

_____

Resource: Magazines or _____

WRITING
Students write response to chart focus.

SPELLING
Select words to spell, team test, complete Word Study Record Sheet.
Papers are dated and filed.

HOMEWORK
Share writing and spell words with a partner.
Notebook signed.

Lesson **67**

Research

LEAD-IN
Teacher introduces the Research Project:
Topic and Focus: Topic selected before or _____
Resource: Varied; selected by students. Or _____

RESEARCH PROJECT
Continue reading to locate additional information. Write the information discovered through reading.

SHARING
During the last ten minutes a third class chart is made from information shared by students.
 Papers are dated and filed.

Recreational Reading

For approximately 30 minutes, all students read books.

CONVERSATIONS
Students read for twenty minutes and then have Book Share for last ten minutes. Students volunteer to share something about the book they are reading. Or _____.

CLIPBOARD NOTES
Teacher notes book selections, willingness to share, and students' reading interests. Or _____.

READ-ALOUD BOOK
Continue current selection or _____.

Writing

MINI-LESSON
Writing comparisons: characters in a book. Or _____.
 Proofreading: capital letters and proper punctuation

COMPOSING
Discuss the likenesses and differences of two seasons. Or _____.

SHARING
Students read, respond to, and proofread partner's paper.
 Papers are dated and filed.

Word Study

CHART DEVELOPMENT
Spelling Emphasis: *dis* or
_____
Other Emphasis: Prefixes or
_____
Resource: Textbooks or _____

WRITING
Students write response to chart focus.

SPELLING
Select words to spell, team test, complete Word Study Record Sheet.
 Papers are dated and filed.

HOMEWORK
Share writing and spell words with a partner.
 Notebook signed.

Research

LEAD-IN
Teacher introduces the Research Project:
Topic and Focus: Topic selected before/Categorizing information or _____
Resource: Class charts made with information shared by students from previous three lessons. Or _____

RESEARCH PROJECT
Students read through the information recorded on charts. As a class, categorize the information. (Use different symbols or magic markers to indicate information belonging to various categories.) This will take the entire module time.

SHARING
This is a whole-class sharing time.
  Papers are dated and filed.

Recreational Reading

For approximately 30 minutes, all students read books.

CONVERSATIONS
Teacher moves from student to student having two to three minute conversations locating words with multiple meanings used in reading selection. Or _____.

CLIPBOARD NOTES
Teacher takes note of students' ability to locate examples of multiple-meaning words or _____.

READ-ALOUD BOOK
Continue current selection or _____

Writing

MINI-LESSON
Writing comparisons: computer/human brain. Or _____.
  Proofreading: subject/verb agreement

COMPOSING
Consider the likenesses and differences of a brain and a computer. Or _____.

SHARING
Students read, respond to, and proofread partner's paper.
  Papers are dated and filed.

Word Study

CHART DEVELOPMENT
Spelling Emphasis: *ful* or
_____

Other Emphasis: Suffixes or
_____

Resource: Magazines or _____

WRITING
Students write response to chart focus.

SPELLING
Select words to spell, team test, complete Word Study Record Sheet.
  Papers are dated and filed.

HOMEWORK
Share writing and spell words with a partner.
  Notebook signed.

171

Lesson 69

Research

LEAD-IN
Teacher introduces the Research Project:
Topic and Focus: Topic selected before or _____
Resource: Language textbooks or _____

RESEARCH PROJECT
Begin writing individual reports.

SHARING
Read and discuss information discovered with a self-selected partner.
Papers are dated and filed.

Recreational Reading

For approximately 30 minutes, all students read books.

CONVERSATIONS
Teacher moves from student to student having two to three minute conversations locating words with multiple meanings used in reading selection. Or _____.

CLIPBOARD NOTES
Teacher takes note of students' ability to locate examples of multiple-meaning words or _____.

READ-ALOUD BOOK
Continue current selection or _____.

Writing

MINI-LESSON
Writing comparisons: day/night. Or _____.
Proofreading: adverbs

COMPOSING
Discuss the likenesses and differences of day and night. Or _____.

SHARING
Students read, respond to, and proofread partner's paper.
Papers are dated and filed.

Word Study

CHART DEVELOPMENT
Spelling Emphasis: *ian* or _____

Other Emphasis: Suffixes or _____

Resource: Health textbooks or _____

WRITING
Students write response to chart focus.

SPELLING
Select words to spell, team test, complete Word Study Record Sheet.
Papers are dated and filed.

HOMEWORK
Share writing and spell words with a partner.
Notebook signed.

Research

LEAD-IN
Teacher introduces the Research Project:
Topic and Focus: Topic selected before or _____
Resource: Language textbooks or _____

RESEARCH PROJECT
Students complete their reports.

SHARING
Read and discuss information discovered with a self-selected partner.
    Papers are dated and filed.

Recreational Reading

For approximately 30 minutes, all students read books.

CONVERSATIONS
Teacher moves from student to student having two to three minute conversations locating words with multiple meanings used in reading selection. Or _____.

CLIPBOARD NOTES
Teacher takes note of students' ability to locate examples of multiple-meaning words or _____.

READ-ALOUD BOOK
Continue current selection or _____.

Writing

MINI-LESSON
Editing and revision. Or _____.
    Proofreading: Proofreading foci from previous lessons.

COMPOSING
Editing and revising a selected paper from previous lessons. Or _____.

SHARING
Students read, respond to, and proofread partner's paper.
    Papers are dated and filed.

Word Study

CHART DEVELOPMENT
Spelling Emphasis: *ed* or _____
Other Emphasis: Suffixes or

_____
Resource: Science textbooks or _____

WRITING
Students write response to chart focus.

SPELLING
Select words to spell, team test, complete Word Study Record Sheet.
    Papers are dated and filed.

HOMEWORK
Share writing and spell words with a partner.
    Notebook signed.

Lesson 71

Research

LEAD-IN
Teacher introduces the Research Project:
Topic and Focus: Current topic of study in health or social studies or science/Main idea or _____
Resource: Newspapers or _____

RESEARCH PROJECT
Teacher reads list of related words, and students group words and provide appropriate categorical headings. Students read to find key words that can be added to the lists. Write main idea headings with several items under each heading.

SHARING
Read and discuss information discovered with a self-selected partner.
Papers are dated and filed.

Recreational Reading

For approximately 30 minutes, all students read books.

CONVERSATIONS
Teacher has seven to ten minute conversations with students to determine recognition of paragraph structure; topic sentence (main idea) and supporting details. Or _____.

CLIPBOARD NOTES
Teacher takes note of students' ability to know main ideas and supporting details. Or _____.

READ-ALOUD BOOK
Rascal by Sterling North or _____

Writing

MINI-LESSON
Anger and times when you have felt angry. Or _____.
Proofreading: paragraph development: topic sentence

COMPOSING
Write a paragraph about a time when you have been angry. Or _____.

SHARING
Read, discuss, and proofread paragraphs with partners.
Papers are dated and filed.

Word Study

CHART DEVELOPMENT
Spelling Emphasis: *ous* or
_____
Other Emphasis: Anger or
_____
Resource: Newspapers or _____

WRITING
Students write response to chart focus.

SPELLING
Select words to spell, team test, complete Word Study Record Sheet.
Papers are dated and filed.

HOMEWORK
Share writing and spell words with a partner.
Notebook signed.

Research

LEAD-IN
Teacher introduces the Research Project:
Topic and Focus: Nutrition or current topic of study/Main idea or _____

Resource: Social Studies, Health, or Science textbooks or _____

RESEARCH PROJECT
Read information about topic. Write the main idea of each paragraph.

SHARING
Read and discuss information discovered with a self-selected partner.
Papers are dated and filed.

Recreational Reading

For approximately 30 minutes, all students read books.

CONVERSATIONS
Teacher has seven to ten minute conversations with students to determine recognition of paragraph structure; topic sentence (main idea) and supporting details. Or _____.

CLIPBOARD NOTES
Teacher takes note of students' ability to know main ideas and supporting details. Or _____.

READ-ALOUD BOOK
Continue current selection or _____.

Writing

MINI-LESSON
Foods or Hobbies (class choice). Or _____.
Proofreading: verbs that add _ed_ to form past tense

COMPOSING
Develop at least one paragraph about one of the topics. Or _____.

SHARING
Read, discuss, and proofread with partners.
Papers are dated and filed.

Word Study

CHART DEVELOPMENT
Spelling Emphasis: _un_ or _____

Other Emphasis: Food, hobbies, or _____

Resource: Magazines or _____

WRITING
Students write response to chart focus.

SPELLING
Select words to spell, team test, complete Word Study Record Sheet.
Papers are dated and filed.

HOMEWORK
Share writing and spell words with a partner.
Notebook signed.

Lesson 73

Research

LEAD-IN
Teacher introduces the Research Project:
Topic and Focus: Poetry/Main idea
or _____
Resource: English textbooks or basal
readers or _____

RESEARCH PROJECT
Read several poems. Write the main idea
of each poem in a sentence.

SHARING
Read and discuss information discovered
with a self-selected partner.
    Papers are dated and filed.

Recreational Reading

For approximately 30 minutes, all students read books.

CONVERSATIONS
Teacher has seven to ten minute conversations with students to determine recognition of paragraph structure; topic
sentence (main idea) and supporting details. Or _____.

CLIPBOARD NOTES
Teacher takes note of students' ability to
know main ideas and supporting details.
Or _____.

READ-ALOUD BOOK
Continue current selection or _____.

Writing

MINI-LESSON
Write "Saturday is my favorite day of the
week." Or _____.
    Proofreading: Indent beginning of
paragraph.

COMPOSING
Develop at least one paragraph on your
favorite day of the week. Or _____.

SHARING
Read, discuss, and proofread with
partners.
    Papers are dated and filed.

Word Study

CHART DEVELOPMENT
Spelling Emphasis: *in* or _____
Other Emphasis: Leisure or
_____
Resource: Health textbooks or
_____

WRITING
Students write response to chart focus.

SPELLING
Select words to spell, team test, complete
Word Study Record Sheet.
    Papers are dated and filed.

HOMEWORK
Share writing and spell words with a
partner.
    Notebook signed.

Research

LEAD-IN
Teacher introduces the Research Project:
Topic and Focus: Weather/Main idea
or _____
Resource: Science textbook, news-
papers or _____

RESEARCH PROJECT
Locate information about weather. Write
the main idea of the articles or paragraphs you read.

SHARING
Read and discuss information discovered
with a self-selected partner.
Papers are dated and filed.

Recreational Reading

For approximately 30 minutes, all students read books.

CONVERSATIONS
Teacher has seven to ten minute conversations with students to determine recognition of paragraph structure; topic
sentence (main idea) and supporting details. Or _____.

CLIPBOARD NOTES
Teacher takes note of students' ability to
know main ideas and supporting details.
Or _____.

READ-ALOUD BOOK
Continue current selection or _____.

Writing

MINI-LESSON
Rainy days: developing paragraphs. Or
_____.
Proofreading: Underline topic sentences.

COMPOSING
Develop paragraphs about a rainy day.
Or _____.

SHARING
Read, discuss, and proofread with
partners.
Papers are dated and filed.

Word Study

CHART DEVELOPMENT
Spelling Emphasis: *im* or
_____

Other Emphasis: Weather or
_____

Resource: Basal readers or
_____

WRITING
Students write response to chart focus.

SPELLING
Select words to spell, team test, complete
Word Study Record Sheet.
Papers are dated and filed.

HOMEWORK
Share writing and spell words with a
partner.
Notebook signed.

Lesson 75

Research

LEAD-IN
Teacher introduces the Research Project:
Topic and Focus: Making predictions or _____
Resource: Teacher-selected book or _____

RESEARCH PROJECT
Read a section of a book to the students and let them predict outcomes. Ask students to work in pairs to select and read to each other a section of a book they have read previously. Each student should predict the outcome from the other's book.

SHARING
One team should share their readings/predictions with another team.
  Papers are dated and filed.

Recreational Reading

For approximately 30 minutes, all students read books.

CONVERSATIONS
Teacher has seven to ten minute conversations with students to determine recognition of paragraph structure; topic sentence (main idea) and supporting details. Or _____.

CLIPBOARD NOTES
Teacher takes note of students' ability to know main ideas and supporting details. Or _____.

READ-ALOUD BOOK
Continue current selection or _____

Writing

MINI-LESSON
Movies: developing paragraphs. Or _____.
  Proofreading: Capitalize the first and important words in titles.

COMPOSING
Develop paragraphs about any movie or movies you select.

SHARING
Read, discuss, and proofread with a partner.
  Papers are dated and filed.

Word Study

CHART DEVELOPMENT
Spelling Emphasis: *dis* or _____

Other Emphasis: Movies or _____

Resource: Newspapers or _____

WRITING
Students write response to chart focus.

SPELLING
Select words to spell, team test, complete Word Study Record Sheet.
  Papers are dated and filed.

HOMEWORK
Share writing and spell words with a partner.
  Notebook signed.

Research

LEAD-IN
Teacher introduces the Research Project:
Topic and Focus: Making predictions or _____
Resource: Picture books or _____

RESEARCH PROJECT
Picture books for students to select from should be available. Working in pairs, students read the book together and take turns predicting what will happen on the next pages. *Good Dog Carl* books and *Will's Mammoth* are books you might consider.

SHARING
One team shares with another their favorite picture book.
Papers are dated and filed.

Recreational Reading

For approximately 30 minutes, all students read books.

CONVERSATIONS
Teacher has seven to ten minute conversations with students to determine recognition of paragraph structure; topic sentence (main idea) and supporting details. Or _____.

CLIPBOARD NOTES
Teacher takes note of students' ability to know main ideas and supporting details. Or _____.

READ-ALOUD BOOK
Just So Stories by Rudyard Kipling or _____

Writing

MINI-LESSON
Discuss the importance of mail, postal employees, the post office. Or _____.
Proofreading: Indent for each new paragraph.

COMPOSING
Write paragraphs about any aspect of mail/postage delivery or topic of your choice. Or _____.

SHARING
Read, discuss, and proofread with a partner.
Papers are dated and filed.

Word Study

CHART DEVELOPMENT
Spelling Emphasis: *ld* or _____
Other Emphasis: Postal service/mail or _____
Resource: Newspapers or _____

WRITING
Students write response to chart focus.

SPELLING
Select words to spell, team test, complete Word Study Record Sheet.
Papers are dated and filed.

HOMEWORK
Share writing and spell words with a partner.
Notebook signed.

Lesson 77

Research

LEAD-IN
Teacher introduces the Research Project:
Topic and Focus: Making predictions or _____
Resource: Picture books, comics or _____

RESEARCH PROJECT
Students select picture books and expand previous day's lesson by writing their own scripts, or they locate a comic strip from the newspaper and write the next day's script sequence.

SHARING
Read and discuss information discovered with a self-selected partner.
Papers are dated and filed.

Recreational Reading

For approximately 30 minutes, all students read books.

CONVERSATIONS
Teacher has seven to ten minute conversations with students to determine recognition of paragraph structure; topic sentence (main idea) and supporting details. Or _____.

CLIPBOARD NOTES
Teacher takes note of students' ability to know main ideas and supporting details.

READ-ALOUD BOOK
Continue current selection or _____.

Writing

MINI-LESSON
Discuss forests. Make a list of facts and make-believe things about a forest. Or _____.
Proofreading: proper punctuation

COMPOSING
Write a factual or fictional paper about the forest. Or _____.

SHARING
Read, discuss, and proofread with a partner.
Papers are dated and filed.

Word Study

CHART DEVELOPMENT
Spelling Emphasis: *ga* or _____

Other Emphasis: Forests or _____

Resource: Social studies textbook or _____

WRITING
Students write response to chart focus.

SPELLING
Select words to spell, team test, complete Word Study Record Sheet.
Papers are dated and filed.

HOMEWORK
Share writing and spell words with a partner.
Notebook signed.

Lesson 78

Research

LEAD-IN
Teacher introduces the Research Project:
Topic and Focus: Foods/food advertisements/Making comparisons or
_____

Resource: Newspapers or _____

RESEARCH PROJECT
Read in newspapers to find food advertisements and make comparisons of costs and effect of advertisement. List food item, cost, store you would choose.

SHARING
Compare your list with that of a self-selected partner.
   Papers are dated and filed.

Recreational Reading

For approximately 30 minutes, all students read books.

CONVERSATIONS
Teacher models reading for first 20 minutes. Teacher invites four or five students at the beginning of the reading time to gather for an oral reading session during the last ten minutes. Each student chooses a selection from a book read previously or one they will read that day. Or _____.

CLIPBOARD NOTES
Teacher records observations made about oral reading fluency or _____.

READ-ALOUD BOOK
Continue current selection or _____.

Writing

MINI-LESSON
Discuss "Changing Myself." If I could change, I would be _____. Or
_____.
   Proofreading: use of suffixes *er, est*

COMPOSING
Write a paragraph about physical changes, and one about personality changes. Or _____.

SHARING
Read, discuss, and proofread with a partner.
   Papers are dated and filed.

Word Study

CHART DEVELOPMENT
Spelling Emphasis: *tt* or _____
Other Emphasis: Foods or
_____

Resource: Food ads and labels or
_____

WRITING
Students write response to chart focus.

SPELLING
Select words to spell, team test, complete Word Study Record Sheet.
   Papers are dated and filed.

HOMEWORK
Share writing and spell words with a partner.
   Notebook signed.

Lesson **79**

Research

LEAD-IN
Teacher introduces the Research Project:
Topic and Focus: Population/Making
Comparisons or _____
Resource: Atlases, encyclopedias, or
_____

RESEARCH PROJECT
Read in atlas or encyclopedia to locate information on the population of several states or countries. Make comparison statements about population information.

SHARING
Read and discuss information discovered with a self-selected partner.
  Papers are dated and filed.

Recreational Reading

For approximately 30 minutes, all students read books.

CONVERSATIONS
Teacher models reading for first 20 minutes. Teacher invites four or five students at the beginning of the reading time to gather for an oral reading session during the last ten minutes. Each student chooses a selection from a book read previously or one they will read that day. Or _____.

CLIPBOARD NOTES
Teacher records observations made about oral reading fluency or _____.

READ-ALOUD BOOK
Just So Stories by Rudyard Kipling or _____

Writing

MINI-LESSON
Discuss beauty and what being beautiful means. Read from *Sleeping Ugly* by Jane Yolen. Or _____.
  Proofreading: adjectives that describe feelings

COMPOSING
Write about your thoughts about beauty. Or write the beginning of a story about a beautiful person. Or _____.

SHARING
Read, discuss, and proofread with a group of three or four.
  Papers are dated and filed.

Word Study

CHART DEVELOPMENT
Spelling Emphasis: *la* or _____
Other Emphasis: Populations or _____

Resource: Encyclopedias or _____

WRITING
Students write response to chart focus.

SPELLING
Select words to spell, team test, complete Word Study Record Sheet.
  Papers are dated and filed.

HOMEWORK
Share writing and spell words with a partner.
  Notebook signed.

Research

LEAD-IN
Teacher introduces the Research Project:
Topic and Focus: Advertising/
Making Comparisons or _____
Resource: Newspapers or _____

RESEARCH PROJECT
Read in newspaper to locate display ads
and classified ads. Cut out an example of
each. Compare and contrast. Describe the
purpose of each.

SHARING
Read and discuss information discovered
with a self-selected partner.
   Papers are dated and filed.

Recreational Reading

For approximately 30 minutes, all students read books.

CONVERSATIONS
Teacher models reading for first 20
minutes. Teacher invites four or five students at the beginning of the reading
time to gather for an oral reading session
during the last ten minutes. Each student
chooses a selection from a book read
previously or one they will read that day.
Or _____.

CLIPBOARD NOTES
Teacher records observations made about
oral reading fluency or _____.

READ-ALOUD BOOK
The Stranger by Chris Van Allsburg or
_____

Writing

MINI-LESSON
Editing. Select paper to edit and revise.
Or _____.
   Proofreading: paragraph structure, in-
denting, topic sentences

COMPOSING
Read and begin editing your selected paper. Or _____.

SHARING
Read, discuss, and proofread with selected
partner.
   Papers are dated and filed.

Word Study

CHART DEVELOPMENT
Spelling Emphasis: cc or _____
Other Emphasis: Homes or

_____
Resource: Magazines or _____

WRITING
Students write response to chart focus.

SPELLING
Select words to spell, team test, complete
Word Study Record Sheet.
   Papers are dated and filed.

HOMEWORK
Share writing and spell words with a
partner.
   Notebook signed.

Lesson 81

Research

LEAD-IN
Teacher introduces the Research Project:
Topic and Focus: Inventions/
Drawing conclusions or _____
Resource: Social Studies, Health,
Science textbooks, or _____

RESEARCH PROJECT
Students read to locate information about
inventions and write the conclusion
reached about the contribution this inven-
tion has made.

SHARING
Read and discuss information discovered
with a self-selected partner.
   Papers are dated and filed.

Recreational Reading

For approximately 30 minutes, all students read books.

CONVERSATIONS
Teacher moves from student to student
having two to three minute conversations
about main characters and story plots.

CLIPBOARD NOTES
Teacher makes notes about students'
recognition and identification of plot and
character analysis. Or _____.

READ-ALOUD BOOK
Sounder by William Armstrong or
_____

Writing

MINI-LESSON
This is an editing and revising day. Students select from previous papers the one
they will edit and revise. Or _____.
   Proofreading: paragraph structure, in-
denting, and any other previous proofreading focus

COMPOSING
Students edit and revise selected papers.
Or _____.

SHARING
Read, discuss, and proofread with a
partner.
   Papers are dated and filed.

Word Study

CHART DEVELOPMENT
Spelling Emphasis: *ss* or _____
Other Emphasis: Conversations or

_____
Resource: Books from Recreational
Reading or _____

WRITING
Students write response to chart focus.

SPELLING
Select words to spell, team test, complete
Word Study Record Sheet.
   Papers are dated and filed.

HOMEWORK
Share writing and spell words with a
partner.
   Notebook signed.

Research

LEAD-IN
Teacher introduces the Research Project:
Topic and Focus: Reading and/or
watching TV/Surveys or _____
Resource: Sample surveys (Gallup
poll), TV Guide, or _____

RESEARCH PROJECT
Discuss surveys, how they are conducted,
and their value to decision makers/con-
sumers. Discuss reading and watching
TV. In groups of three or four, students
decide what they want to know, what
questions to ask on the survey (oral or
written), and what to do with the results.

SHARING
Groups share their questions. Design a
survey with the students to be conducted
with either oral or written responses.
Whole class involved in determining the
basic construction of the survey. Some
students may take a different approach or
wish to investigate a different topic. Students begin conducting the survey as
homework.
   Papers are dated and filed.

Recreational Reading

For approximately 30 minutes, all students read books.

CONVERSATIONS
Teacher moves from student to student
having two to three minute conversations
about main characters and story plots. Or
_____.

CLIPBOARD NOTES
Teacher makes notes about students'
recognition and identification of plot and
character analysis. Or _____.

READ-ALOUD BOOK
Continue current selection or _____.

Writing

MINI-LESSON
This is Sharing Day. Teacher and students determine if this is to be whole
class or small groups. Or _____.

COMPOSING
Sharing Day or _____.

SHARING
Sharing Day
   Papers are dated and filed.

Word Study

CHART DEVELOPMENT
Spelling Emphasis: *spl* or
_____
Other Emphasis: Synonyms or
_____
Resource: Textbooks or _____

WRITING
Students write response to chart focus.

SPELLING
Select words to spell, team test, complete
Word Study Record Sheet.
   Papers are dated and filed.

HOMEWORK
Share writing and spell words with a
partner.
   Notebook signed.

Lesson 83

Research

LEAD-IN
Teacher introduces the Research Project:
Topic and Focus: Reading and/or watching TV/Surveys or _____
Resource: Classmates, families, friends, school personnel, or _____

RESEARCH PROJECT
Students continue to work in same group as in previous lesson to look at the results of their surveys. Begin to compile results, draw conclusions, and perhaps take some action.

SHARING
Each group should share summary of information discovered with the class. Continue to conduct the surveys as homework.
Papers are dated and filed.

Recreational Reading

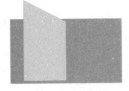

For approximately 30 minutes, all students read books.

CONVERSATIONS
Teacher moves from student to student having two to three minute conversations about main characters and story plots. Or _____.

CLIPBOARD NOTES
Teacher makes notes about students' recognition and identification of plot and character analysis. Or _____.

READ-ALOUD BOOK
Continue current selection or _____.

Writing

MINI-LESSON
Teacher discusses story settings. Students brainstorm topics for a story and discuss possible settings for the story ideas. Or

_____.
Proofreading: descriptive words

COMPOSING
Students begin writing a story about their selected idea and describe in "picture words" the setting for their story. Or
_____.

SHARING
Read, discuss, and proofread with a partner.
Papers are dated and filed.

Word Study

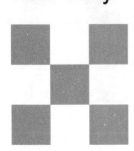

CHART DEVELOPMENT
Spelling Emphasis: *spr* or
_____

Other Emphasis: Synonyms or
_____

Resource: Books from Recreational Reading or _____

WRITING
Students write response to chart focus.

SPELLING
Select words to spell, team test, complete Word Study Record Sheet.
Papers are dated and filed.

HOMEWORK
Share writing and spell words with a partner.
Notebook signed.

Research

LEAD-IN
Teacher introduces the Research Project:
Topic and Focus: Reading and/or
watching TV/Surveys or _____
Resource: Classmates, friends, parents, school personnel, or _____

RESEARCH PROJECT
Again meet in same groups to consider,
compile, and summarize information
learned through surveys. Each group
should make suggestions about how they
want to share the information discovered
with others outside classroom and what
they would like to see happen as a result
of the survey.

SHARING
Groups share with entire class. Class decides how to compile and share results
(charts, graphs, narratives). Class then
decides whether to take action or make
suggestions for change.
  Papers are dated and filed.

Recreational Reading

For approximately 30 minutes, all students read books.

CONVERSATIONS
Teacher has seven to ten minute conversations with students to determine students' abilities to make inferences and
see relationships in reading selection. Or
_____.

CLIPBOARD NOTES
Teacher takes notes about any weaknesses that may need follow-up instruction or _____.

READ-ALOUD BOOK
Continue current selection or _____.

Writing

MINI-LESSON
Continue with story begun in previous
lesson. Discuss sequence and plot. Or
_____.
  Proofreading: sequence words

COMPOSING
Students continue writing their stories.
Or _____.

SHARING
Read, discuss, and proofread stories with
a partner.
  Papers are dated and filed.

Word Study

CHART DEVELOPMENT
Spelling Emphasis: *ses* or
_____

Other Emphasis: Synonyms or
_____

Resource: Basal readers or
_____

WRITING
Students write response to chart focus.

SPELLING
Select words to spell, team test, complete
Word Study Record Sheet.
  Papers are dated and filed.

HOMEWORK
Share writing and spell words with a
partner.
  Notebook signed.

Lesson 85

Research

LEAD-IN
Teacher introduces the Research Project:
Topic and Focus: Economy, taxes, money/Interpreting graphs or _____
Resource: Mathematics textbook, business magazines, or _____

RESEARCH PROJECT
Students read to locate a graph and write the information presented by the graph. Students draw one conclusion from reading the graph.

SHARING
Read and discuss information discovered with a self-selected partner.
Papers are dated and filed.

Recreational Reading

For approximately 30 minutes, all students read books.

CONVERSATIONS
Teacher has seven to ten minute conversations with students to determine students' abilities to make inferences and see relationships in reading selection. Or _____.

CLIPBOARD NOTES
Teacher takes notes about any weaknesses that may need follow-up instruction or _____.

READ-ALOUD BOOK
Continue current selection or _____

Writing

MINI-LESSON
Teacher reads a description of a character from book. Discuss the addition of a character to the story. Or _____.
Proofreading: proper nouns

COMPOSING
Students continue writing stories adding a character and developing the plot. Or _____.

SHARING
Read, discuss, and proofread stories with a partner.
Papers are dated and filed.

Word Study

CHART DEVELOPMENT
Spelling Emphasis: *em* or
_____

Other Emphasis: Homonyms or
_____

Resource: Spelling books or
_____

WRITING
Students write response to chart focus.

SPELLING
Select words to spell, team test, complete Word Study Record Sheet.
Papers are dated and filed.

HOMEWORK
Share writing and spell words with a partner.
Notebook signed.

Lesson 86

Research

LEAD-IN
Teacher introduces the Research Project:
Topic and Focus: Economy, taxes, money/Interpreting graphs or _____
Resource: Social Studies textbooks, business magazines, or _____

RESEARCH PROJECT
Students read to locate graphs they can associate with the topic and write the information learned from reading the graph. Write a conclusion drawn from reading the graph.

SHARING
Read and discuss information discovered with a self-selected partner.
    Papers are dated and filed.

Recreational Reading

For approximately 30 minutes, all students read books.

CONVERSATIONS
Teacher has seven to ten minute conversations with students to determine students' abilities to make inferences and see relationships in reading selection. Or _____.

CLIPBOARD NOTES
Teacher takes notes about any weaknesses that may need follow-up instruction or _____.

READ-ALOUD BOOK
Ramona the Pest by Beverly Cleary or _____

Writing

MINI-LESSON
Class discusses problems encountered by writers and the problems of saying what you want to say clearly. Discuss problems students may be having with the development of their stories. Or _____.
    Proofreading: correct verb usage

COMPOSING
Continue developing stories. Or _____.

SHARING
Read, discuss, and proofread stories with a partner.
    Papers are dated and filed.

Word Study

CHART DEVELOPMENT
Spelling Emphasis: *nd* or _____

Other Emphasis: Homonyms or _____

Resource: Newspapers or _____

WRITING
Students write response to chart focus.

SPELLING
Select words to spell, team test, complete Word Study Record Sheet.
    Papers are dated and filed.

HOMEWORK
Share writing and spell words with a partner.
    Notebook signed.

Lesson 87

Research

LEAD-IN
Teacher introduces the Research Project:
Topic and Focus: Economy, taxes, money/Interpreting graphs or _____
Resource: Encyclopedias, newspapers, or _____

RESEARCH PROJECT
Students read to locate a graph and write a summary of the information learned from the graph. How is the graph useful in giving information?

SHARING
Read and discuss information discovered with a self-selected partner.
Papers are dated and filed.

Recreational Reading

For approximately 30 minutes, all students read books.

CONVERSATIONS
Teacher has seven to ten minute conversations with students to determine students' abilities to make inferences and see relationships in reading selection. Or _____.

CLIPBOARD NOTES
Teacher takes notes about any weaknesses that may need follow-up instruction or _____.

READ-ALOUD BOOK
Continue current selection or _____.

Writing

MINI-LESSON
Discuss endings and conclusions to stories. Or _____.
Proofreading: sequence words that denote time and closure

COMPOSING
Students write the ending to their stories. Or _____.

SHARING
Read, discuss, and proofread story endings with a partner.
Papers are dated and filed.

Word Study

CHART DEVELOPMENT
Spelling Emphasis: *ve* or _____
Other Emphasis: Homonyms or
_____
Resource: Magazines or _____

WRITING
Students write response to chart focus.

SPELLING
Select words to spell, team test, complete Word Study Record Sheet.
Papers are dated and filed.

HOMEWORK
Share writing and spell words with a partner.
Notebook signed.

Research

LEAD-IN
Teacher introduces the Research Project:
Topic and Focus: Economy, money, taxes/Graphing information or _____
Resource: Student- and teacher-selected or _____

RESEARCH PROJECT
Make a graph with the class to show the amount of money students spend in the cafeteria per day of the week. Students begin reading to locate information they can present through a graph (e.g., amount of money in state or federal budget spent on education, defense, environment, etc.). Work in groups of two or three.

SHARING
Groups share information discovered.
  Papers are dated and filed.

Recreational Reading

For approximately 30 minutes, all students read books.

CONVERSATIONS
Teacher has seven to ten minute conversations with students to determine students' abilities to make inferences and see relationships in reading selection. Or _____.

CLIPBOARD NOTES
Teacher takes notes about any weaknesses that may need follow-up instruction or _____.

READ-ALOUD BOOK
Continue current selection or _____.

Writing

MINI-LESSON
Editing and revision process begins. Or _____.
  Proofreading: story development and flow

COMPOSING
Students edit and revise papers. Or _____.

SHARING
Read, discuss, and offer suggestions in groups of three or four.
  Papers are dated and filed.

Word Study

CHART DEVELOPMENT
Spelling Emphasis: *ry* or _____
Other Emphasis: Compound words or _____

Resource: Encyclopedias or _____

WRITING
Students write response to chart focus.

SPELLING
Select words to spell, team test, complete Word Study Record Sheet.
  Papers are dated and filed.

HOMEWORK
Share writing and spell words with a partner.
  Notebook signed.

Lesson 89

Research

LEAD-IN
Teacher introduces the Research Project:
Topic and Focus: Economy, taxes,
money/Graphing information or
_____

Resource: Student/teacher-selected
material or _____

RESEARCH PROJECT
Students continue reading to collect data
about topic to be presented in a graph.
Work in same groups of two or three.

SHARING
Groups share and discuss information
discovered.
    Papers are dated and filed.

Recreational Reading

For approximately 30 minutes, all students read books.

CONVERSATIONS
Teacher has seven to ten minute conversations with students to determine students' abilities to make inferences and
see relationships in reading selection.

CLIPBOARD NOTES
Teacher takes notes about any weaknesses that may need follow-up instruction or _____.

READ-ALOUD BOOK
Continue current selection or _____.

Writing

MINI-LESSON
Editing and revision process continues.
Or _____.
    Proofreading: story development and
flow

COMPOSING
Students continue to edit and revise
papers. Or _____.

SHARING
Read, discuss, and offer suggestions in
groups of three or four.
    Papers are dated and filed.

Word Study

CHART DEVELOPMENT
Spelling Emphasis: *rt* or _____
Other Emphasis: Compound words or
_____

Resource: Dictionaries or _____

WRITING
Students write response to chart focus.

SPELLING
Select words to spell, team test, complete
Word Study Record Sheet.
    Papers are dated and filed.

HOMEWORK
Share writing and spell words with a
partner.
    Notebook signed.

Research

LEAD-IN
Teacher introduces the Research Project:
Topic and Focus: Economy, taxes, money/Graphing information or _____

Resource: Student/teacher-selected materials or _____

RESEARCH PROJECT
Students make a graph presenting the information learned about the topic investigated. Students put graphs on charts to share with entire class.

SHARING
Whole class shares. Each group presents their final graph.
   Papers are dated and filed.

Recreational Reading

For approximately 30 minutes, all students read books.

CONVERSATIONS
Teacher has seven to ten minute conversations with students to determine students' abilities to make inferences and see relationships in reading selection. Or _____.

CLIPBOARD NOTES
Teacher takes notes about any weaknesses that may need follow-up instruction or _____.

READ-ALOUD BOOK
Continue current selection or _____.

Writing

MINI-LESSON
Stories rewritten, students share stories either with whole class or in small groups of five or six. Or _____.

COMPOSING
Sharing Day or _____.

SHARING
Sharing Day
   Papers are dated and filed.

Word Study

CHART DEVELOPMENT
Spelling Emphasis: _iz_ or _____
Other Emphasis: Compound words or _____

Resource: Basal readers or _____

WRITING
Students write response to chart focus.

SPELLING
Select words to spell, team test, complete Word Study Record Sheet.
   Papers are dated and filed.

HOMEWORK
Share writing and spell words with a partner.
   Notebook signed.

Lesson 91

Research

Six-day Research Project.

LEAD-IN
Teacher introduces the Research Project:
Topic and Focus: Music/musicians/
Selecting references and resources or
_____

Resource: Student-selected materials
or _____

RESEARCH PROJECT
Students decide references to be used for
a six-day reporting cycle on music and/or
musicians. Students begin locating information on a selected musician or music-
related topic in a reference of their
choice.

SHARING
Read and discuss information discovered
with a partner.
  Papers are dated and filed.

Recreational Reading

For approximately 30 minutes, all students read books.

CONVERSATIONS
Students read for twenty minutes and
then have Book Share for last ten
minutes. Students volunteer to share
something about the book they are reading. Or _____.

CLIPBOARD NOTES
Teacher notes book selections, willingness
to share, and students' reading interest.
Or _____.

READ-ALOUD BOOK
Song and Dance Man by Karen Ackerman or _____

Writing

MINI-LESSON
Writing a Mystery: Discuss the unique
features of mysteries. Visualize a mystery
story by drawing a story map that begins
with the idea, adds characters, animals,
objects, draws conclusions, and adds suspense before ending. Or _____.
  Proofreading: adjectives—"words that
paint a picture"

COMPOSING
Begin story by describing the setting to
create the suspense for the mystery to unfold. Or _____.

SHARING
Read, discuss, and proofread with a
partner.
  Papers are dated and filed.

Word Study

CHART DEVELOPMENT
Spelling Emphasis: *po* or _____
Other Emphasis: Multiple-meaning
words or _____
Resource: Spelling books or
_____

WRITING
Students write response to chart focus.

SPELLING
Select words to spell, team test, complete
Word Study Record Sheet.
  Papers are dated and filed.

HOMEWORK
Share writing and spell words with a
partner.
  Notebook signed.

Research

LEAD-IN
Teacher introduces the Research Project:
Topic and Focus: Music/musicians/
Locating information or _____
Resource: Student-selected materials
or _____

RESEARCH PROJECT
Students read in self-selected references
to locate information on music-related
topic or musician. Write the most important and most interesting information.

SHARING
Read and discuss information located
with a partner.
　Papers are dated and filed.

Recreational Reading

For approximately 30 minutes, all students read books.

CONVERSATIONS
Students read for twenty minutes and
then have Book Share for last ten
minutes. Students volunteer to share
something about the book they are reading. Or _____.

CLIPBOARD NOTES
Teacher notes book selections, willingness
to share, and students' reading interest.
Or _____.

READ-ALOUD BOOK
The Philharmonic Gets Dressed by Marc
Simont or _____

Writing

MINI-LESSON
Mystery: Discuss the excitement that develops in a mystery and how adding a
character to the story could help develop
the plot and add suspense. Or
_____.
　Proofreading: character descriptions

COMPOSING
Students continue writing their mystery
stories and add a character to the story.
Or _____.

SHARING
Read, discuss, and proofread with a part-
ner or small group.
　Papers are dated and filed.

Word Study

CHART DEVELOPMENT
Spelling Emphasis: *dy* or
_____

Other Emphasis: Multiple-meaning
words or _____
Resource: Newspapers or _____

WRITING
Students write response to chart focus.

SPELLING
Select words to spell, team test, complete
Word Study Record Sheet.
　Papers are dated and filed.

HOMEWORK
Share writing and spell words with a
partner.
　Notebook signed.

195

Lesson 93

Research

LEAD-IN
Teacher introduces the Research Project:
Topic and Focus: Music/musicians/
Locating information or _____
Resource: Student-selected materials
or _____

RESEARCH PROJECT
Students read to locate information about
a selected topic and write the most important and interesting information found.

SHARING
Read and discuss information discovered
with a new partner.
    Papers are dated and filed.

Recreational Reading

For approximately 30 minutes, all students read books.

CONVERSATIONS
Teacher moves from student to student
having two to three minute conversations
asking for answers to specific questions
pertaining to their reading selections or
_____.

CLIPBOARD NOTES
Teacher takes notes about students'
literal comprehension of selected reading
material or _____.

READ-ALOUD BOOK
The Philharmonic Gets Dressed by Marc
Simont or _____

Writing

MINI-LESSON
Mystery: Continue discussion of elements
of mystery stories. Discuss the idea of
adding an animal to the story students
are writing. Or _____.
    Proofreading: pronouns

COMPOSING
Students continue writing the mystery
story and add an animal to the story. Or
_____.

SHARING
Read, discuss, and proofread with a partner or small group.
    Papers are dated and filed.

Word Study

CHART DEVELOPMENT
Spelling Emphasis: *gth* or
_____

Other Emphasis: Multiple-meaning
words or _____
Resource: Basal readers or
_____

WRITING
Students write response to chart focus.

SPELLING
Select words to spell, team test, complete
Word Study Record Sheet.
    Papers are dated and filed.

HOMEWORK
Share writing and spell words with a
partner.
    Notebook signed.

Research

LEAD-IN
Teacher introduces the Research Project:
Topic and Focus: Music/musicians/
Organizing information or _____
Resource: Student-selected materials
or _____

RESEARCH PROJECT
Students read through the information
recorded for the past few days and begin
to organize for a final written report.

SHARING
Read and discuss report with a partner.
  Papers are dated and filed.

Recreational Reading

For approximately 30 minutes, all students read books.

CONVERSATIONS
Teacher moves from student to student
having two to three minute conversations
asking for answers to specific questions
pertaining to their reading selections or
_____.

CLIPBOARD NOTES
Teacher takes notes about students'
literal comprehension of selected reading
material or _____.

READ-ALOUD BOOK
A biography of Mozart or Beethoven or
another famous musician or _____

Writing

MINI-LESSON
Mystery: Discuss how often in mystery
stories or books an object becomes the
central focus. Or _____.
  Proofreading: prepositions

COMPOSING
Continue to write the mystery story and
add an object to the story. Or _____.

SHARING
Read, discuss, and proofread with a part-
ner or small group.
  Papers are dated and filed.

Word Study

CHART DEVELOPMENT
Spelling Emphasis: *mb* or
_____

Other Emphasis: Music or
_____

Resource: Music textbooks or
_____

WRITING
Students write response to chart focus.

SPELLING
Select words to spell, team test, complete
Word Study Record Sheet.
  Papers are dated and filed.

HOMEWORK
Share writing and spell words with a
partner.
  Notebook signed.

Lesson 95

Research

LEAD-IN
Teacher introduces the Research Project:
Topic and Focus: Music/musicians/
Writing a first draft of report or
_____

Resource: Student-selected materials
or _____

RESEARCH PROJECT
Students write the first draft of a report
on the topic being researched.

SHARING
Read and discuss the report being
prepared.
   Papers are dated and filed.

Recreational Reading

For approximately 30 minutes, all students read books.

CONVERSATIONS
Teacher moves from student to student
having two to three minute conversations
asking for answers to specific questions
pertaining to their reading selections or
_____.

CLIPBOARD NOTES
Teacher takes notes about students'
literal comprehension of selected reading
material or _____.

READ-ALOUD BOOK
Continue current selection or _____.

Writing

MINI-LESSON
Mystery: Discuss bringing the story to a
conclusion and how mystery authors wait
until the end of the story to solve the
problem or reveal certain connections. Or
_____.
   Proofreading: words that denote
sequence

COMPOSING
Students work on the ending to their stories. Or _____.

SHARING
Read, discuss, and proofread with a part-
ner or in small groups.
   Papers are dated and filed.

Word Study

CHART DEVELOPMENT
Spelling Emphasis: *syn* or
_____

Other Emphasis: Musicians or
_____

Resource: Magazines or _____

WRITING
Students write response to chart focus.

SPELLING
Select words to spell, team test, complete
Word Study Record Sheet.
   Papers are dated and filed.

HOMEWORK
Share writing and spell words with a
partner.
   Notebook signed.

Research

LEAD-IN
Teacher introduces the Research Project:
Topic and Focus: Music/musicians/
Rewrite report or _____
Resource: Student-selected material or
_____

RESEARCH PROJECT
Students write the final version of report
on a musician or a music-related topic.
These reports could be displayed on a
bulletin board or compiled into a booklet
to be shared either in the library or music room.

SHARING
Students should determine how to share
their reports: orally with whole class or
in small groups or with another class or
with their music teacher.
   Papers are dated and filed.

Recreational Reading

For approximately 30 minutes, all students read books.

CONVERSATIONS
Teacher has seven to ten minute conversations with students to identify
strengths and weaknesses in word attack
or comprehension skills or _____.

CLIPBOARD NOTES
Teacher takes notes concerning the above
or _____.

READ-ALOUD BOOK
Continue current selection or _____.

Writing

MINI-LESSON
Mystery: Review the editing and revision
process and the elements of mystery stories. Or _____.
   Proofreading: all previous proofreading
suggestions

COMPOSING
Students read their stories carefully, editing and revising their stories. Or
_____.

SHARING
Read, discuss, and proofread with a
partner.
   Papers are dated and filed.

Word Study

CHART DEVELOPMENT
Spelling Emphasis: *hy* or

_____
Other Emphasis: Body or _____
Resource: Health textbooks or

_____

WRITING
Students write response to chart focus.

SPELLING
Select words to spell, team test, complete
Word Study Record Sheet.
   Papers are dated and filed.

HOMEWORK
Share writing and spell words with a
partner.
   Notebook signed.

Lesson **97**

Research

LEAD-IN
Teacher introduces the Research Project:
Topic and Focus: Recognizing similes, metaphors, and analogies or
_____

Resource: Recreational Reading books or _____

RESEARCH PROJECT
Discuss the differences and importance of these conventions of written English. Students read to locate examples of any or all of the above and explain in their own words the comparisons made and why the writer used these comparisons.

SHARING
With a partner share the similes, metaphors, and/or analogies located and explained.
Papers are dated and filed.

Recreational Reading

For approximately 30 minutes, all students read books.

CONVERSATIONS
Teacher has seven to ten minute conversations with students to identify strengths and weaknesses in word attack or comprehension skills or _____.

CLIPBOARD NOTES
Teacher takes notes concerning the above or _____.

READ-ALOUD BOOK
Cricket in Times Square by George Selden or _____

Writing

MINI-LESSON
Sharing Day. Ask students to work in small groups of three or four at the beginning of this lesson. Each student should read his/her mystery story aloud. Group members should respond to the writing by telling what they like best and sharing any ideas for changes. Or
_____.

COMPOSING
This is a group editing day. Students should be given time after above group work to make any final changes. Or
_____.

SHARING
Sharing Day
Papers are dated and filed.

Word Study

CHART DEVELOPMENT
Spelling Emphasis: _iv_ or _____
Other Emphasis: Safety or
_____

Resource: Newspapers or _____

WRITING
Students write response to chart focus.

SPELLING
Select words to spell, team test, complete Word Study Record Sheet.
Papers are dated and filed.

HOMEWORK
Share writing and spell words with a partner.
Notebook signed.

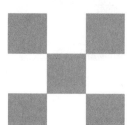

Research

LEAD-IN
Teacher introduces the Research Project:
Topic and Focus: Recognizing similes, metaphors, and analogies or
_____

Resource: Recreational Reading books or _____

RESEARCH PROJECT
Same as Lesson 97.

SHARING
Same as Lesson 97.
Papers are dated and filed.

Recreational Reading

For approximately 30 minutes, all students read books.

CONVERSATIONS
Teacher has seven to ten minute conversations with students to identify strengths and weaknesses in word attack or comprehension skills or _____.

CLIPBOARD NOTES
Teacher takes notes concerning the above or _____.

READ-ALOUD BOOK
Continue current selection or _____.

Writing

MINI-LESSON
Discuss the completion of mystery stories. Focus on neatness and spelling errors in this final rewrite. Or _____.

COMPOSING
Students complete the rewriting of their stories. If there is time, some students may wish to add illustrations. Or _____.

SHARING
Students' stories are placed in a binding and are available for everyone to read during Recreational Reading time. You may decide to make multiple copies of the collection.
Papers are dated and filed.

Word Study

CHART DEVELOPMENT
Spelling Emphasis: _mp_ or _____

Other Emphasis: Breakfast or _____

Resource: Magazines or _____

WRITING
Students write response to chart focus.

SPELLING
Select words to spell, team test, complete Word Study Record Sheet.
Papers are dated and filed.

HOMEWORK
Share writing and spell words with a partner.
Notebook signed.

Lesson 99

Research

LEAD-IN
Teacher introduces the Research Project:
Topic and Focus: Using similes, metaphors, and analogies or _____
Resource: Magazines or _____

RESEARCH PROJECT
Read to locate two products or items that you can compare using a simile, a metaphor, and/or an analogy. Cut these out of the magazine, paste on a sheet of paper, and write the comparison on the paper.

SHARING
In groups of three or four share your comparisons.
   Papers are dated and filed.

Recreational Reading

For approximately 30 minutes, all students read books.

CONVERSATIONS
Teacher has seven to ten minute conversations with students to identify strengths and weaknesses in word attack or comprehension skills or _____.

CLIPBOARD NOTES
Teacher takes notes concerning the above or _____.

READ-ALOUD BOOK
Continue current selection or _____.

Writing

MINI-LESSON
Begin by asking students to select a previously revised story for publication. This may take ten to fifteen minutes. Discuss the title page of a book and what is found on this page. Or _____.
   Proofreading: capital letters

COMPOSING
Students design the title page of their book. Or _____.

SHARING
Read, discuss, and proofread with a partner.
   Papers are dated and filed.

Word Study

CHART DEVELOPMENT
Spelling Emphasis: _nt_ or _____
Other Emphasis: Prehistoric times or _____

Resource: Recreational Reading books or _____

WRITING
Students write response to chart focus.

SPELLING
Select words to spell, team test, complete Word Study Record Sheet.
   Papers are dated and filed.

HOMEWORK
Share writing and spell words with a partner.
   Notebook signed.

Research

LEAD-IN
Teacher introduces the Research Project:
Topic and Focus: Categorizing similes, metaphors, and analogies or
_____

Resource: Library books, textbooks or basal readers, magazines, or _____

RESEARCH PROJECT
Make a chart with SIMILES, METAPHORS and ANALOGIES RESOURCE, and PAGES as headings. Read to locate examples of each and give the resource and pages where the example is found.

SHARING
Share charts in small groups and then ask for volunteers to make a class chart for display.
Papers are dated and filed.

Recreational Reading

For approximately 30 minutes, all students read books.

CONVERSATIONS
Teacher has seven to ten minute conversations with students to identify strengths and weaknesses in word attack or comprehension skills or _____.

CLIPBOARD NOTES
Teacher takes notes concerning the above or _____.

READ-ALOUD BOOK
Continue current selection or _____.

Writing

MINI-LESSON
Discuss the layout of books (dividing manuscript into pages) and the importance of illustrations. Or _____.

COMPOSING
Using folded paper, students do a "dummy" layout of their book. Or _____.

SHARING
Discuss the layout with a partner and suggest any changes. Or _____.
Papers are dated and filed.

Word Study

CHART DEVELOPMENT
Spelling Emphasis: ey or _____
Other Emphasis: Bees, birds, flying objects or _____
Resource: Science textbooks or _____

WRITING
Students write response to chart focus.

SPELLING
Select words to spell, team test, complete Word Study Record Sheet.
Papers are dated and filed.

HOMEWORK
Share writing and spell words with a partner.
Notebook signed.

Lesson 101

Research

LEAD-IN
Teacher introduces the Research Project:
Topic and Focus: Population/Using maps and reading map symbols or _____

Resource: Social Studies books or _____

RESEARCH PROJECT
Discuss the various uses of maps. Students read population maps in the Social Studies books and write the information provided by the map.

SHARING
Read and discuss information discovered with a self-selected partner.
Papers are dated and filed.

Recreational Reading

For approximately 30 minutes, all students read books.

CONVERSATIONS
Teacher has seven to ten minute conversations with students to identify strengths and weaknesses in word attack or comprehension skills or _____.

CLIPBOARD NOTES
Teacher takes notes concerning the above or _____.

READ-ALOUD BOOK
Continue current selection or _____.

Writing

MINI-LESSON
Students should work for the next three days completing their writing and arranging pages with illustrations. Or _____.

COMPOSING
Continue copying the manuscript onto the final pages of the book. Or _____.

SHARING
Consider eliminating the share time for the three days and devote all this time to completing the book.
Papers are dated and filed.

Word Study

CHART DEVELOPMENT
Spelling Emphasis: _cy_ or _____
Other Emphasis: Weather, seasons, or _____
Resource: Social Studies textbooks or _____

WRITING
Students write response to chart focus.

SPELLING
Select words to spell, team test, complete Word Study Record Sheet.
Papers are dated and filed.

HOMEWORK
Share writing and spell words with a partner.
Notebook signed.

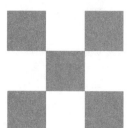

Research

LEAD-IN
Teacher introduces the Research Project:
Topic and Focus: Landforms/Using
and understanding maps or _____
Resource: Encyclopedias, atlases, or
_____

RESEARCH PROJECT
Read to locate landform maps and interpret the information provided.

SHARING
Read and discuss information discovered
with a self-selected partner.
   Papers are dated and filed.

Recreational Reading

For approximately 30 minutes, all students read books.

CONVERSATIONS
Teacher has seven to ten minute conversations with students to identify
strengths and weaknesses in word attack
or comprehension skills or _____.

CLIPBOARD NOTES
Teacher takes notes concerning the above
or _____.

READ-ALOUD BOOK
Wayside School Is Falling Down by Louis
Sachar or _____

Writing

MINI-LESSON
Continue as in Lesson 101. Or
_____.

COMPOSING
Continue as in Lesson 101. Or
_____.

SHARING
Continue as in lesson 101. Or _____.
   Papers are dated and filed.

Word Study

CHART DEVELOPMENT
Spelling Emphasis: *ap* or
_____

Other Emphasis: Things that move,
motion, or _____
Resource: Newspapers or _____

WRITING
Students write response to chart focus.

SPELLING
Select words to spell, team test, complete
Word Study Record Sheet.
   Papers are dated and filed.

HOMEWORK
Share writing and spell words with a
partner.
   Notebook signed.

Lesson **103**

Research

LEAD-IN
Teacher introduces the Research Project:
Topic and Focus: Travel/Using a
map mileage scale and legend or
_____

Resource: An assortment of road maps
or _____

RESEARCH PROJECT
In groups of two or three, students read
maps and plan a trip. On a chart, record
the mileage from one town to another
along the route, the road numbers for the
trip and the important scenic or historic
sites along the route.

SHARING
One group shares their trip plans with
another group.
  Papers are dated and filed.

Recreational Reading

For approximately 30 minutes, all students read books.

CONVERSATIONS
Teacher models reading for first 20
minutes. Teacher invites four or five students at the beginning of the reading
time to gather for an oral reading session
during the last ten minutes. Each student
chooses a selection from a book read
previously or one they will read that day.
Or _____.

CLIPBOARD NOTES
Teacher records observations made about
oral reading fluency or _____.

READ-ALOUD BOOK
Wayside School Is Falling Down by Louis
Sachar or _____

Writing

MINI-LESSON
Continue as in Lesson 101. Or
_____.

COMPOSING
Continue as in Lesson 101. Or
_____.

SHARING
Continue as in Lesson 101. Or
_____.
  Papers are dated and filed.

Word Study

CHART DEVELOPMENT
Spelling Emphasis: _sis_ or
_____

Other Emphasis: Families or
_____

Resource: Magazines or _____

WRITING
Students write response to chart focus.

SPELLING
Select words to spell, team test, complete
Word Study Record Sheet.
  Papers are dated and filed.

HOMEWORK
Share writing and spell words with a
partner.
  Notebook signed.

Research

LEAD-IN
Teacher introduces the Research Project:
Topic and Focus: Reading and using maps or _____
Resource: Varied; student-selected materials or _____

RESEARCH PROJECT
Read to locate any kind of map and relate the information discovered to a current event. Write the associations you are making. (e.g., weather maps and current weather conditions locally, nationally, or around the world)

SHARING
Share information and associations in small groups. Each small group then selects one student's discovery to share with the class.
  Papers are dated and filed.

Recreational Reading

For approximately 30 minutes, all students read books.

CONVERSATIONS
Teacher models reading for first 20 minutes. Teacher invites four or five students at the beginning of the reading time to gather for an oral reading session during the last ten minutes. Each student chooses a selection from a book read previously or one they will read that day. Or _____.

CLIPBOARD NOTES
Teacher records observations made about oral reading fluency or _____.

READ-ALOUD BOOK
Continue current selection or _____.

Writing

MINI-LESSON
On this day the actual construction of the book (putting it together) begins. It will be helpful if you have volunteers who can assist the students with this process. Or _____.

COMPOSING
Book construction day. Or _____.

SHARING
Book construction day. Or _____.
  Papers are dated and filed.

Word Study

CHART DEVELOPMENT
Spelling Emphasis: *sne* or _____

Other Emphasis: Sleeping, night time, or _____
Resource: Health books or _____

WRITING
Students write response to chart focus.

SPELLING
Select words to spell, team test, complete Word Study Record Sheet.
  Papers are dated and filed.

HOMEWORK
Share writing and spell words with a partner.
  Notebook signed.

Lesson **105**

Research

LEAD-IN
Teacher introduces the Research Project:
Topic and Focus: Drawing a map or
_____

Resource: School and school grounds
or _____

RESEARCH PROJECT
Students draw maps of classroom, school,
or school grounds and make a legend for
their maps.

SHARING
Share maps with other students. Compare
those made of the same area.
   Papers are dated and filed.

Recreational Reading

For approximately 30 minutes, all students read books.

CONVERSATIONS
Teacher models reading for first 20
minutes. Teacher invites four or five students at the beginning of the reading
time to gather for an oral reading session
during the last ten minutes. Each student
chooses a selection from a book read
previously or one they will read that day.
Or _____.

CLIPBOARD NOTES
Teacher records observations made about
oral reading fluency or _____.

READ-ALOUD BOOK
Continue current selection or _____.

Writing

MINI-LESSON
Complete book construction. Or
_____.

COMPOSING
Complete book construction. Or
_____.

SHARING
Every student should have a "published"
book to share. This can be done in small
groups or as a whole class in place of the
current suggested Read-Aloud selection. If
students agree, the books can be shared
with students in another class or placed
in the library for others to read.
   Papers are dated and filed.

Word Study

CHART DEVELOPMENT
Spelling Emphasis: *url* or

Other Emphasis: Television or
_____

Resource: TV Guides or _____

WRITING
Students write response to chart focus.

SPELLING
Select words to spell, team test, complete
Word Study Record Sheet.
   Papers are dated and filed.

HOMEWORK
Share writing and spell words with a
partner.
   Notebook signed.

Lesson 106

Research

Five-day integrated lessons: Mathematics

LEAD-IN
Teacher introduces the Research Project:
Topic and Focus: Mathematics/Time and world time zones or _____
Resource: Encyclopedias, Social Studies books, library books, or _____

RESEARCH PROJECT
Read to locate information about the time zones in the United States and throughout the world. How many time zones are there? Name a state/country or city in each of these time zones.

SHARING
Have a whole-class share to identify as many time zones as possible, especially the five in the US and the different locations identified.
　Papers are dated and filed.

Recreational Reading

For approximately 30 minutes, all students read books.

CONVERSATIONS
Teacher moves from student to student having two to three minute conversations about fact and/or opinion statement found in students' reading selections. Or _____.

CLIPBOARD NOTES
Teacher takes notes about the above or _____.

READ-ALOUD BOOK
The Man Who Tried to Save Time by Phyllis Krasilousky or _____

Writing

MINI-LESSON
Discuss the everyday connections of mathematics to our lives. Time, measurement, money, geometric shapes, numbers, and counting. Or _____.
　Proofread: use of examples to support points

COMPOSING
Students select one of the connections discussed and write a paragraph about the importance of that particular aspect of math in their lives. Or _____.

SHARING
Read, discuss, and proofread with a small group.
　Papers are dated and filed.

Word Study

CHART DEVELOPMENT
Spelling Emphasis: *flo* or _____

Other Emphasis: Math, time or _____

Resource: Math textbooks, encyclopedias, or _____

WRITING
Students write response to chart focus.

SPELLING
Select words to spell, team test, complete Word Study Record Sheet.
　Papers are dated and filed.

HOMEWORK
Share writing and spell words with a partner.
　Notebook signed.

Lesson **107**

Research

LEAD-IN
Teacher introduces the Research Project:
Topic and Focus: Math/Geometric
shapes and architecture or _____
Resource: Magazines, Social Studies
books, encyclopedias, or _____

RESEARCH PROJECT
Students work in groups of two or three
to read to locate examples of modern architecture and architecture from another
period of history. Identify geometric
shapes in the buildings and compare the
two types of architecture using geometric
shapes.

SHARING
One group shares discoveries with another small group.
    Papers are dated and filed.

Recreational Reading

For approximately 30 minutes, all students read books.

CONVERSATIONS
Teacher moves from student to student
having two to three minute conversations
about fact and/or opinion statements
found in students' reading selections. Or
_____.

CLIPBOARD NOTES
Teacher takes notes about the above or
_____.

READ-ALOUD BOOK
Shapes, Shapes, Shapes by Tana Hoban
or _____

Writing

MINI-LESSON
Continue to discuss the connections between mathematics and life. Focus on geometry and nature or geometry and the
classroom. Students should be given time
for observation either in the classroom or
outdoors. Or _____.
    Proofreading: mathematical terms

COMPOSING
Write a paragraph about the connections
observed between geometry and nature or
geometry to the classroom. Or
_____.

SHARING
Read, discuss, and proofread with a small
group.
    Papers are dated and filed.

Word Study

CHART DEVELOPMENT
Spelling Emphasis: _opt_ or
_____

Other Emphasis: Math concepts, geometry, or _____
Resource: Science textbooks or
_____

WRITING
Students write response to chart focus.

SPELLING
Select words to spell, team test, complete
Word Study Record Sheet.
    Papers are dated and filed.

HOMEWORK
Share writing and spell words with a
partner.
    Notebook signed.

Research

LEAD-IN
Teacher introduces the Research Project:
Topic and Focus: Mathematics/
Money or _____
Resource: Advertisement section of
newspaper or _____

RESEARCH PROJECT
Students read to locate information about
the prices for houses, automobiles, or ap-
pliances for sale. Compare the most expensive to the least expensive.

SHARING
Students share their findings in groups of
three or four.
    Papers are dated and filed.

Recreational Reading

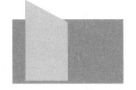

For approximately 30 minutes, all students read books.

CONVERSATIONS
Teacher moves from student to student
having two to three minute conversations
about fact and/or opinion statements
found in students' reading selections. Or
_____.

CLIPBOARD NOTES
Teacher takes notes about the above or
_____.

READ-ALOUD BOOK
How Much Is A Million? by David
Schwartz or _____

Writing

MINI-LESSON
Discuss money as it applies to allowances
and wages or salaries and budgets. Or
_____.
    Proofreading: money terms

COMPOSING
Students write about having or wanting
to have an allowance and how they
spend, save, or would like to use an allowance. Or _____.

SHARING
Read, discuss, and proofread with a small
group.
    Papers are dated and filed.

Word Study

CHART DEVELOPMENT
Spelling Emphasis: *exp* or
_____
Other Emphasis: Business, money, or
_____
Resource: Magazines, newspapers, or
_____

WRITING
Students write response to chart focus.

SPELLING
Select words to spell, team test, complete
Word Study Record Sheet.
    Papers are dated and filed.

HOMEWORK
Share writing and spell words with a
partner.
    Notebook signed.

Lesson **109**

Research

LEAD-IN
Teacher introduces the Research Project:
Topic and Focus: Mathematical con-
cepts or _____
Resource: Magazines or _____

RESEARCH PROJECT
Students read in magazines to locate any
information related in mathematical
terms. They interpret and rewrite this information in their own words.

SHARING
Students select partners to share informa-
tion discovered.
Papers are dated and filed.

Recreational Reading

For approximately 30 minutes, all students read books.

CONVERSATIONS
Teacher has seven to ten minute conversations with students about cause-and-
effect relationships in their reading selections or _____.

CLIPBOARD NOTES
Teacher takes notes about the above or
_____.

READ-ALOUD BOOK
Roosevelt Grady by Louisa Shotwell, *How
Many Snails* by Paul Giganti, or
_____

Writing

MINI-LESSON
Discuss learning mathematical concepts.
Why do some students have problems and
for others math comes easy? How should
math be taught? What helps you to learn
math? Or _____.
Proofreading: pronouns

COMPOSING
Students write about their experiences
and feelings (confidence, fear, anxiety)
about math. Or _____.

SHARING
Read, discuss, and proofread in small
groups.
Papers are dated and filed.

Word Study

CHART DEVELOPMENT
Spelling Emphasis: *eg* or _____
Other Emphasis: Numbers or
_____
Resource: Mathematics textbooks or
_____

WRITING
Students write response to chart focus.

SPELLING
Select words to spell, team test, complete
Word Study Record Sheet.
Papers are dated and filed.

HOMEWORK
Share writing and spell words with a
partner.
Notebook signed.

Research

LEAD-IN
Teacher introduces the Research Project:
Topic and Focus: Mathematics symbols or _____
Resource: Student-selected resource or _____

RESEARCH PROJECT
Read to locate all the math symbols you can find. Then tell what each symbol means or represents.

SHARING
Groups of three to four students compare their symbols and develop one combined list. Each group then reports the number located.
   Papers are dated and filed.

Recreational Reading

For approximately 30 minutes, all students read books.

CONVERSATIONS
Teacher has seven to ten minute conversations with students about cause-and-effect relationships in their reading selections or _____.

CLIPBOARD NOTES
Teacher takes notes about the above or _____.

READ-ALOUD BOOK
Sideways Arithmetic from Wayside School by Louis Sachar or _____

Writing

MINI-LESSON
Discuss mathematical concepts and terms. Have students brainstorm a list of the above. Discuss becoming one of these terms or having a conversation between a square and a circle or an argument between a dollar sign ($) and a decimal (.) about who is most important. Or _____.
   Proofreading: proper punctuation

COMPOSING
Students write about one of the sugges-
tions discussed or an idea of their own that illustrates a creative connection with math and their composition. Or _____.

SHARING
Read, discuss, and proofread in small groups.
   Papers are dated and filed.

Word Study

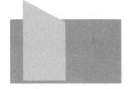

CHART DEVELOPMENT
Spelling Emphasis: *som* or _____

Other Emphasis: Mathematical symbols or entertainment or _____
Resource: Magazines or _____

WRITING
Students write response to chart focus.

SPELLING
Select words to spell, team test, complete Word Study Record Sheet.
   Papers are dated and filed.

HOMEWORK
Share writing and spell words with a partner.
   Notebook signed.

Lesson 111

Research

LEAD-IN
Teacher introduces the Research Project:
Topic and Focus: Art/Fact or opinion or _____
Resource: Art prints, books about art, or _____

RESEARCH PROJECT
Discuss the difference between a fact and an opinion. How do we tell one from the other? Students read or observe and then write fact and opinion statements pertaining to what they read in books about art or their observations of a piece of art. They should identify their statements by an F or O.

SHARING
Share with a partner your discoveries and see if they agree.
Papers are dated and filed.

Recreational Reading

For approximately 30 minutes, all students read books.

CONVERSATIONS
Teacher has seven to ten minute conversations with students about cause-and-effect relationships in their reading selections or _____.

CLIPBOARD NOTES
Teacher takes notes about the above or _____.

READ-ALOUD BOOK
Continue current selection or _____.

Writing

MINI-LESSON
Short stories (two days). Discuss "A Forest Fire" as a title for the short story. Or _____.
    Proofreading: contractions

COMPOSING
Students write the beginning of a short story about "A Forest Fire." Or _____.

SHARING
Read, discuss, and proofread with a partner.
Papers are dated and filed.

Word Study

CHART DEVELOPMENT
Spelling Emphasis: *spa* or _____

Other Emphasis: Forests, parks, or _____

Resource: Science textbooks, library books, newspapers, or _____

WRITING
Students write response to chart focus.

SPELLING
Select words to spell, team test, complete Word Study Record Sheet.
Papers are dated and filed.

HOMEWORK
Share writing and spell words with a partner.
Notebook signed.

Research

LEAD-IN
Teacher introduces the Research Project:
Topic and Focus: Art/Fact or opinion
_____

Resource: Encyclopedias

RESEARCH PROJECT
Read to locate information about a
famous artist. Write statements of fact
and statements of opinion based on the
information read. Identify statements by
an F or O.

SHARING
Read and discuss information discovered
with a self-selected partner.
    Papers are dated and filed.

Recreational Reading

For approximately 30 minutes, all students read books.

CONVERSATIONS
Teacher has seven to ten minute conversations with individual students about
cause-and-effect relationships in their
reading selections or _____.

CLIPBOARD NOTES
Teacher takes notes about the above or
_____.

READ-ALOUD BOOK
Sideways Arithmetic from Wayside School
by Louis Sachar or _____.

Writing

MINI-LESSON
Discuss forest fires and the use of
descriptions in writing. Or _____.
    Proofreading: use of "If" at the
beginning of a sentence.

COMPOSING
Students continue writing the short story
"A Forest Fire." Or _____.

SHARING
Read, discuss, and proofread with a
partner.
    Papers are dated and filed.

Word Study

CHART DEVELOPMENT
Spelling Emphasis: _za_ or
_____

Other Emphasis: Radio or
_____

Resource: Newspapers or _____

WRITING
Students write response to chart focus.

SPELLING
Select words to spell, team test, complete
Word Study Record Sheet.
    Papers are dated and filed.

HOMEWORK
Share writing and spell words with a
partner.
    Notebook signed.

Lesson **113**

Research

LEAD-IN
Teacher introduces the Research Project:
Topic and Focus: Art/Fact and opinion or _____
Resource: Magazines or _____

RESEARCH PROJECT
Students read to locate information or find pictures of what they consider or define as art. They write opinion statements and factual statements about this art.

SHARING
Read and discuss information discovered and written with a partner.
  Papers are dated and filed.

Recreational Reading

For approximately 30 minutes, all students read books.

CONVERSATIONS
Teacher has seven to ten minute conversations with students about cause-and-effect relationships in their reading selections or _____.

CLIPBOARD NOTES
Teacher takes notes about the above or _____.

READ-ALOUD BOOK
Laura Ingalls Wilder by Gwenda Blair or _____

Writing

MINI-LESSON
Write a short story about "A Flock of Birds." Discuss story settings. Or _____.
  Proofreading: sentences beginning with _when_

COMPOSING
Students begin a short story about "A Flock of Birds." Or _____.

SHARING
Read, discuss, and proofread with a partner.
  Papers are dated and filed.

Word Study

CHART DEVELOPMENT
Spelling Emphasis: _bom_ or _____

Other Emphasis: Birds or _____

Resource: Magazines or _____

WRITING
Students write response to chart focus.

SPELLING
Select words to spell, team test, complete Word Study Record Sheet.
  Papers are dated and filed.

HOMEWORK
Share writing and spell words with a partner.
  Notebook signed.

Lesson 114

Research

LEAD-IN
Teacher introduces the Research Project:
Topic and Focus: Art/Fact and opinion or _____
Resource: Other people: interviews or _____

RESEARCH PROJECT
Discuss people as a resource. Students should interview other persons about the subject art. The class may wish to decide three or four questions that each student would ask. Students will determine whether the answers given are fact or opinion.

SHARING
As a class students read and discuss the responses to their interview questions.
Papers are dated and filed.

Recreational Reading

For approximately 30 minutes, all students read books.

CONVERSATIONS
Teacher has seven to ten minute conversations with students about cause-and-effect relationships in their reading selections or _____.

CLIPBOARD NOTES
Teacher takes notes about the above or _____.

READ-ALOUD BOOK
Continue current selection or _____.

Writing

MINI-LESSON
Discuss the "Flock of Birds" short story begun yesterday. Ask students to volunteer to read their favorite sentence aloud. Discuss motion words. Or _____.
 Proofreading: verbs

COMPOSING
Complete the short story about "A Flock of Birds." Or _____.

SHARING
Read, discuss, and proofread with a partner.
Papers are dated and filed.

Word Study

CHART DEVELOPMENT
Spelling Emphasis: *hyp* or _____

Other Emphasis: Disease or _____

Resource: Magazines or _____

WRITING
Students write response to chart focus.

SPELLING
Select words to spell, team test, complete Word Study Record Sheet.
Papers are dated and filed.

HOMEWORK
Share writing and spell words with a partner.
Notebook signed.

Lesson **115**

Research

LEAD-IN
Teacher introduces the Research Project:
Topic and Focus: Art/Fact and opinion or _____
Resource: Student-selected materials or _____

RESEARCH PROJECT
Discuss all the aspects of art investigated. Raise the question "What is Art?" Students write their answers to this question using both fact and opinion statements and identifying an example of each.

SHARING
In groups of three or four read and discuss your responses.
Papers are dated and filed.

Recreational Reading

For approximately 30 minutes, all students read books.

CONVERSATIONS
Teacher has seven to ten minute conversations with students about cause-and-effect relationships in their reading selections or _____.

CLIPBOARD NOTES
Teacher takes note of the above or
_____.

READ-ALOUD BOOK
Continue current selection or _____.

Writing

MINI-LESSON
Discuss something "Slick and Slimy." Discuss use of "picture words"—adjectives. Or
_____.
  Proofreading: adjectives

COMPOSING
Students begin a short story on something that is "Slick and Slimy." Or
_____.

SHARING
Read, discuss, and proofread with two other persons.
Papers are dated and filed.

Word Study

CHART DEVELOPMENT
Spelling Emphasis: *nst* or
_____

Other Emphasis: Mythology or
_____

Resource: Encyclopedias or
_____

WRITING
Students write response to chart focus.

SPELLING
Select words to spell, team test, complete Word Study Record Sheet.
  Papers are dated and filed.

HOMEWORK
Share writing and spell words with a partner.
  Notebook signed.

Lesson 116

Research

LEAD-IN
Teacher introduces the Research Project:
Topic and Focus: Emergencies/Symbolism or _____
Resource: Telephone books, first aid pamphlets, signs in public buildings, or _____

RESEARCH PROJECT
Students read to locate symbols that can be associated with emergencies. Draw the symbols and explain the relationships.

SHARING
Test with a partner to see if you know symbols located by your partner.
Papers are dated and filed.

Recreational Reading

For approximately 30 minutes, all students read books.

CONVERSATIONS
Students read for twenty minutes and then have Book Share for last ten minutes. Students volunteer to share something about the book they are reading. Or _____.

CLIPBOARD NOTES
Teacher notes book selections, willingness to share, and students' reading interest. Or _____.

READ-ALOUD BOOK
Continue current selection or _____.

Writing

MINI-LESSON
Discuss the use of senses in describing something "Slick and Slimy." Or _____.
Proofreading: prepositions

COMPOSING
Continue writing short story about something "Slick and Slimy." Or _____.

SHARING
Continue discussions and proofreading with the same two persons as yesterday.
Papers are dated and filed.

Word Study

CHART DEVELOPMENT
Spelling Emphasis: *ric* or _____

Other Emphasis: Prehistoric times or _____

Resource: Science textbooks, Social Studies textbooks, or _____

WRITING
Students write response to chart focus.

SPELLING
Select words to spell, team test, complete Word Study Record Sheet.
Papers are dated and filed.

HOMEWORK
Share writing and spell words with a partner.
Notebook signed.

Lesson 117

Research

LEAD-IN
Teacher introduces the Research Project:
Topic and Focus: Advertising/Symbolism or _____
Resource: Magazines and newspapers or _____

RESEARCH PROJECT
Students read advertisements to locate symbols. Cut out the symbols and write what each symbolizes.

SHARING
Read and discuss the symbols located and what they mean.
Papers are dated and filed.

Recreational Reading

For approximately 30 minutes, all students read books.

CONVERSATIONS
Students read for twenty minutes and then have Book Share for last ten minutes. Students volunteer to share something about the book they are reading. Or _____.

CLIPBOARD NOTES
Teacher notes book selections, willingness to share, and students' reading interest. Or _____.

READ-ALOUD BOOK
Continue current selection or _____.

Writing

MINI-LESSON
Discuss "Prehistoric Adventures." Discuss historical perspectives of authors. Or
_____.
    Proofreading: adverbs

COMPOSING
Students begin short story about "Prehistoric Adventures." Include details you know about factual events or animals. Or _____.

SHARING
Read, discuss, and proofread with a partner.
Papers are dated and filed.

Word Study

CHART DEVELOPMENT
Spelling Emphasis: *ist* or
_____
Other Emphasis: Time or _____
Resource: Newspapers or _____

WRITING
Students write response to chart focus.

SPELLING
Select words to spell, team test, complete Word Study Record Sheet.
Papers are dated and filed.

HOMEWORK
Share writing and spell words with a partner.
Notebook signed.

Research

LEAD-IN
Teacher introduces the Research Project:
Topic and Focus: Symbolism or
_____
Resource: Student/Teacher-selected or
_____

RESEARCH PROJECT
Students read to locate words they can
identify with a symbol, (e.g., love—heart)
Students make a chart to show this.
Charts will have three headings: WORD,
SYMBOL, OBJECT. Using the example
above, *Love* will be written in the WORD
column, a picture of a heart under SYM-
BOL, and the word *heart* under OBJECT.

SHARING
Students share their charts in small
groups and groups with entire class.
Make a classroom chart.
   Papers are dated and filed.

Recreational Reading

For approximately 30 minutes, all students read books.

CONVERSATIONS
Teacher moves from student to student
having two to three minute conversations
about symbolism in their reading selection or _____.

CLIPBOARD NOTES
Teacher takes notes about the above or
_____.

READ-ALOUD BOOK
Did You Carry the Flag Today, Charley?
by Caudill or _____

Writing

MINI-LESSON
Discuss "Prehistoric Adventures." Discuss
use of imagination to fill in the gaps of
knowledge. Or _____.
   Proofreading: adverbs

COMPOSING
Students complete their short story on
"Prehistoric Adventures."

SHARING
Read, discuss, and proofread with a
partner.
   Papers are dated and filed.

Word Study

CHART DEVELOPMENT
Spelling Emphasis: *ld* or _____
Other Emphasis: Movies or
_____
Resource: Newspapers or _____

WRITING
Students write response to chart focus.

SPELLING
Select words to spell, team test, complete
Word Study Record Sheet.
   Papers are dated and filed.

HOMEWORK
Share writing and spell words with a
partner.
   Notebook signed.

Lesson **119**

Research

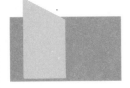

LEAD-IN
Teacher introduces the Research Project:
Topic and Focus: Seasons/Inferences or _____
Resource: Magazines or _____

RESEARCH PROJECT
Read in magazines to locate pictures related to seasons. Cut and paste pictures on a sheet of paper. Write a list of the clues in the picture that suggest a season.

SHARING
Read and discuss your pictures with a partner.
  Papers are dated and filed.

Recreational Reading

For approximately 30 minutes, all students read books.

CONVERSATIONS
Teacher moves from student to student having two to three minute conversations about symbolism in their reading selection or _____.

CLIPBOARD NOTES
Teacher takes notes about the above or _____.

READ-ALOUD BOOK
Continue current selection or _____.

Writing

MINI-LESSON
Review the editing and revision processes. Or _____.
  Proofreading: all the proofreading foci in the short story lessons

COMPOSING
Select a paper to edit and revise. Two days are devoted to this because some students may want to add more to their selected story before they begin to edit. Or _____.

SHARING
Read, discuss, and proofread with a partner.
  Papers are dated and filed.

Word Study

CHART DEVELOPMENT
Spelling Emphasis: *li* or _____
Other Emphasis: Publications or _____

Resource: Library books or _____

WRITING
Students write response to chart focus.

SPELLING
Select words to spell, team test, complete Word Study Record Sheet.
  Papers are dated and filed.

HOMEWORK
Share writing and spell words with a partner.
  Notebook signed.

Research

LEAD-IN
Teacher introduces the Research Project:
Topic and Focus: Outdoor activity/People's feelings/inferences or
_____

Resource: Magazines or _____

RESEARCH PROJECT
Read in a magazine to select a picture showing an outdoor activity involving people. Write your interpretation of what is happening and how the people are feeling.

SHARING
Read, discuss and compare your pictures and writing.
Papers are dated and filed.

Recreational Reading

For approximately 30 minutes, all students read books.

CONVERSATIONS
Teacher moves from student to student having two to three minute conversations about symbolism in their reading selection or _____.

CLIPBOARD NOTES
Teacher takes notes about the above or _____.

READ-ALOUD BOOK
Continue current selection or _____.

Writing

MINI-LESSON
Discuss editing and revising stories, especially any problems students may want to share. Or _____.

COMPOSING
Students continue to edit and revise short stories. Or _____.

SHARING
Read, discuss, and proofread with a new partner.
Papers are dated and filed.

Word Study

CHART DEVELOPMENT
Spelling Emphasis: *le* or _____
Other Emphasis: Any unfamiliar word or _____
Resource: Newspapers or _____

WRITING
Students write response to chart focus.

SPELLING
Select words to spell, team test, complete Word Study Record Sheet.
Papers are dated and filed.

HOMEWORK
Share writing and spell words with a partner.
Notebook signed.

Lesson 121

Research

LEAD-IN
Teacher introduces the Research Project:
Topic and Focus: Emotions/Inference
or _____
Resource: Basal readers or
_____

RESEARCH PROJECT
Read a story to find examples of emotional expression. What emotion is being expressed and how do you know? Write about these passages explaining the clues that helped you know what was happening.

SHARING
Read, discuss, and explain your writing. Papers are dated and filed.

Recreational Reading

For approximately 30 minutes, all students read books.

CONVERSATIONS
Teacher has seven to ten minute conversations with students about predicting outcomes or next part of story using context of students' reading selections. Or _____.

CLIPBOARD NOTES
Teacher takes notes about the above or _____.

READ-ALOUD BOOK
Continue current selection or _____.

Writing

MINI-LESSON
Discuss illustrations and rewriting the final copy of the short story in good handwriting. Or _____.

COMPOSING
Students rewrite short story as final copy. If time permits, students should be given a clean white sheet of paper on which to draw an illustration for their story. Or _____.

SHARING
Read, discuss, and proofread stories. Papers are dated and filed.

Word Study

CHART DEVELOPMENT
Spelling Emphasis: *ta* or _____
Other Emphasis: Eyes or _____
Resource: Health books or _____

WRITING
Students write response to chart focus.

SPELLING
Select words to spell, team test, complete Word Study Record Sheet.
Papers are dated and filed.

HOMEWORK
Share writing and spell words with a partner.
Notebook signed.

Lesson 122

Research

LEAD-IN
Teacher introduces the Research Project:
Topic and Focus: Authors techniques/Tone and mood or _____
Resource: Basal readers, Recreational Reading books, or _____

RESEARCH PROJECT
Students read to locate passages that are clues to the tone or mood the author is trying to create. Write the words or phrases that are the clues.

SHARING
Read, discuss, and explain your writing.
Papers are dated and filed.

Recreational Reading

For approximately 30 minutes, all students read books.

CONVERSATIONS
Teacher has seven to ten minute conversations with students about predicting outcomes or next part of story using context of students' reading selections. Or _____.

CLIPBOARD NOTES
Teacher takes notes about the above or _____.

READ-ALOUD BOOK
Continue current selection or _____.

Writing

MINI-LESSON
Discuss sharing time and the importance of being a good listener. Or _____.

COMPOSING
Sharing Day: The class may decide to put all the short stories in a book entitled "Collection of Short Stories" by _____ class. Include illustrations. Or _____.

SHARING
In groups of five or six, students read their stories aloud. Each group member responds with a positive comment.
Papers are dated and filed.

Word Study

CHART DEVELOPMENT
Spelling Emphasis: pa or _____

Other Emphasis: Patriotism or _____

Resource: Social Studies textbooks or _____

WRITING
Students write response to chart focus.

SPELLING
Select words to spell, team test, complete Word Study Record Sheet.
Papers are dated and filed.

HOMEWORK
Share writing and spell words with a partner.
Notebook signed.

Lesson 123

Research

LEAD-IN
Teacher introduces the Research Project:
Topic and Focus: Authors' techniques/Alliteration or _____
Resource: Basal readers or Recreational Reading books or _____

RESEARCH PROJECT
Students read to locate examples of alliteration and write as many examples as they can find.

SHARING
Read, discuss, and compare with a partner.
 Papers are dated and filed.

Recreational Reading

For approximately 30 minutes, all students read books.

CONVERSATIONS
Teacher has seven to ten minute conversations with students about predicting outcomes or next part of story using context of students' reading selections. Or _____.

CLIPBOARD NOTES
Teacher takes notes about the above or _____.

READ-ALOUD BOOK
The Talking Eggs by Robert D. San Souci or _____

Writing

MINI-LESSON
Discuss written book reports and making an outline of interesting things about the book to share. Or _____.
 Proofreading: adjectives

COMPOSING
Students select a book they have particularly enjoyed reading and begin a written book report. Write an outline and a first draft. Or _____.

SHARING
Read, discuss, and proofread with a partner.
 Papers are dated and filed.

Word Study

CHART DEVELOPMENT
Spelling Emphasis: *la* or _____
Other Emphasis: Cities or towns or _____

Resource: Travel Brochures, magazines, or _____

WRITING
Students write response to chart focus.

SPELLING
Select words to spell, team test, complete Word Study Record Sheet.
 Papers are dated and filed.

HOMEWORK
Share writing and spell words with a partner.
 Notebook signed.

Research

LEAD-IN
Teacher introduces the Research Project:
Topic and Focus: Authors' techniques/Imagery or _____
Resource: Basal readers, Recreational Reading books, or _____

RESEARCH PROJECT
Students read to locate examples of imagery that convey the author's sense of the topic or scene being described. Write the examples you locate.

SHARING
Read, discuss, and explain your writing to a partner.
  Papers are dated and filed.

Recreational Reading

For approximately 30 minutes, all students read books.

CONVERSATIONS
Teacher has seven to ten minute conversations with students about predicting outcomes or next part of story using context of students' reading selections. Or _____.

CLIPBOARD NOTES
Teacher takes notes about the above or _____.

READ-ALOUD BOOK
Continue current selection or _____.

Writing

MINI-LESSON
Book Reports: Include any examples of author's techniques (mood, tone, imagery) that make the book a favorite. Or _____.

COMPOSING
Continue writing book report. Or _____.

SHARING
Read, discuss, and proofread with a partner.
  Papers are dated and filed.

Word Study

CHART DEVELOPMENT
Spelling Emphasis: *ra* or _____
Other Emphasis: Acronyms or _____

Resource: Newspapers or _____

WRITING
Students write response to chart focus.

SPELLING
Select words to spell, team test, complete Word Study Record Sheet.
  Papers are dated and filed.

HOMEWORK
Share writing and spell words with a partner.
  Notebook signed.

Lesson 125

Research

LEAD-IN
Teacher introduces the Research Project:
Topic and Focus: Authors' techniques/Purpose or intent. Or _____
Resource: Basal readers or other short story collections. Or _____

RESEARCH PROJECT
Students read (skim) to find examples of stories in which the author's purpose is 1) to inform 2) to describe 3) to entertain 4) to persuade. Write the title of the short story and the author's name.

SHARING
Read and discuss discoveries with a partner.
Papers are dated and filed.

Recreational Reading

For approximately 30 minutes, all students read books.

CONVERSATIONS
Teacher has seven to ten minute conversations with students about predicting outcomes or next part of story using context of students' reading selections. Or _____

CLIPBOARD NOTES
Teacher takes notes about the above or _____.

READ-ALOUD BOOK
Sleeping Ugly by Jane Yolen or _____

Writing

MINI-LESSON
Discuss the purposes of book reports. Or _____.

Proofreading: prepositions

COMPOSING
Edit and revise the book report. Or _____.

SHARING
In groups of five or six share book reports. (The class may decide to display these when completed along with the book on a bulletin board or shelf or in a file for reference by other students.)
Papers are dated and filed.

Word Study

CHART DEVELOPMENT
Spelling Emphasis: *rp* or _____
Other Emphasis: Unfamiliar words or _____
Resource: Basal readers, library books, or _____

WRITING
Students write response to chart focus.

SPELLING
Select words to spell, team test, complete Word Study Record Sheet.
Papers are dated and filed.

HOMEWORK
Share writing and spell words with a partner.
Notebook signed.

Research

Five-day integrated lessons: The environment

LEAD-IN
Teacher introduces the Research Project:
Topic and Focus: Environment/Recycling or _____
Resource: Magazines, newspapers, or _____

RESEARCH PROJECT
Read to locate information about recycling projects or an environmental issue that should be considered. Write a description of the project or the issue.

SHARING
Read and discuss the projects or issues you've identified with a partner. (These lessons offer opportunties for outdoor activity and resource persons as additional sources of information on this topic.)
Papers are dated and filed.

Recreational Reading

For approximately 30 minutes, all students read books.

CONVERSATIONS
Teacher has seven to ten minute conversations with students about predicting outcomes or next part of story using context of students' reading selections. Or _____.

CLIPBOARD NOTES
Teacher takes notes about the above or _____.

READ-ALOUD BOOK
The Magic School Bus Inside the Human Body by Joanna Cole or _____

Writing

MINI-LESSON
Discuss recycling of waste. Discuss opinions and facts. Or _____.
Proofreading: subject/verb agreement

COMPOSING
Write your opinion of the efforts being made to recycle matter or your opinion of what needs to be considered for recycling. Reinforce your opinions with facts. Or _____.

SHARING
Read, discuss, and explain your positions.
Papers are dated and filed.

Word Study

CHART DEVELOPMENT
Spelling Emphasis: *ma* or _____

Other Emphasis: Recycling or _____

Resource: Magazines or _____

WRITING
Students write response to chart focus.

SPELLING
Select words to spell, team test, complete Word Study Record Sheet.
Papers are dated and filed.

HOMEWORK
Share writing and spell words with a partner.
Notebook signed.

Lesson **127**

Research

LEAD-IN
Teacher introduces the Research Project:
Topic and Focus: Environmental issues/Natural resources or _____
Resource: Student-selected materials or _____

RESEARCH PROJECT
Read to locate information about the protection of natural resources. Describe the efforts being made, how, when, and where to protect these resources.

SHARING
Read and discuss your discoveries with a partner.
Papers are dated and filed.

Recreational Reading

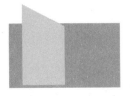

For approximately 30 minutes, all students read books.

CONVERSATIONS
Teacher has seven to ten minute conversations with students about predicting outcomes or next part of story using context of students' reading selections. Or _____.

CLIPBOARD NOTES
Teacher takes notes about the above or _____.

READ-ALOUD BOOK
The Giving Tree by Shel Silverstein or _____

Writing

MINI-LESSON
Discuss beauty in nature. Go outdoors or observe from a window a tree or the landscape or the playground. Or _____.
  Proofreading: adjectives

COMPOSING
Write a description of an outdoor scene. Describe either the beauty viewed or the ugliness of the scene. Or _____.

SHARING
Read, discuss, and proofread with a partner.
Papers are dated and filed.

Word Study

CHART DEVELOPMENT
Spelling Emphasis: *ca* or _____
Other Emphasis: Natural resources or _____
Resource: Science textbooks, music books, or _____

WRITING
Students write response to chart focus.

SPELLING
Select words to spell, team test, complete Word Study Record Sheet.
Papers are dated and filed.

HOMEWORK
Share writing and spell words with a partner.
Notebook signed.

Research

LEAD-IN
Teacher introduces the Research Project:
Topic and Focus: Environment/Ecology or _____
Resource: Science textbooks, library books about ecology or _____

RESEARCH PROJECT
Read to locate information about the interrelations between living organisms and their environments. Make a list of the essential elements of life and the impact of an environment on these. (water: desert, drought, etc.)

SHARING
Read, discuss, and explain your discoveries.
Papers are dated and filed.

Recreational Reading

For approximately 30 minutes, all students read books.

CONVERSATIONS
Teacher models reading for first 20 minutes. Teacher invites four or five students at the beginning of the reading time to gather for an oral reading session during the last ten minutes. Each student chooses a selection from a book read previously or one they will read that day. Or _____.

CLIPBOARD NOTES
Teacher records observations made about oral reading fluency or _____.

READ-ALOUD BOOK
The Magic School Bus at the Waterworks by Joanna Cole or _____

Writing

MINI-LESSON
Discuss Ecological issues in your area. Discuss solutions to problems or potential problems. Or _____.
Proofreading: correct letter form

COMPOSING
Write a letter to the editor or to the CEO of a business that is either contributing to pollution or has made a special effort to be a responsible industry and not pollute. Or _____.

SHARING
Select students with similar issues to share their writing, proofread letters, etc. Students may decide to mail letters, in which case they should be edited and revised and rewritten.
Papers are dated and filed.

Word Study

CHART DEVELOPMENT
Spelling Emphasis: *ri* or _____
Other Emphasis: Pollution or

_____
Resource: Newspapers or _____

WRITING
Students write response to chart focus.

SPELLING
Select words to spell, team test, complete Word Study Record Sheet.
Papers are dated and filed.

HOMEWORK
Share writing and spell words with a partner.
Notebook signed.

Lesson **129**

Research

LEAD-IN
Teacher introduces the Research Project:
Topic and Focus: Environmental Issues/Wildlife or _____
Resource: Student-selected materials or _____

RESEARCH PROJECT
Read to locate information about the protection of wildlife. Make a list of the things people do to harm wildlife, wildlife habitats, and the things people are doing to protect wildlife.

SHARING
Read and discuss your discoveries with a partner.
Papers are dated and filed.

Recreational Reading

For approximately 30 minutes, all students read books.

CONVERSATIONS
Teacher models reading for first 20 minutes. Teacher invites four or five students at the beginning of the reading time to gather for an oral reading session during the last ten minutes. Each student chooses a selection from a book read previously or one they will read that day. Or _____.

CLIPBOARD NOTES
Teacher records observations made about oral reading fluency or _____.

READ-ALOUD BOOK
Owl Moon by Jane Yolen or _____

Writing

MINI-LESSON
Discuss wildlife habitats. Or _____.
Proofreading: subject/verb agreement

COMPOSING
Pretend you are a wild animal and your home is being destroyed by bulldozers clearing land for a new shopping center. Describe how you would feel and what you would do. Or _____.

SHARING
Read, discuss, and proofread with a partner.
Papers are dated and filed.

Word Study

CHART DEVELOPMENT
Spelling Emphasis: *ct* or _____
Other Emphasis: Wildlife or
_____
Resource: Library books, basal readers, or _____

WRITING
Students write response to chart focus.

SPELLING
Select words to spell, team test, complete Word Study Record Sheet.
Papers are dated and filed.

HOMEWORK
Share writing and spell words with a partner.
Notebook signed.

Lesson 130

Research

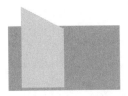

LEAD-IN
Teacher introduces the Research Project:
Topic and Focus: Environmental Issues/Food Chains or _____
Resource: Science textbooks, encyclopedias, or _____

RESEARCH PROJECT
Read to locate information about a food chain. Draw the food chain and explain what might happen if the food chain is broken.

SHARING
Read and discuss your drawings and writing with a partner.
　Papers are dated and filed.

Recreational Reading

For approximately 30 minutes, all students read books.

CONVERSATIONS
Teacher models reading for first 20 minutes. Teacher invites four or five students at the beginning of the reading time to gather for an oral reading session during the last ten minutes. Each student chooses a selection from a book read previously or one they will read that day. Or _____.

CLIPBOARD NOTES
Teacher records observations made about oral reading fluency or _____.

READ-ALOUD BOOK
Bird Watch by Jane Yolen or _____

Writing

MINI-LESSON
Discuss food chains and the predator/prey relationship in nature. Or _____.
　Proofreading: pronouns

COMPOSING
Think about how your life would be if you were either the predator or the prey in a food chain. Write about your life. Or _____.

SHARING
Read, discuss, and proofread with a partner.
　Papers are dated and filed.

Word Study

CHART DEVELOPMENT
Spelling Emphasis: *pt* or _____
Other Emphasis: Food chains or
_____
Resource: Encyclopedias or
_____

WRITING
Students write response to chart focus.

SPELLING
Select words to spell, team test, complete Word Study Record Sheet.
　Papers are dated and filed.

HOMEWORK
Share writing and spell words with a partner.
　Notebook signed.

Lesson **131**

Research

LEAD-IN
Teacher introduces the Research Project:
Topic and Focus: Autobiography/
Time lines or _____
Resource: Teacher's example or
_____

RESEARCH PROJECT
Teacher shares personal autobiographical
time line using board, overhead, or hand-
out. Students create a personal time line.

SHARING
Read and discuss with a partner.
  Papers are dated and filed.

Recreational Reading

For approximately 30 minutes, all students read books.

CONVERSATIONS
Teacher moves from student to student
having two to three minute conversations
about similes, metaphors, and alliteration
or _____.

CLIPBOARD NOTES
Teacher takes notes about students' abilities to recognize the above in their reading selection or _____.

READ-ALOUD BOOK
Continue current selection or _____.

Writing

MINI-LESSON
Display pictures that depict scenes in na-
ture. Discuss similes. Or _____.
  Proofreading: use of *as* or *like*

COMPOSING
Write a paragraph about a picture on display using similes as comparisons. Or
_____.

SHARING
Read, discuss, and proofread with a partner who selected the same picture to
write about.
  Papers are dated and filed.

Word Study

CHART DEVELOPMENT
Spelling Emphasis: *ex* or _____
Other Emphasis: Deserts or
_____
Resource: Library books, Science text-
books, or _____

WRITING
Students write response to chart focus.

SPELLING
Select words to spell, team test, complete
Word Study Record Sheet.
  Papers are dated and filed.

HOMEWORK
Share writing and spell words with a
partner.
  Notebook signed.

234

Research

LEAD-IN
Teacher introduces the Research Project:
Topic and Focus: Presidents/Time lines or _____
Resource: Encyclopedias, history books, biographies, or _____

RESEARCH PROJECT
Students read to make notes on important events in the life of any president they select. This is a two-day lesson.

SHARING
Read and discuss information discovered with a partner.
Papers are dated and filed.

Recreational Reading

For approximately 30 minutes, all students read books.

CONVERSATIONS
Teacher moves from student to student having two to three minute conversations about similes, metaphors, and alliteration or _____.

CLIPBOARD NOTES
Teacher takes notes about students' abilities to recognize the above in their reading selection or _____.

READ-ALOUD BOOK
The Cay by Theodore Taylor or _____

Writing

MINI-LESSON
Discuss parts of the body and human anatomony. Discuss use of similes to compare things that are usually different. Or
_____.
Proofreading: use of *like/as*

COMPOSING
Write similes to compare parts of the body to other things. Or _____.

SHARING
Read, discuss, and proofread with four or five partners.
Papers are dated and filed.

Word Study

CHART DEVELOPMENT
Spelling Emphasis: *est* or
_____
Other Emphasis: Feet, hands or
_____
Resource: Health textbook, magazines, or _____

WRITING
Students write response to chart focus.

SPELLING
Select words to spell, team test, complete Word Study Record Sheet.
Papers are dated and filed.

HOMEWORK
Share writing and spell words with a partner.
Notebook signed.

Lesson 133

Research

LEAD-IN
Teacher introduces the Research Project:
Topic and Focus: Presidents/Time lines or _____
Resource: Encyclopedias, history books, biographies, or _____

RESEARCH PROJECT
Continue with previous day's reading and writing, put the information located in a time line of the president's life.

SHARING
Read, discuss, and compare time lines in groups of two or three. Pair students with the same presidents.
   Papers are dated and filed.

Recreational Reading

For approximately 30 minutes, all students read books.

CONVERSATIONS
Teacher moves from student to student having two to three minute conversations about similes, metaphors, and alliteration or _____.

CLIPBOARD NOTES
Teacher takes notes about students' abilities to recognize the above in their reading selection or _____

READ-ALOUD BOOK
Continue current selection or _____.

Writing

MINI-LESSON
Discuss metaphors. These are comparisons without *like/as*. Read some examples to the students. Or _____.
   Proofreading: correct spelling

COMPOSING
Students write a paragraph or poem about school, the classroom, or learning/studying using metaphors to compare these to other things. Or _____.

SHARING
Read, discuss, and proofread with a partner
   Papers are dated and filed.

Word Study

CHART DEVELOPMENT
Spelling Emphasis: *un* or
_____
Other Emphasis: Illness or
_____
Resource: Newspapers or _____

WRITING
Students write response to chart focus.

SPELLING
Select words to spell, team test, complete Word Study Record Sheet.
   Papers are dated and filed.

HOMEWORK
Share writing and spell words with a partner.
   Notebook signed.

Lesson 134

Research

LEAD-IN
Teacher introduces the Research Project:
Topic and Focus: Storytelling/Recall and sequence or _____
Resource: Collections of short stories and recordings or _____

RESEARCH PROJECT
Discuss the art and the elements of storytelling. Let students listen to a recording of a storyteller. What was effective? Students select favorite short story and reread it.

SHARING
Discuss the short story selected with a partner.
    Papers are dated and filed.

Recreational Reading

For approximately 30 minutes, all students read books.

CONVERSATIONS
Teacher has seven to ten minute conversations with individual students determining literal comprehension or

_____.

CLIPBOARD NOTES
Teacher takes notes about discoveries during conversations or _____.

READ-ALOUD BOOK
Continue current selection or _____.

Writing

MINI-LESSON
Discuss opinions and homework. Or

_____.
    Proofreading: topic sentences

COMPOSING
Students write opinions about homework. Or _____.

SHARING
Read, discuss, and proofread in groups of two or three.
    Papers are dated and filed.

Word Study

CHART DEVELOPMENT
Spelling Emphasis: *ic* or _____
Other Emphasis: Homework or

_____
Resource: Newspapers or _____

WRITING
Students write response to chart focus.

SPELLING
Select words to spell, team test, complete Word Study Record Sheet.
    Papers are dated and filed.

HOMEWORK
Share writing and spell words with a partner.
    Notebook signed.

Lesson 135

Research

LEAD-IN
Teacher introduces the Research Project:
Topic and Focus: Storytelling/Recall and Sequence or _____
Resource: Same short story selected in previous lesson or _____

RESEARCH PROJECT
Storytellers reread their stories several times before they begin to practice telling it without a book or notes. Reread selected short story and make notes about important things you want to include as you retell it. Also make notes so that you get the sequence of events correct.

SHARING
With a partner, begin to retell story using notes.
   Papers are dated and filed.

Recreational Reading

For approximately 30 minutes, all students read books.

CONVERSATIONS
Teacher has seven to ten minute conversations with individual students determining literal comprehension or _____.

CLIPBOARD NOTES
Teacher takes notes about discoveries during conversations or _____.

READ-ALOUD BOOK
Continue current selection or _____.

Writing

MINI-LESSON
Discuss writing opinions. Discuss rights and responsibilities or home and school. Or _____.
   Proofreading: possessive pronouns

COMPOSING
Students write their opinion about rights and responsibilities or a topic of their choice. Or _____.

SHARING
Read, discuss, and proofread in groups of two or three.
   Papers are dated and filed.

Word Study

CHART DEVELOPMENT
Spelling Emphasis: *nom* or
_____
Other Emphasis: Leadership or
_____
Resource: Magazines or _____

WRITING
Students write response to chart focus.

SPELLING
Select words to spell, team test, complete Word Study Record Sheet.
   Papers are dated and filed.

HOMEWORK
Share writing and spell words with a partner.
   Notebook signed.

Lesson **136**

Research

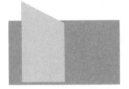

LEAD-IN
Teacher introduces the Research Project:
Topic and Focus: Storytelling/Recall and sequence or _____
Resource: Same short story as selected previously or _____

RESEARCH PROJECT
Students practice retelling their story with a partner. Reread any parts of the story for detail. Discuss the use of voice, dress, or props for effect.

SHARING
Partners pair with another set of partners to retell stories. Students should practice retelling their stories at home.
Papers are dated and filed.

Recreational Reading

For approximately 30 minutes, all students read books.

CONVERSATIONS
Teacher has seven to ten minute conversations with individual students determining literal comprehension or _____.

CLIPBOARD NOTES
Teacher takes notes about discoveries during conversations or _____.

READ-ALOUD BOOK
Continue current selection or _____.

Writing

MINI-LESSON
Discuss local issues and editorials. Or
_____.
Proofreading: words spelled correctly

COMPOSING
Write a letter to the editor about a local issue or write an editorial for a class or school newsletter. Or _____.

SHARING
Read, discuss, and proofread in groups of two or three.
Papers are dated and filed.

Word Study

CHART DEVELOPMENT
Spelling Emphasis: *cip* or
_____
Other Emphasis: College or
_____
Resource: Newspapers or _____

WRITING
Students write response to chart focus.

SPELLING
Select words to spell, team test, complete Word Study Record Sheet.
Papers are dated and filed.

HOMEWORK
Share writing and spell words with a partner.
Notebook signed.

Lesson **137**

Research

LEAD-IN
Teacher introduces the Research Project:
Topic and Focus: Storytelling/Recall and sequence or _____
Resource: Same short story selected previously or _____

RESEARCH PROJECT
In groups of five or six, students tell their stories or segments of a story. Recordings may be made of these and shared with other classes, or students may volunteer to go to other class to be a guest storyteller.

SHARING
Share with other classes. See above.
   Papers are dated and filed.

Recreational Reading

For approximately 30 minutes, all students read books.

CONVERSATIONS
Teacher has seven to ten minute conversations with individual students determining literal comprehension or _____.

CLIPBOARD NOTES
Teacher takes notes about discoveries during conversations or _____.

READ-ALOUD BOOK
Continue current selection or _____.

Writing

MINI-LESSON
Discuss honesty and meaning of honesty in everyday life and the tough decisions that honest people must sometimes make. Or _____.
   Proofreading: *there* and *their*

COMPOSING
Students write about honesty or _____.

SHARING
Read, discuss, and proofread with a partner.
   Papers are dated and filed.

Word Study

CHART DEVELOPMENT
Spelling Emphasis: *fer* or
_____

Other Emphasis: Magic or
_____

Resource: Recreational Reading books or _____

WRITING
Students write response to chart focus.

SPELLING
Select words to spell, team test, complete Word Study Record Sheet.
   Papers are dated and filed.

HOMEWORK
Share writing and spell words with a partner.
   Notebook signed.

S u c c e s **S** u c c e s **S** u c c e s **S** u c c e s **S** u c c e s **S** u c c e s **S** u c c e s **S** u c c e s **S**

Lesson **138**

Research

LEAD-IN
Teacher introduces the Research Project:
Topic and Focus: Advertising/Satire or _____
Resource: Magazines or _____

RESEARCH PROJECT
Discuss satire. Read in magazines to locate food ads. Design a satirical food ad.

SHARING
Discuss examples of satire in groups of five or six. Make a bulletin board of examples of satire.
Papers are dated and filed.

Recreational Reading

For approximately 30 minutes, all students read books.

CONVERSATIONS
Teacher has seven to ten minute conversations with individual students determining literal comprehension or _____

CLIPBOARD NOTES
Teacher takes notes about discoveries during conversations or _____.

READ-ALOUD BOOK
Whoppers, Tall Tales and Other Lies Collected from American Folklore by Alvin Schwartz or _____

Writing

MINI-LESSON
Discuss tall tales and exaggeration. Read examples to class. Or _____.
Proofreading: _was_ and _were_

COMPOSING
Write your own version of a familiar tall tale or write a tall tale about a modern day person or topic. Or _____.

SHARING
Read, discuss, and proofread with a partner.
Papers are dated and filed.

Word Study

CHART DEVELOPMENT
Spelling Emphasis: _sho_ or
_____

Other Emphasis: Exaggeration or
_____

Resource: Basal readers or
_____

WRITING
Students write response to chart focus.

SPELLING
Select words to spell, team test, complete Word Study Record Sheet.
Papers are dated and filed.

HOMEWORK
Share writing and spell words with a partner.
Notebook signed.

Lesson **139**

Research

LEAD-IN
Teacher introduces the Research Project:
Topic and Focus: Advertising/
Techniques of persuasion or _____
Resource: Magazines or _____

RESEARCH PROJECT
Read in magazines to locate advertisements using "techniques of persuasion." Cut out ads and explain persuasive techniques used.

SHARING
Read and discuss in groups of three or four examples of persuasion in advertising.
    Papers are dated and filed.

Recreational Reading

For approximately 30 minutes, all students read books.

CONVERSATIONS
Teacher has seven to ten minute conversations with individual students determining literal comprehension or _____.

CLIPBOARD NOTES
Teacher takes notes about discoveries during conversations or _____.

READ-ALOUD BOOK
The Iron Giant by Ted Hughes or _____

Writing

MINI-LESSON
Continue discussion of tall tales and use of exaggeration. Or _____.
    Proofreading: *is* and *are*

COMPOSING
Complete composition begun in previous lesson. Or _____.

SHARING
Read, discuss, and proofread with a partner. You may want to have a class share time or put all tall tales in a booklet.
    Papers are dated and filed.

Word Study

CHART DEVELOPMENT
Spelling Emphasis: *eth* or _____

Other Emphasis: Furniture or _____

Resource: Newspapers or _____

WRITING
Students write response to chart focus.

SPELLING
Select words to spell, team test, complete Word Study Record Sheet.
    Papers are dated and filed.

HOMEWORK
Share writing and spell words with a partner.
    Notebook signed.

Lesson **140**

Research

LEAD-IN
Teacher introduces the Research Project:
Topic and Focus: Advertising/
Techniques of persuasion or _____
Resource: TV Guide and recall of com-
mercials, or _____

RESEARCH PROJECT
Using TV schedules, ask students to recall commercials or show ads that use
techniques of persuasion. Write the name
of show or product. Explain what was
used to persuade them to watch the show
or buy the product.

SHARING
Read and discuss with partner.
  Papers are dated and filed.

Recreational Reading

For approximately 30 minutes, all students read books.

CONVERSATIONS
Teacher has seven to ten minute conversations with individual students determining literal comprehension.

CLIPBOARD NOTES
Teacher takes notes about discoveries
during conversations or _____.

READ-ALOUD BOOK
Continue current selection or _____.

Writing

MINI-LESSON
Discuss elements of science fiction stories.
Or _____.
  Proofreading: *do* and *did*

COMPOSING
Write your version of a favorite science
fiction story or comic strip or write your
own science fiction story. Or _____.

SHARING
Read, discuss, and proofread with a
partner.
  Papers are dated and filed.

Word Study

CHART DEVELOPMENT
Spelling Emphasis: *own* or
_____
Other Emphasis: Antiques or
_____
Resource: Magazines or _____

WRITING
Students write response to chart focus.

SPELLING
Select words to spell, team test, complete
Word Study Record Sheet.
  Papers are dated and filed.

HOMEWORK
Share writing and spell words with a
partner.
  Notebook signed.

Lesson **141**

Research

Six-day Research Project

LEAD-IN
Teacher introduces the Research Project:
Topic and Focus: Authors/Selecting
a report topic and resources or
_____

Resource: Student-selected materials
or _____

RESEARCH PROJECT
Students select an author they would like
to learn more about by doing a report on
that person. Students collect resources

and begin reading for information and
taking notes.

SHARING
Read and discuss information discovered.
Papers are dated and filed.

Recreational Reading

For approximately 30 minutes, all students read books.

CONVERSATIONS
Teacher reads for 20 minutes modeling
reading. Book Share: Students volunteer
to share something about the books they
are reading during the last ten minutes.
Or _____.

CLIPBOARD NOTES
Teacher notes who eagerly volunteers,
what kind of books they are reading, and
who seems interested in the book after
the sharing time. Or _____.

READ-ALOUD BOOK
Good Dog Carl or *Carl Goes Shopping* by
Alexandra Day or _____

Writing

MINI-LESSON
Discuss "Wordless books": books that tell
stories without words or with very few
words. Or _____.
  Proofreading: vivid descriptions

COMPOSING
Students select a "wordless book" they
would like to rewrite using words. Discuss with a partner what you might want
to write. Make notes for use when you begin rewriting. Or _____.

SHARING
See above.
  Papers are dated and filed.

Word Study

CHART DEVELOPMENT
Spelling Emphasis: *ive* or
_____

Other Emphasis: Hospitals or
_____

Resource: Newspapers or _____

WRITING
Students write response to chart focus.

SPELLING
Select words to spell, team test, complete
Word Study Record Sheet.
  Papers are dated and filed.

HOMEWORK
Share writing and spell words with a
partner.
  Notebook signed.

Research

LEAD-IN
Teacher introduces the Research Project:
Topic and Focus: Authors/Selecting
resources and locating information or
_____

Resource: Student-selected materials
or _____

RESEARCH PROJECT
Students continue to read and record information about their selected author.

SHARING
Read and discuss information discovered.
   Papers are dated and filed.

Recreational Reading

For approximately 30 minutes, all students read books.

CONVERSATIONS
Teacher models reading for ten minutes.
Book Share: Students volunteer to share
something about the books they are reading during the last 20 minutes. Or
_____.

CLIPBOARD NOTES
Teacher notes who eagerly volunteers,
what kind of books they are reading, and
who seems interested in the book after
the sharing time. Or _____.

READ-ALOUD BOOK
Will's Mammoth by Rafe Martin or
_____

Writing

MINI-LESSON
Continue discussion of telling stories
without words. Or _____.
   Proofreading: correct punctuation in
conversation

COMPOSING
Students begin to rewrite their selected
"wordless book." Or _____.

SHARING
Read, discuss, and proofread with a
partner.
   Papers are dated and filed.

Word Study

CHART DEVELOPMENT
Spelling Emphasis: *dem* or
_____

Other Emphasis: Unfamiliar words
or _____
Resource: Newspapers or _____

WRITING
Students write response to chart focus.

SPELLING
Select words to spell, team test, complete
Word Study Record Sheet.
   Papers are dated and filed.

HOMEWORK
Share writing and spell words with a
partner.
   Notebook signed.

Lesson **143**

Research

LEAD-IN
Teacher introduces the Research Project:
Topic and Focus: Authors/Locating information or _____
Resource: Student-selected materials or _____

RESEARCH PROJECT
Students continue to read and collect information on their selected author.

SHARING
Read and discuss information discovered with a partner.
   Papers are dated and filed.

Recreational Reading

For approximately 30 minutes, all students read books.

CONVERSATIONS
Teacher moves from student to student having two to three minute conversations about their favorite authors or _____

CLIPBOARD NOTES
Teacher notes favorite authors for future reference when recommending books or _____.

READ-ALOUD BOOK
A Boy, a Dog, and a Frog by Mercer Mayer or _____

Writing

MINI-LESSON
Continue to share and discuss the wonderful world of the "wordless book." Or _____.

   Proofreading: adjectives

COMPOSING
Continue to rewrite the selected "wordless book." Or _____.

SHARING
Read, discuss, and proofread with a partner.
   Papers are dated and filed.

Word Study

CHART DEVELOPMENT
Spelling Emphasis: *the* or _____

Other Emphasis: Prisons or _____

Resource: Newspapers or _____

WRITING
Students write response to chart focus.

SPELLING
Select words to spell, team test, complete Word Study Record Sheet.
   Papers are dated and filed.

HOMEWORK
Share writing and spell words with a partner.
   Notebook signed.

Lesson **144**

Research

LEAD-IN
Teacher introduces the Research Project:
Topic and Focus: Authors/Organizing information or _____
Resource: Student-selected materials or _____

RESEARCH PROJECT
Students begin to organize information into report and find any other facts or interesting bits of information about their author to complete their information gathering.

SHARING
Read and discuss information discovered with a partner.
Papers are dated and filed.

Recreational Reading

For approximately 30 minutes, all students read books.

CONVERSATIONS
Teacher moves from student to student having two to three minute conversations about their favorite authors or _____.

CLIPBOARD NOTES
Teacher notes favorite authors for future reference when recommending books or _____.

READ-ALOUD BOOK
Rain by Peter Spier or _____

Writing

MINI-LESSON
Discuss editing and revision. Or _____.
    Proofreading: misspelled words

COMPOSING
Match pages of writing and dialogue with the picture pages of the "wordless book" you are rewriting. Or _____.

SHARING
Read, discuss, and proofread with a partner.
Papers are dated and filed.

Word Study

CHART DEVELOPMENT
Spelling Emphasis: *van* or _____

Other Emphasis: Skin care or _____

Resource: Magazines or _____

WRITING
Students write response to chart focus.

SPELLING
Select words to spell, team test, complete Word Study Record Sheet.
Papers are dated and filed.

HOMEWORK
Share writing and spell words with a partner.
Notebook signed.

Lesson **145**

Research

LEAD-IN
Teacher introduces the Research Project:
Topic and Focus: Authors/Writing first draft of report or _____
Resource: Student-selected materials or _____

RESEARCH PROJECT
Students write the first draft of their report on their selected author.

SHARING
Read and discuss your report with a partner.
 Papers are dated and filed.

Recreational Reading

For approximately 30 minutes, all students read books.

CONVERSATIONS
Teacher moves from student to student having two to three minute conversations about their favorite authors or _____.

CLIPBOARD NOTES
Teacher notes favorite authors for future reference when recommending books or _____.

READ-ALOUD BOOK
Sebastian and the Mushroom by Fernando Krahn or _____

Writing

MINI-LESSON
Discuss final copy of rewritten story. Or _____.
 Proofreading: all previous proofreading suggestions

COMPOSING
Students write the final copy of their words for the "wordless book." Or _____.

SHARING
With the "wordless book" in hand, read words written for the book in groups of three or four.
 Papers are dated and filed.

Word Study

CHART DEVELOPMENT
Spelling Emphasis: *ric* or
_____
Other Emphasis: Cartoons or
_____
Resource: Newspapers or _____

WRITING
Students write response to chart focus.

SPELLING
Select words to spell, team test, complete Word Study Record Sheet.
 Papers are dated and filed.

HOMEWORK
Share writing and spell words with a partner.
 Notebook signed.

Research

LEAD-IN
Teacher introduces the Research Project:
Topic and Focus: Authors/Completing and sharing reports or _____
Resource: Student-selected materials or _____

RESEARCH PROJECT
Students rewrite their reports, and class decides how to share reports. (e.g., oral reading, bulletin board display, small-group presentations, video tapes, etc.)

SHARING
See above.
 Papers are dated and filed.

Recreational Reading

For approximately 30 minutes, all students read books.

CONVERSATIONS
Teacher has seven to ten minute conversations with students about authors' literary techniques and styles or _____.

CLIPBOARD NOTES
Teacher takes notes about discoveries during conversations or _____.

READ-ALOUD BOOK
Roll of Thunder, Hear My Cry by Mildred Taylor or _____

Writing

MINI-LESSON
Discuss feature or book reviews and book reports. Or _____.
 Proofreading: capital letters and underlining names of books.

COMPOSING
Students select a favorite book they have read and begin writing a book report or review about it. Or _____.

SHARING
Read, discuss, and proofread with a partner.
 Papers are dated and filed.

Word Study

CHART DEVELOPMENT
Spelling Emphasis: *pon* or
_____
Other Emphasis: Authors or
_____
Resource: Textbooks or basal Readers or _____

WRITING
Students write response to chart focus.

SPELLING
Select words to spell, team test, complete Word Study Record Sheet.
 Papers are dated and filed.

HOMEWORK
Share writing and spell words with a partner.
 Notebook signed.

Lesson **147**

Research

LEAD-IN
Teacher introduces the Research Project:
Topic and Focus: Bees/Relating information or _____
Resource: Science textbooks or _____

RESEARCH PROJECT
Students read in a science textbook about bees. Relate information on how bees are helpful to man; how harmful.

SHARING
Read and discuss information discovered with a partner.
Papers are dated and filed.

Recreational Reading

For approximately 30 minutes, all students read books.

CONVERSATIONS
Teacher has seven to ten minute conversations with students about authors' literary techniques and styles or _____.

CLIPBOARD NOTES
Teacher takes notes about discoveries during conversations or _____.

READ-ALOUD BOOK
Continue current selection or _____

Writing

MINI-LESSON
Discuss progress by asking some students to randomly share parts of their book reviews or reports. Or _____.
Proofreading: adjectives, adverbs, prepositions

COMPOSING
Students continue to write their book review or report. Or _____.

SHARING
Read, discuss, and proofread with a partner.
Papers are dated and filed.

Word Study

CHART DEVELOPMENT
Spelling Emphasis: *ect* or _____

Other Emphasis: Unfamiliar Words or _____
Resource: Recreational Reading books or _____

WRITING
Students write response to chart focus.

SPELLING
Select words to spell, team test, complete Word Study Record Sheet.
Papers are dated and filed.

HOMEWORK
Share writing and spell words with a partner.
Notebook signed.

Lesson 148

Research

LEAD-IN
Teacher introduces the Research Project:
Topic and Focus: Pollution/Relating
information or _____
Resource: Student-selected materials
or _____

RESEARCH PROJECT
Read to locate information you can relate
to pollution. Write about the connection
and associations you can make.

SHARING
Read and discuss information discovered
with a partner.
  Papers are dated and filed.

Recreational Reading

For approximately 30 minutes, all students read books.

CONVERSATIONS
Teacher has seven to ten minute conversations with students about authors' literary techniques and styles or _____.

CLIPBOARD NOTES
Teacher takes notes about discoveries
during conversations or _____.

READ-ALOUD BOOK
Continue current selection or _____.

Writing

MINI-LESSON
Discuss editing and revising book reports
and reviews. Or _____.
  Proofreading: paragraph structure

COMPOSING
Students begin to rewrite reports.

SHARING
Read, discuss, and proofread with a
partner.
  Papers are dated and filed.

Word Study

CHART DEVELOPMENT
Spelling Emphasis: *sta* or

_____
Other Emphasis: Investments or

_____
Resource: Newspapers or _____

WRITING
Students write response to chart focus.

SPELLING
Select words to spell, team test, complete
Word Study Record Sheet.
  Papers are dated and filed.

HOMEWORK
Share writing and spell words with a
partner.
  Notebook signed.

Lesson **149**

Research

LEAD-IN
Teacher introduces the Research Project:
Topic and Focus: First Aid/Relating information or _____
Resource: Student-selected materials or _____

RESEARCH PROJECT
Read to locate information you can relate to first aid. Write your findings.

SHARING
Read and discuss your discoveries with a partner.
  Papers are dated and filed.

Recreational Reading

For approximately 30 minutes, all students read books.

CONVERSATIONS
Teacher has seven to ten minute conversations with students about authors' literary techniques and styles or _____.

CLIPBOARD NOTES
Teacher takes notes about discoveries during conversations or _____.

READ-ALOUD BOOK
Continue current selection or _____.

Writing

MINI-LESSON
Discuss completing the book review or report. Or _____.
  Proofreading: handwriting

COMPOSING
Students should complete final copy of their book reports. Or _____.

SHARING
Read, discuss, and proofread with a partner.
  Papers are dated and filed.

Word Study

CHART DEVELOPMENT
Spelling Emphasis: *lop* or

_____

Other Emphasis: First aid or

_____

Resource: Student-selected or

_____

WRITING
Students write response to chart focus.

SPELLING
Select words to spell, team test, complete Word Study Record Sheet.
  Papers are dated and filed.

HOMEWORK
Share writing and spell words with a partner.
  Notebook signed.

Lesson 150

Research

LEAD-IN
Teacher introduces the Research Project:
Topic and Focus: Oceans/Relating
Information or _____
Resource: Student-selected materials
or _____

RESEARCH PROJECT
Read to locate information you can relate
to oceans. Use more than one resource.
Write the name of resource and information found. Write the connections between
the information in the two different
resources.

SHARING
Read and discuss the information you dis-
covered with a partner.
   Papers are dated and filed.

Recreational Reading

For approximately 30 minutes, all students read books.

CONVERSATIONS
Teacher has seven to ten minute conversations with students about authors' literary techniques and styles or _____.

CLIPBOARD NOTES
Teacher takes notes about discoveries
during conversations or _____.

READ-ALOUD BOOK
Continue current selection or _____.

Writing

MINI-LESSON
This is a sharing day for book reports or
reviews. Or _____.

COMPOSING
Sharing Day. Or _____.

SHARING
Sharing Day.
   Papers are dated and filed.

Word Study

CHART DEVELOPMENT
Spelling Emphasis: *res* or

_____

Other Emphasis: Oceans or

_____

Resource: Student-selected or

_____

WRITING
Students write response to chart focus.

SPELLING
Select words to spell, team test, complete
Word Study Record Sheet.
   Papers are dated and filed.

HOMEWORK
Share writing and spell words with a
partner.
   Notebook signed.

Lesson **151**

Research

LEAD-IN
Teacher introduces the Research Project:
Topic and Focus: Computers/
Relating Information or _____
Resource: Student-selected materials
or _____

RESEARCH PROJECT
Read to locate information you can relate
to computers. Explain your associations
and connections.

SHARING
Read and discuss information discovered
with a partner.
　Papers are dated and filed.

Recreational Reading

For approximately 30 minutes, all students read books.

CONVERSATIONS
Teacher has seven to ten minute conversations with students about authors' literary techniques and styles or _____.

CLIPBOARD NOTES
Teacher takes notes about discoveries
during conversations or _____.

READ-ALOUD BOOK
The Lost Garden by Laurence Yep or
_____

Writing

MINI-LESSON
Discuss autobiographies and time lines.
Or _____.
　Proofreading: words that denote
sequence

COMPOSING
Students make a time line of their lives
to use as a guide for writing their autobiographies. Or _____.

SHARING
Read, discuss, and proofread with a
partner.
　Papers are dated and filed.

Word Study

CHART DEVELOPMENT
Spelling Emphasis: *don* or

_____

Other Emphasis: Games or

_____

Resource: Newspapers or _____

WRITING
Students write response to chart focus.

SPELLING
Select words to spell, team test, complete
Word Study Record Sheet.
　Papers are dated and filed.

HOMEWORK
Share writing and spell words with a
partner.
　Notebook signed.

Lesson **152**

Research

LEAD-IN
Teacher introduces the Research Project:
Topic and Focus: Opera, musicals, broadway productions/Relating information or _____
Resource: Student-selected materials or _____

RESEARCH PROJECT
Read to locate information you can associate with opera, musical, and broadway productions. Explain the associations and connections.

SHARING
Read and discuss information discovered in groups of three or four.
  Papers are dated and filed.

Recreational Reading

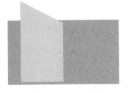

For approximately 30 minutes, all students read books.

CONVERSATIONS
Teacher has seven to ten minute conversations with students about authors' literary techniques and styles or _____.

CLIPBOARD NOTES
Teacher takes notes about discoveries during conversations or _____.

READ-ALOUD BOOK
Continue current selection or _____.

Writing

MINI-LESSON
Discuss autobiographies. Or _____.
  Proofreading: use of comma in words in a series

COMPOSING
Students begin to write their autobiographies. Or _____.

SHARING
Read, discuss, and proofread with a partner.
  Papers are dated and filed.

Word Study

CHART DEVELOPMENT
Spelling Emphasis: *bra* or
_____
Other Emphasis: Bravery, courage, or _____
Resource: Basal readers or _____

WRITING
Students write response to chart focus.

SPELLING
Select words to spell, team test, complete Word Study Record Sheet.
  Papers are dated and filed.

HOMEWORK
Share writing and spell words with a partner.
  Notebook signed.

Lesson 153

Research

LEAD-IN
Teacher introduces the Research Project:
Topic and Focus: Personal health
and care/Relating information or
_____

Resource: Student-selected materials
or _____

RESEARCH PROJECT
Read to locate any information related to
the health and care of the body. Explain
the associations and connections to your
own personal health and care of your
body.

SHARING
Read and discuss information discovered
in groups of two or three.
   Papers are dated and filed.

Recreational Reading

For approximately 30 minutes, all students read books.

CONVERSATIONS
Teacher reads for first fifteen minutes.
Teacher invites four or five students at
the beginning of the reading time to
gather for an oral reading session during
the last fifteen minutes. Each student
chooses a selection from a book read
previously or one they will read that day.
Or _____.

CLIPBOARD NOTES
Teacher takes notes about students' abilities to listen and respond in a peer reading group or _____.

READ-ALOUD BOOK
Continue current selection or _____.

Writing

MINI-LESSON
Continue discussion of autobiographies.
Or _____.
   Proofreading: capital letters for proper
nouns

COMPOSING
Students continue to write their autobiographies. Or _____.

SHARING
Read, discuss, and proofread with a
partner.
   Papers are dated and filed.

Word Study

CHART DEVELOPMENT
Spelling Emphasis: _min_ or
_____

Other Emphasis: Heroes or
_____

Resource: Newspapers or _____

WRITING
Students write response to chart focus.

SPELLING
Select words to spell, team test, complete
Word Study Record Sheet.
   Papers are dated and filed.

HOMEWORK
Share writing and spell words with a
partner.
   Notebook signed.

Research

LEAD-IN
Teacher introduces the Research Project:
Topic and Focus: Vacations/Relating
information or _____
Resource: Student-selected materials
or _____

RESEARCH PROJECT
Read to locate information you associate
with vacations. Explain the relationship
of the information to vacations.

SHARING
Read and discuss in groups of three or
four the information you discovered.
  Papers are dated and filed.

Recreational Reading

For approximately 30 minutes, all students read books.

CONVERSATIONS
Teacher reads for first fifteen minutes.
Teacher invites four or five students at
the beginning of the reading time to
gather for an oral reading session during
the last fifteen minutes. Each student
chooses a selection from a book read
previously or one they will read that day.
Or _____.

CLIPBOARD NOTES
Teacher takes notes about students' abilities to listen and respond in a peer reading group.

READ-ALOUD BOOK
Continue current selection or _____.

Writing

MINI-LESSON
Discuss the editing and revision of autobiographies. Or _____.
  Proofreading: all previous proofreading
suggestions

COMPOSING
Students begin to edit and revise
autobiographies.

SHARING
Read, discuss, and proofread with a
partner.
  Papers are dated and filed.

Word Study

CHART DEVELOPMENT
Spelling Emphasis: *dre* or
_____
Other Emphasis: Dogs, cats or
_____
Resource: Student-selected materials
or _____

WRITING
Students write response to chart focus.

SPELLING
Select words to spell, team test, complete
Word Study Record Sheet.
  Papers are dated and filed.

HOMEWORK
Share writing and spell words with a
partner.
  Notebook signed.

Lesson 155

Research

Six-day Research Project

LEAD-IN
Teacher introduces the Research Project:
Topic and Focus: Current world is-
sues/Locating information or _____
Resource: Magazines, newspapers, or
_____

RESEARCH PROJECT
Students through discussion and brainstorming identify a list of current world
issues. Divide into groups of three or four
for this project. Each groups selects an issue to research. Read to locate information about the issue and to locate information related to the issue.

SHARING
Read and discuss information discovered
with another group.
   Papers are dated and filed.

Recreational Reading

For approximately 30 minutes, all students read books.

CONVERSATIONS
Teacher moves from student to student
having two to three minute conversations
about story settings, plots, and character
analysis or _____.

CLIPBOARD NOTES
Teacher takes notes about the above or
_____.

READ-ALOUD BOOK
Continue current selection or _____.

Writing

MINI-LESSON
Discuss final copy of autobiographies and
any problem of concerns related. Or
_____.

COMPOSING
Students complete the final copy of their
autobiographies. Or _____.

SHARING
Read and discuss with a partner. These
can be put in a class booklet, on a bulletin board with photographs of students, or
read on an additional day during a class
share time.
   Papers are dated and filed.

Word Study

CHART DEVELOPMENT
Spelling Emphasis: *con* or
_____
Other Emphasis: Unfamiliar words
or _____
Resource: Student-selected materials
or _____

WRITING
Students write response to chart focus.

SPELLING
Select words to spell, team test, complete
Word Study Record Sheet.
   Papers are dated and filed.

HOMEWORK
Share writing and spell words with a
partner.
   Notebook signed.

Lesson 156

Research

LEAD-IN
Teacher introduces the Research Project:
Topic and Focus: Current issues/
Locating and relating information or

Resource: Student-selected materials
or _____

RESEARCH PROJECT
Students working in previously designated groups, continue to locate and draw
relationships of information to the current issue they are investigating.

SHARING
Read and discuss information discovered
with another group.
  Papers are dated and filed.

Recreational Reading

For approximately 30 minutes, all students read books.

CONVERSATIONS
Teacher moves from student to student
having two to three minute conversations
about story settings, plots, and character
analysis or _____.

CLIPBOARD NOTES
Teacher takes notes about the above or
_____.

READ-ALOUD BOOK
Be a Perfect Person in Just Three Days by
Stephen Manes or _____

Writing

MINI-LESSON
Read the two books *Miss Rumphius* and
Legend of Blue Bonnets or two other
books for comparison of likenesses and
differences. Or _____.

COMPOSING
Students take notes as the teacher reads
these two books. Or _____.

SHARING
Read and discuss your ideas of the likenesses and differences with two other
students.
  Papers are dated and filed.

Word Study

CHART DEVELOPMENT
Spelling Emphasis: *com* or

Other Emphasis: Art or _____
Resource: Encyclopedias or
_____

WRITING
Students write response to chart focus.

SPELLING
Select words to spell, team test, complete
Word Study Record Sheet.
  Papers are dated and filed.

HOMEWORK
Share writing and spell words with a
partner.
  Notebook signed.

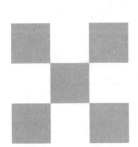

Lesson **157**

Research

LEAD-IN
Teacher introduces the Research Project:
Topic and Focus: Current issues/
Locating and relating information or

_____

Resource: Student-selected materials
or _____

RESEARCH PROJECT
Students continue to work in groups to locate information about the current issue
selected for investigation and to write
about the connections or effects this issue
may have on other issues.

SHARING
Read and discuss information located
with another group.
   Papers are dated and filed.

Recreational Reading

For approximately 30 minutes, all students read books.

CONVERSATIONS
Teacher moves from student to student
having two to three minute conversations
about story settings, plots, and character
analysis or _____.

CLIPBOARD NOTES
Teacher takes notes about the above or

_____.

READ-ALOUD BOOK
Babe: the Gallant Pig by Dick King-Smith
or _____

Writing

MINI-LESSON
Discuss the notes students took in previous lessons as books were read. Or

_____.

   Proofreading: paragraph structure and
topic sentences

COMPOSING
Students write papers describing the likenesses and differences of the two books
being compared. Or _____.

SHARING
Read, discuss, and proofread with a
partner.
   Papers are dated and filed.

Word Study

CHART DEVELOPMENT
Spelling Emphasis: *cau* or

_____

Other Emphasis: World issues or

_____

Resource: Newspapers, magazines, or

_____

WRITING
Students write response to chart focus.

SPELLING
Select words to spell, team test, complete
Word Study Record Sheet.
   Papers are dated and filed.

HOMEWORK
Share writing and spell words with a
partner.
   Notebook signed.

Research

LEAD-IN
Teacher introduces the Research Project:
Topic and Focus: Current world issues/Organizing information or

_____
Resource: Student-selected materials or _____

RESEARCH PROJECT
Groups begin the process of orgainizing the information they have discovered for a report to be shared with class. Each student should have a written report and the group will develop a plan for the presentation.

SHARING
Read and discuss in own group the organizing of information for reports.
　Papers are dated and filed.

Recreational Reading

For approximately 30 minutes, all students read books.

CONVERSATIONS
Teacher has seven to ten minute conversations with students, tailoring these conversations to each student's reading needs or _____.

CLIPBOARD NOTES
Teacher takes notes about discoveries during conversations or _____.

READ-ALOUD BOOK
Continue current selection or _____.

Writing

MINI-LESSON
Discuss illustrators Barbara Coney and Tommy de Paula or other selected illustrators. Share the illustrations of the two books previously used or others. Or

_____.
　Proofreading: use of *their, they're, there*

COMPOSING
Write how the two illustrators are alike and different. Or _____.

SHARING
Read, discuss, and proofread with a partner.
　Papers are dated and filed.

Word Study

CHART DEVELOPMENT
Spelling Emphasis: *try* or

_____
Other Emphasis: Airports, train or bus stations or _____
Resource: Student-selected materials or _____

WRITING
Students write response to chart focus.

SPELLING
Select words to spell, team test, complete Word Study Record Sheet.
　Papers are dated and filed.

HOMEWORK
Share writing and spell words with a partner.
　Notebook signed.

Lesson 159

Research

LEAD-IN
Teacher introduces the Research Project:
Topic and Focus: Current world issues/Presenting information or
_____

Resource: Student-selected materials or _____

RESEARCH PROJECT
Groups meet to plan a presentation of the issue they have investigated to the class. The most important thing to keep in mind is that this presentation is to inform others.

SHARING
Work within groups to prepare for presentations.
Papers are dated and filed.

Recreational Reading

For approximately 30 minutes, all students read books.

CONVERSATIONS
Teacher has seven to ten minute conversations with students tailoring these conversations to each student's reading needs or _____.

CLIPBOARD NOTES
Teacher takes notes about discoveries during conversations or _____.

READ-ALOUD BOOK
Continue current selection or _____.

Writing

MINI-LESSON
Discuss comparison of books and authors. Students share their own examples. Or
_____.
   Proofreading: use of commas with conjunctions _and_ and _or_

COMPOSING
Write a comparison of two self-selected books or authors. Or _____.

SHARING
Read, discuss, and proofread with a partner.
Papers are dated and filed.

Word Study

CHART DEVELOPMENT
Spelling Emphasis: _gen_ or
_____

Other Emphasis: Food products or
_____

Resource: Magazines or _____

WRITING
Students write response to chart focus.

SPELLING
Select words to spell, team test, complete Word Study Record Sheet.
Papers are dated and filed.

HOMEWORK
Share writing and spell words with a partner.
Notebook signed.

Research

LEAD-IN
Teacher introduces the Research Project:
Topic and Focus: Current world issues/Sharing information or _____
Resource: Student-selected materials
or _____

RESEARCH PROJECT
Groups present information discovered to class.

SHARING
Class Share Day
  Papers are dated and filed.

Recreational Reading

For approximately 30 minutes, all students read books.

CONVERSATIONS
Teacher has seven to ten minute conversations with students tailoring these conversations to each student's reading needs
or _____ .

CLIPBOARD NOTES
Teacher takes notes about discoveries during conversations or _____.

READ-ALOUD BOOK
The Fairy Rebel by Lynne Reid Banks or
_____

Writing

MINI-LESSON
Discuss favorite books. Or _____.
  Proofreading: Capitalize title of books and underline.

COMPOSING
Write about your favorite book read in the fourth grade. Or _____.

SHARING
Read, discuss, and proofread with a partner.
  Papers are dated and filed.

Word Study

CHART DEVELOPMENT
Spelling Emphasis: *sha* or
_____
Other Emphasis: Unfamiliar words
or _____
Resource: Newspapers or _____

WRITING
Students write response to chart focus.

SPELLING
Select words to spell, team test, complete Word Study Record Sheet.
  Papers are dated and filed.

HOMEWORK
Share writing and spell words with a partner.
  Notebook signed.

Lesson **161**

Research

Ten-day Research Project

LEAD-IN
Teacher introduces the Research Project:
Topic and Focus: Real life issues/Becoming problem solvers or _____
Resource: Teacher- and student-selected materials or _____

RESEARCH PROJECT
Through class discussion, identify a list of problems facing your community, town, state, or country. Discuss possible steps for solving such problems: identification of problem, becoming informed, considering all aspects of an issue, and deciding how to take action. Divide into groups of four or five (based on interest) for gathering information and suggesting solutions to the problems.

SHARING
Group/class sharing of ideas related to problem identification.
    Papers are dated and filed.

Recreational Reading

For approximately 30 minutes, all students read books.

CONVERSATIONS
Teacher has seven to ten minute conversations with students tailoring these conversations to each student's reading needs. Or _____.

CLIPBOARD NOTES
Teacher takes notes about discoveries during conversations or _____.

READ-ALOUD BOOK
Continue current selection or _____.

Writing

MINI-LESSON
Discuss fourth grade and a favorite day in the fourth grade. Or _____.
    Proofreading: relative pronouns—*who, that, which*

COMPOSING
Write about "My Favorite Day in 4th Grade." Or _____.

SHARING
Read, discuss, and proofread in groups of two or three.
    Papers are dated and filed.

Word Study

CHART DEVELOPMENT
Spelling Emphasis: *men* or _____

Other Emphasis: Fourth grade or _____

Resource: Health textbooks or _____

WRITING
Students write response to chart focus.

SPELLING
Select words to spell, team test, complete Word Study Record Sheet.
    Papers are dated and filed.

HOMEWORK
Share writing and spell words with a partner.
    Notebook signed.

Lesson 162

Research

LEAD-IN
Teacher introduces the Research Project:
Topic and Focus: Real life issues/Becoming informed, gathering information
or _____
Resource: Student-selected materials
or _____

RESEARCH PROJECT
Students read to locate information about the problem identified and to answer any questions they may have. Write notes about information located and make a plan as a group for what information may be needed. Learn about all aspects of the problem and begin to think of possible solutions.

SHARING
Groups share among themselves information discovered and how it relates to their problem.
   Papers are dated and filed.

Recreational Reading

For approximately 30 minutes, all students read books.

CONVERSATIONS
Teacher has seven to ten minute conversations with students tailoring these conversations to each student's reading needs. Or _____.

CLIPBOARD NOTES
Teacher takes notes about discoveries during conversations or _____.

READ-ALOUD BOOK
Continue current selection or _____.

Writing

MINI-LESSON
Discuss unpleasant days in one's life and what makes a day a bad day. Or _____.
   Proofreading: writing dates correctly

COMPOSING
Write about "My Worse Day in Fourth Grade." Or _____.

SHARING
Read, discuss, and proofread in groups of three or four.
   Papers are dated and filed.

Word Study

CHART DEVELOPMENT
Spelling Emphasis: *cin* or
_____
Other Emphasis: Books or
_____
Resource: Magazines or _____

WRITING
Students write response to chart focus.

SPELLING
Select words to spell, team test, complete Word Study Record Sheet.
   Papers are dated and filed.

HOMEWORK
Share writing and spell words with a partner.
   Notebook signed.

Lesson **163**

Research

LEAD-IN
Teacher introduces the Research Project:
Topic and Focus: Real life issues/
Gathering information or _____
Resource: Student-selected materials
or _____

RESEARCH PROJECT
Students working in groups continue to
read to locate information related to the
problem identified.

SHARING
Group sharing of information located.
  Papers are dated and filed.

Recreational Reading

For approximately 30 minutes, all students read books.

CONVERSATIONS
Teacher has seven to ten minute conversations with students tailoring these conversations to each student's reading
needs. Or _____.

CLIPBOARD NOTES
Teacher takes notes about discoveries
during conversations or _____.

READ-ALOUD BOOK
Continue current selection or _____.

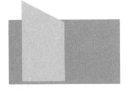

Writing

MINI-LESSON
Discuss friends. Or _____.
  Proofreading: pronouns

COMPOSING
Write about "My Best Friend in Fourth
Grade." Or _____.

SHARING
Read, discuss, and proofread with your
best friend in the class.
  Papers are dated and filed.

Word Study

CHART DEVELOPMENT
Spelling Emphasis: *rin* or

_____
Other Emphasis: Friends or

_____
Resource: Recreational Reading books
or _____

WRITING
Students write response to chart focus.

SPELLING
Select words to spell, team test, complete
Word Study Record Sheet.
  Papers are dated and filed.

HOMEWORK
Share writing and spell words with a
partner.
  Notebook signed.

Lesson **164**

Research

LEAD-IN
Teacher introduces the Research Project:
Topic and Focus: Real life issues/Developing a "plan of action" or _____
Resource: Student-selected materials or _____

RESEARCH PROJECT
Students in groups discuss the audience they need to address, how to approach this audience, and what action to take to solve the identified problem (e.g., new school playground equipment; principal, PTA, school board; letters, meetings, presentations; have a PTA bake sale, encourage school board to put in budget, write letters to newspapers, build the equipment as a class project with help from community)

SHARING
Students discuss and share ideas within their groups.
   Papers are dated and filed.

Recreational Reading

For approximately 30 minutes, all students read books.

CONVERSATIONS
Teacher has seven to ten minute conversations with students tailoring these conversations to each student's reading needs. Or _____.

CLIPBOARD NOTES
Teacher takes notes about discoveries during conversations or _____.

READ-ALOUD BOOK
Continue current selection or _____.

Writing

MINI-LESSON
Discuss personal growth and improvements. Or _____.
   Proofreading: plurals

COMPOSING
Write about "My Personal Improvements During Fourth Grade." Or _____.

SHARING
Read, discuss, and proofread with partner.
   Papers are dated and filed.

Word Study

CHART DEVELOPMENT
Spelling Emphasis: *tec* or _____
Other Emphasis: Writing or _____
Resource: Magazines or _____

WRITING
Students write response to chart focus.

SPELLING
Select words to spell, team test, complete Word Study Record Sheet.
   Papers are dated and filed.

HOMEWORK
Share writing and spell words with a partner.
   Notebook signed.

Lesson **165**

Research

LEAD-IN
Teacher introduces the Research Project:
Topic and Focus: Real life issues/Developing a plan of action or _____
Resource: Student-selected materials or _____

RESEARCH PROJECT
Students in groups develop in written form a plan of action that includes identification of problem, facts pertaining to problem and solutions, and plans for presentations.

SHARING
Groups report to the entire class their preliminary plans.
    Papers are dated and filed.

Recreational Reading

For approximately 30 minutes, all students read books.

CONVERSATIONS
Teacher reads for fifteen minutes. Book Share: Students volunteer to share something about the books they are reading during the last fifteen minutes. Or _____.

CLIPBOARD NOTES
Teacher notes any changes in attitudes, willingness to share, or enthusiasm about books or reading. Or _____.

READ-ALOUD BOOK
Heidi by Johanna Spyri or _____

Writing

MINI-LESSON
Discuss teachers and students and their relationships. Or _____.
    Proofreading: poetry forms

COMPOSING
Write in any kind of poetry form a poem about "Teachers," "Students," or "Teachers and Students." Or _____.

SHARING
Whole Class Share
    Papers are dated and filed.

Word Study

CHART DEVELOPMENT
Spelling Emphasis: *lab* or
_____
Other Emphasis: Imaginations or
_____
Resource: Recreational Reading books or _____

WRITING
Students write response to chart focus.

SPELLING
Select words to spell, team test, complete Word Study Record Sheet.
    Papers are dated and filed.

HOMEWORK
Share writing and spell words with a partner.
    Notebook signed.

Research

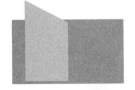

LEAD-IN
Teacher introduces the Research Project:
Topic and Focus: Real life issues/
Organizing information or _____
Resource: Student-selected materials
or _____

RESEARCH PROJECT
Students begin to organize information
and gather materials needed for presentations to the class and any other group as
part of their action plan for solving their
identified problem. Students will have
three days for gathering materials, putting together visuals, practicing presentations, etc.

SHARING
Students share within groups.
    Papers are dated and filed.

Recreational Reading

For approximately 30 minutes, all students read books.

CONVERSATIONS
Teacher reads for fifteen minutes. Book
Share: Students volunteer to share something about the books they are reading
during the last fifteen minutes. Or
_____.

CLIPBOARD NOTES
Teacher notes any changes in attitudes,
willingness to share, or enthusiasm about
books or reading. Or _____.

READ-ALOUD BOOK
Continue current selection or _____.

Writing

MINI-LESSON
Discuss money. Or _____.
    Proofreading: uses of commas

COMPOSING
Write about "If I had a million dol-
lars. . . . " Or _____.

SHARING
Read, discuss, and proofread in groups of
three or four.
    Papers are dated and filed.

Word Study

CHART DEVELOPMENT
Spelling Emphasis: *tri* or
_____

Other Emphasis: Mountains or
_____

Resource: Social Studies textbooks or
_____

WRITING
Students write response to chart focus.

SPELLING
Select words to spell, team test, complete
Word Study Record Sheet.
    Papers are dated and filed.

HOMEWORK
Share writing and spell words with a
partner.
    Notebook signed.

Lesson **167**

Research

LEAD-IN
Teacher introduces the Research Project:
Topic and Focus: Real life issues/
Solving problems (Preparing presenta-
tions) or _____
Resource: Student-selected material or
_____

RESEARCH PROJECT
Continue as in previous lesson.

SHARING
Students share within groups.
    Papers are dated and filed.

Recreational Reading

For approximately 30 minutes, all students read books.

CONVERSATIONS
Teacher moves from student to student
having two to three minute conferences
discussing reading interests and changes
in interests and attitudes since the beginning of the year. Or _____.

CLIPBOARD NOTES
Teacher takes notes about things re-
vealed during these conversations or
_____.

READ-ALOUD BOOK
Continue current selection or _____.

Writing

MINI-LESSON
Discuss fantasy and wishes. Or
_____.
    Proofreading: possessives

COMPOSING
Write about "If I had three wishes. . . . "
Or _____.

SHARING
Read, discuss, and proofread in groups of
three or four.
    Papers are dated and filed.

Word Study

CHART DEVELOPMENT
Spelling Emphasis: *ild* or
_____

Other Emphasis: Vegetables or
_____

Resource: Health textbooks or
_____

WRITING
Students write response to chart focus.

SPELLING
Select words to spell, team test, complete
Word Study Record Sheet.
    Papers are dated and filed.

HOMEWORK
Share writing and spell words with a
partner.
    Notebook signed.

Research

LEAD-IN
Teacher introduces the Research Project:
Topic and Focus: Real life issues/
Solving problems (Preparing presenta-
tions) or _____
Resource: Student-selected materials
or _____

RESEARCH PROJECT
Continue as in previous lesson.

SHARING
Students share within groups.
  Papers are dated and filed.

Recreational Reading

For approximately 30 minutes, all students read books.

CONVERSATIONS
Teacher moves from student to student
having two to three minute conferences
discussing reading interests and changes
in interests and attitudes since the beginning of the year. Or _____.

CLIPBOARD NOTES
Teacher takes notes about things re-
vealed during these conversations or
_____.

READ-ALOUD BOOK
Continue current selection or _____.

Writing

MINI-LESSON
Discuss metamorphosis or decisions to
make changes in one's personality or life.
Or _____.
  Proofreading: subject/verb agreement

COMPOSING
Write about "If I could change, I
would. . . . " Or _____.

SHARING
Read, discuss, and proofread with a
partner.
  Papers are dated and filed.

Word Study

CHART DEVELOPMENT
Spelling Emphasis: *age* or

_____

Other Emphasis: Birthdays or

_____

Resource: Recreational Reading books
or _____

WRITING
Students write response to chart focus.

SPELLING
Select words to spell, team test, complete
Word Study Record Sheet.
  Papers are dated and filed.

HOMEWORK
Share writing and spell words with a
partner.
  Notebook signed.

Lesson **169**

Research

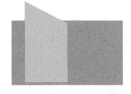

LEAD-IN
Teacher introduces the Research Project:
Topic and Focus: Real life issues/
Group presentations or _____
Resource: Student-selected materials
or _____

RESEARCH PROJECT
For two days students will be presenting
their "real life issue" problems and solutions. Parents, school administrators,
city/county officials, or other selected persons could be invited; the presentations

could be video taped for use later; or
presentations could be made at meetings
of above groups.

SHARING
This will be whole-class share.
   Papers are dated and filed.

Recreational Reading

For approximately 30 minutes, all students read books.

CONVERSATIONS
Teacher moves from student to student
having two to three minute conferences
discussing reading interests and changes
in interests and attitudes since the beginning of the year. Or _____.

CLIPBOARD NOTES
Teacher takes notes about things re-
vealed during these conversations or
_____.

READ-ALOUD
Continue current selection or _____.

Writing

MINI-LESSON
Discuss animals and people and their
relationships. Or _____.
   Proofreading: run-on sentences

COMPOSING
Write about "My favorite animal is . . . . "
or "My Pet." Or _____.

SHARING
Read, discuss, and proofread in groups of
three or four.
   Papers are dated and filed.

Word Study

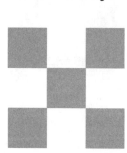

CHART DEVELOPMENT
Spelling Emphasis: *der* or
_____
Other Emphasis: Problems or
_____
Resource: Student-selected materials
or _____

WRITING
Students write response to chart focus.

SPELLING
Select words to spell, team test, complete
Word Study Record Sheet.
   Papers are dated and filed.

HOMEWORK
Share writing and spell words with a
partner.
   Notebook signed.

Lesson **170**

Research

LEAD-IN
Teacher introduces the Research Project:
Topic and Focus: Real life issues/
Group presentations or _____
Resource: Student-selected materials
or _____

RESEARCH PROJECT
Same as previous lesson

SHARING
Same as previous lesson
  Papers are dated and filed.

Recreational Reading

For approximately 30 minutes, all students read books.

CONVERSATIONS
Teacher has seven to ten minute assessment conversations with students discussing progress and setting goals for summer reading. Or _____.

CLIPBOARD NOTES
Teacher makes notes of summarizing comments of student progress or
_____.

READ-ALOUD BOOK
Continue current selection or _____.

Writing

MINI-LESSON
Discuss formulas and potions as they are used in stories to create suspense and make magic things happen. Or
_____.
  Proofreading: detail in stories

COMPOSING
Write about "Secret Formula X-19" or
_____.

SHARING
Read, discuss, and proofread with three or four students.
  Papers are dated and filed.

Word Study

CHART DEVELOPMENT
Spelling Emphasis: *vic* or
_____

Other Emphasis: Boys or _____
Resource: Newspapers or _____

WRITING
Students write response to chart focus.

SPELLING
Select words to spell, team test, complete Word Study Record Sheet.
  Papers are dated and filed.

HOMEWORK
Share writing and spell words with a partner.
  Notebook signed.

Lesson 171

Research

Ten-day Research Project

LEAD-IN
Teacher introduces the Research Project:
Topic and Focus: Summer camps/
Locating information or _____
Resource: Newspapers, magazines,
brochures, tourist/travel guides, or

_____

RESEARCH PROJECT
Students read to locate information on
summer camps. They write about the features of the camps that appeal to them.

SHARING
Read and discuss information discovered
with a partner.
  Papers are dated and filed.

Recreational Reading

For approximately 30 minutes, all students read books.

CONVERSATIONS
Teacher has seven to ten minute assessment conversations with students discussing progress and setting goals for summer
reading.

CLIPBOARD NOTES
Teacher takes notes about summarizing
comments of student progress.

READ-ALOUD BOOK
The Sign of the Beaver by Elizabeth
George Speare or _____

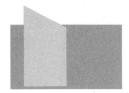

Writing

MINI-LESSON
Discuss summer vacations. Or

_____.

  Proofreading: prepositions

COMPOSING
Write about your summer vacation plans.
Or _____.

SHARING
Read, discuss, and proofread with three or
four students.
  Papers are dated and filed.

Word Study

CHART DEVELOPMENT
Spelling Emphasis: *oth* or

_____

Other Emphasis: Media or _____

_____

Resource: Newspapers or _____

WRITING
Students write response to chart focus.

SPELLING
Select words to spell, team test, complete
Word Study Record Sheet.
  Papers are dated and filed.

HOMEWORK
Share writing and spell words with a
partner.
  Notebook signed.

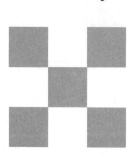

Research

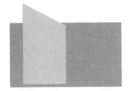

LEAD-IN
Teacher introduces the Research Project:
Topic and Focus: Summer camps/
Designing a camp or _____
Resource: Student-selected materials
or _____

RESEARCH PROJECT
Brainstorm with class the kinds of possible summer camps: music, nature, literary, sports. Students form groups according to the type of camp they want to design. After groups are formed, students begin to design their own summer camp: kind, location, special attractions.

SHARING
Students share within groups.
　Papers are dated and filed.

Recreational Reading

For approximately 30 minutes, all students read books.

CONVERSATIONS
Teacher has seven to ten minute assessment conversations with students discussing progress and setting goals for summer reading. Or _____.

CLIPBOARD NOTES
Teacher takes notes about summarizing comments of student progress or

_____.

READ-ALOUD BOOK
Continue current selection or _____.

Writing

MINI-LESSON
Discuss what happens when you become bored during the summer vacation time. Or _____.
　Proofreading: Sentences beginning with *if, when, during,* etc.; use of commas

COMPOSING
Write about a time when you were bored during summer vacation or what you will do if you become bored this summer. Or _____.

SHARING
Read, discuss, and proofread in groups of three or four.
　Papers are dated and filed.

Word Study

CHART DEVELOPMENT
Spelling Emphasis: *fer* or

_____

Other Emphasis: Death, dying or

_____

Resource: Recreational Reading books
or _____

WRITING
Students write response to chart focus.

SPELLING
Select words to spell, team test, complete Word Study Record Sheet.
　Papers are dated and filed.

HOMEWORK
Share writing and spell words with a partner.
　Notebook signed.

Lesson 173

Research

LEAD-IN
Teacher introduces the Research Project:
Topic and Focus: Summer camps/
Planning a schedule or _____
Resource: Math books, calendars,
student-selected materials or _____

RESEARCH PROJECT
Plan the schedule for a five-day camp.
Write the schedule.

SHARING
Students plan and discuss in groups.
   Papers are dated and filed.

Recreational Reading

For approximately 30 minutes, all students read books.

CONVERSATIONS
Teacher has seven to ten minute assessment conversations with students discussing progress and setting goals for summer
reading. Or _____.

CLIPBOARD NOTES
Teacher takes notes about summarizing
comments of student progress or

_____.

READ-ALOUD BOOK
Continue current selection or _____.

Writing

MINI-LESSON
Discuss editing and revising and publishing. Or _____.
   Proofreading: all previous proofreading
suggestions

COMPOSING
Students select any previous writing for
editing, revision, and publication. Begin
the process. Books will be completed by
lesson 180. Or _____.

SHARING
Read, discuss, and proofread with a
partner.
   Papers are dated and filed.

Word Study

CHART DEVELOPMENT
Spelling Emphasis: *eau* or

_____

Other Emphasis: Peace or

_____

Resource: Magazines or _____

WRITING
Students write response to chart focus.

SPELLING
Select words to spell, team test, complete
Word Study Record Sheet.
   Papers are dated and filed.

HOMEWORK
Share writing and spell words with a
partner.
   Notebook signed.

Research

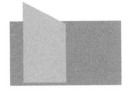

LEAD-IN
Teacher introduces the Research Project:
Topic and Focus: Summer camps/
Planning a budget and costs or
_____

Resource: Math books, student-
selected materials or _____

RESEARCH PROJECT
Groups plan costs and budgets for their
camps.

SHARING
Students share within groups.
  Papers are dated and filed.

Recreational Reading

For approximately 30 minutes, all students read books.

CONVERSATIONS
Teacher has seven to ten minute assessment conversations with students discussing progress and setting goals for summer
reading. Or _____.

CLIPBOARD NOTES
Teacher takes notes about summarizing
comments of student progress or
_____.

READ-ALOUD BOOK
Continue current selection or _____.

Writing

MINI-LESSON
For the next seven days students will be
editing, revising, illustrating, and preparing their stories for publication. Daily discussion time will be as needed.

COMPOSING
Students continue to work on their books.

SHARING
Read, discuss, and proofread with
partner.
  Papers are dated and filed.

Word Study

CHART DEVELOPMENT
Spelling Emphasis: *ser* or
_____

Other Emphasis: Supermarkets or
_____

Resource: Newspapers or _____

WRITING
Students write response to chart focus.

SPELLING
Select words to spell, team test, complete
Word Study Record Sheet.
  Papers are dated and filed.

HOMEWORK
Share writing and spell words with a
partner.
  Notebook signed.

Lesson **175**

Research

LEAD-IN
Teacher introduces the Research Project:
Topic and Focus: Summer camps/
Designing a brochure or _____
Resource: Student-selected materials
or _____

RESEARCH PROJECT
Students work in groups to design a
brochure for their camp. Remember purpose of brochures is to inform. Give all
the basic information needed.

SHARING
Students share within groups.
    Papers are dated and filed.

Recreational Reading

For approximately 30 minutes, all students read books.

CONVERSATIONS
Teacher has seven to ten minute assessment conversations with students discussing progress and setting goals for summer
reading. Or _____.

CLIPBOARD NOTES
Teacher takes notes about summarizing
comments of student progress or
_____.

READ-ALOUD BOOK
Continue current selection or _____.

Writing

MINI-LESSON
Continue as in previous lesson. Or
_____.

COMPOSING
Continue as in previous lesson. Or
_____.

SHARING
Read, discuss, and proofread with a
partner.
    Papers are dated and filed.

Word Study

CHART DEVELOPMENT
Spelling Emphasis: *ink* or

_____
Other Emphasis: Girls or _____
Resource: Magazines or _____

WRITING
Students write response to chart focus.

SPELLING
Select words to spell, team test, complete
Word Study Record Sheet.
    Papers are dated and filed.

HOMEWORK
Share writing and spell words with a
partner.
    Notebook signed.

Research

LEAD-IN
Teacher introduces the Research Project:
Topic and Focus: Summer camps/
Advertising the camp or _____
Resource: Student-selected materials
or _____

RESEARCH PROJECT
Groups decide when, where, and how they
will advertise their camp. Write the plan
and designs.

SHARING
Students share within groups.
Papers are dated and filed.

Recreational Reading

For approximately 30 minutes, all students read books.

CONVERSATIONS
Teacher has seven to ten minute assessment conversations with students discussing progress and setting goals for summer
reading. Or _____.

CLIPBOARD NOTES
Teacher takes notes about summarizing
comments of student progress or
_____.

READ-ALOUD BOOK
Continue current selection or _____.

Writing

MINI-LESSON
Same as previous lesson. Or _____.

COMPOSING
Same as previous lesson. Or _____.

SHARING
Read, discuss, and proofread with
partner.
Papers are dated and filed.

Word Study

CHART DEVELOPMENT
Spelling Emphasis: *fic* or
_____

Other Emphasis: Television or
_____

Resource: Newspapers or _____

WRITING
Students write response to chart focus.

SPELLING
Select words to spell, team test, complete
Word Study Record Sheet.
Papers are dated and filed.

HOMEWORK
Share writing and spell words with a
partner.
Notebook signed.

Lesson 177

Research

LEAD-IN
Teacher introduces the Research Project:
Topic and Focus: Summer camps/
Letters of invitation or _____
Resource: Language Arts books or
_____

RESEARCH PROJECT
Groups write a letter of invitation to be
mailed to prospective campers along with
the brochure.

SHARING
Students discuss and share within groups.
Papers are dated and filed.

Recreational Reading

For approximately 30 minutes, all students read books.

CONVERSATIONS
Teacher and students select a passage
from their favorite book read during the
year. Each has a turn to read a chapter
or chosen section to the class. Or
_____.

CLIPBOARD NOTES
Teacher notes how students respond to
the books being shared. Or _____.

READ-ALOUD BOOK
Dear Mr. Henshaw by Beverly Cleary or
_____

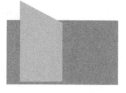

Writing

MINI-LESSON
Same as previous lesson. Or _____.

COMPOSING
Same as previous lesson. Or _____.

SHARING
Read, discuss, and proofread with a
partner.
Papers are dated and filed.

Word Study

CHART DEVELOPMENT
Spelling Emphasis: *sim* or
_____

Other Emphasis: Unfamiliar words
or _____
Resource: Social Studies textbooks or
_____

WRITING
Students write response to chart focus.

SPELLING
Select words to spell, team test, complete
Word Study Record Sheet.
Papers are dated and filed.

HOMEWORK
Share writing and spell words with a
partner.
Notebook signed.

Research

LEAD-IN
Teacher introduces the Research Project:
Topic and Focus: Summer camps/
Planning a presentation or _____
Resource: Student-selected materials
or _____

RESEARCH PROJECT
Groups plan the presentation of their
camp to the rest of the class.

SHARING
Discussions and planning within groups.
  Papers are dated and filed.

Recreational Reading

For approximately 30 minutes, all students read books.

CONVERSATIONS
Teacher and students select a passage
from their favorite book read during the
year. Each has a turn to read a chapter
or chosen section to the class. Or
_____.

CLIPBOARD NOTES
Teacher notes how students respond to
the books being shared or _____.

READ-ALOUD BOOK
Continue current selection or _____.

Writing

MINI-LESSON
Students should be into the actual book
writing and illustrating stages of publishing a book. Or _____.

COMPOSING
Continue to work on book. Or
_____.

SHARING
Whatever is needed.
  Papers are dated and filed.

Word Study

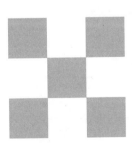

CHART DEVELOPMENT
Spelling Emphasis: *ear* or
_____
Other Emphasis: Unfamiliar words
or _____
Resource: Health textbooks or
_____

WRITING
Students write response to chart focus.

SPELLING
Select words to spell, team test, complete
Word Study Record Sheet.
  Papers are dated and filed.

HOMEWORK
Share writing and spell words with a
partner.
  Notebook signed.

Lesson 179

Research

LEAD-IN
Teacher introduces the Research Project:
Topic and Focus: Summer camps/
Group presentations or _____
Resource: Student-selected materials
or _____

RESEARCH PROJECT
Groups begin their presentations.

SHARING
Each group presents to the class.
  Papers are dated and filed.

Recreational Reading

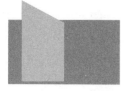

For approximately 30 minutes, all students read books.

CONVERSATIONS
Teacher and students select a passage from their favorite book read during the year. Each has a turn to read a chapter or chosen section to the class. Or _____.

CLIPBOARD NOTES
Teacher notes how students respond to the books being shared or _____.

READ-ALOUD BOOK
Continue current selection or _____.

Writing

MINI-LESSON
Final stages of completing the books. Or _____.

COMPOSING
Continue work on books. Or _____.

SHARING
Whatever is needed.
  Papers are dated and filed.

Word Study

CHART DEVELOPMENT
Spelling Emphasis: *sus* or
_____

Other Emphasis: Unfamiliar words
or _____
Resource: Science textbooks or
_____

WRITING
Students write response to chart focus.

SPELLING
Select words to spell, team test, complete Word Study Record Sheet.
  Papers are dated and filed.

HOMEWORK
Share writing and spell words with a partner.
  Notebook signed.

Research

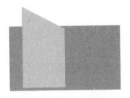

LEAD-IN
Teacher introduces the Research Project:
Topic and Focus: Summer camps/
Complete group presentations or
_____

Resource: Student-selected materials

RESEARCH PROJECT
Groups continue to present their summer
camp designs.

SHARING
Groups with whole class.
   Papers are dated and filed.

Recreational Reading

For approximately 30 minutes, all students read books.

CONVERSATIONS
Teacher and students select a passage
from their favorite book read during the
year. Each has a turn to read a chapter
or chosen section to the class. Or
_____.

CLIPBOARD NOTES
Teacher notes how students respond to
the books being shared or _____.

READ-ALOUD BOOK
Continue current selection or _____.

Writing

MINI-LESSON
Books must be completed. Or _____.

COMPOSING
Students complete books and share as
much as time allows. Or _____.

SHARING
As time allows. Consider having a "last
day of school tea" and share books with
parents and other invited guests.
   Papers are dated and filed.

Word Study

CHART DEVELOPMENT
Spelling Emphasis: _ary_ or
_____

Other Emphasis: Unfamiliar words
or _____
Resource: Newspapers or _____

WRITING
Students write response to chart focus.

SPELLING
Select words to spell, team test, complete
Word Study Record Sheet.
   Papers are dated and filed.

HOMEWORK
Share writing and spell words with a
partner.
   Notebook signed.

▶ Appendix

Sources for Further Reading

Atwell, Nancie, ed. *Coming to Know: Writing to Learn in the Intermediate Grades.* Portsmouth, NH. Heinemann, 1990.

———. *In the Middle: Writing, Reading, and Learning with Adolescents.* Portsmouth, NH: Boynton/Cook, 1987.

Calkins, Lucy McCormick. *The Art of Teaching Writing.* Portsmouth, NH: Heinemann, 1986.

Hansen, Jane; Newkirk, Thomas; and Graves, Donald, eds. *Breaking Ground: Teachers Relate Reading and Writing in the Elementary School.* Portsmouth, NH: Heinemann, 1985.

Kimmel, Mary Margaret and Segel, Elizabeth. *For Reading Out Loud: A Guide to Sharing Books with Children.* New York: Delacorte Press, 1988.

Landsberg, Michele. *Reading for the Love of It: Best Books for Young Readers.* New York: Prentice Hall, 1987.

Murray, Donald M. *Expecting the Unexpected.* Portsmouth, NH: Boynton/Cook, 1989.

Olson, Carol Booth, ed. *Practical Ideas for Teaching Writing as a Process.* Sacramento, CA: California State Department of Education, 1986.

Routman, Regie. *Transitions: From Literature to Literacy.* Portsmouth, NH: Heinemann, 1988.

Smith, Frank. *Insult to Intelligence.* Portsmouth, NH: Heinemann, 1986.

Trelease, Jim. *The Read-Aloud Handbook.* New York: Penguin Books, 1982.

Research Module Sequence

Lesson	Topic/Focus	Resource
1	People/Alphabetizing	student handbook
2	People/Alphabetizing	Social Studies text
3	People/Alphabetizing	newspapers
4	People/Alphabetizing	magazines
5	People/Alphabetizing	Fiction/nonfiction
6	Food/Locating information	encyclopedias
7	Food/Locating information	dictionaries
8	Animals/Locating information	textbooks
9	Animals/Locating information	Readers' Guide to Periodicals, etc.
10	People, Food, Animals/locating information	student-selected

Five-Day Integrated Lessons: Machines

Lesson	Topic/Focus	Resource
11	Machines/Selecting topic	Science textbooks, magazines
12	Machines/Gathering information	student/teacher-selected
13	Machines/Gathering information	student/teacher-selected
14	Machines/Organizing reports	Language textbook
15	Machines/Writing reports	Language textbook
16	Recipes/Sequence	labels from food packages, recipe cards/books
17	Television/Sequence	TV Guide
18	Experiments/Sequence	Science textbooks
19	History/Sequence	Social Studies textbooks
20	Travel/Making charts	maps
21	Travel/Information in charts	travel folders, advertisements
22	Transportation/Information in charts	newspapers
23	Transportation/Information in charts	Science/Health textbooks
24	Transportation/Information in charts	Social Studies textbooks
25	Transportation/Information in charts	newspapers
26	Transportation and people/ Information in charts	newspapers, magazines
27	Occupations/Reading pictures	magazines
28	Work/Information in pictures	encyclopedias
29	Technology/Information in pictures	magazines
30	Advertising/Information in pictures	catalogues
31	Space exploration/Selecting resources	student-selected
32	Space exploration/Selecting resources	student-selected
33	Solar system/Selecting resources	student-selected
34	Astronauts/Selecting resources	student-selected
35	Space vehicles/Selecting resources	student-selected
36	Space/Selecting resources	student-selected
37	TV Personalities/Listening skills	TV Guides
38	Famous people/Listening skills	biographies/ autobiographies
39	Current events/Listening skills	newspapers/news magazines

Lesson	Topic/Focus	Resource
40	Short stories/Listening skills	basal readers
41	Animals/Classifying	brainstorming
42	Animals/Classifying	magazines
43	Animals/Classifying	reference materials and textbooks
44	Animals/Classifying	fiction books
45	Animals/Classifying	reference books, textbooks
46	Sports/Notetaking	newspapers, Language textbooks
47	Sports/Notetaking	autobiography/ biography
48	Sports/Notetaking	magazines
49	Sports/Notetaking	encyclopedias

Ten-Day Research Project

Lesson	Topic/Focus	Resource
50	Countries/Locating and organizing information	student-selected
51	Countries/Locating and organizing information	student-selected
52	Countries/Locating and organizing information	student-selected
53	Countries/Locating and organizing information	student-selected
54	Countries/Locating and organizing information	student-selected
55	Countries/Group work, presentation planning	student-selected
56	Countries/Group work, presentation planning	student-selected
57	Countries/Group work, presentation planning	student-selected
58	Countries/Group work, making reports	none
59	Countries/Group work, making reports	none

Five-Day Integrated Lessons: Reading and Literacy

Lesson	Topic/Focus	Resource
60	Reading/literacy/Interviews	classmates, others
61	Reading/literacy/Interviews	classmates, others
62	Reading/literacy/Interviews	students from other classes
63	reading/literacy/Summarizing information	notes and writings from interviews
64	Reading/literacy/Media	newspapers, magazines

Six-Day Research Project

Lesson	Topic/Focus	Resource
65	Student-selected/Selecting Resources	student-selected
66	Student-selected/Locating Information	student-selected
67	Student-selected/Locating Information	student-selected

Lesson	Topic/Focus	Resource
68	Student-selected/Categorizing Information	none
69	Student-selected/Writing Reports	Language texts
70	Student-selected/Writing Reports	Language texts
71	Topic being studied in health, social studies, science/ Main Idea	newspapers
72	Nutrition/Main Idea	Health, Science textbooks
73	Poetry/Main Idea	Language texts, basal readers
74	Weather/Main Idea	Science textbooks, newspapers
75	Making predications	teacher-selected
76	Making predications	picture books
77	Making predications	picture books, comics
78	Foods/Making comparisons	newspapers
79	Population/Making comparisons	atlases, encyclope-dias
80	Advertising/Making comparisons	newspapers
81	Inventions/Drawing conclusions	Social Studies, Health, Science textbooks
82	Reading and/or watching TV/Surveys	Gallup poll, TV Guide
83	Reading and/or watching TV/Surveys	classmates, friends, family, school personnel
84	Reading and/or watching TV/Surveys	(same as above)

Six-Day Research Project

Lesson	Topic/Focus	Resource
85	Economy, taxes, money/ interpreting graphs	Math texts, business magazines
86	Economy, taxes, money/ Interpreting graphs	Social Studies textbooks
87	Economy, taxes, money/ Interpreting graphs	encyclopedias, newspapers
88	Economy, taxes, money/ Graphing information	student/teacher-selected
89	Economy, taxes, money/ Graphing information	student/teacher-selected
90	Economy, taxes, money/ Graphing information	student/teacher-selected

Six-Day Research Project

Lesson	Topic/Focus	Resource
91	Music/Musicians/Selecting resources	student-selected
92	Music/Musicians/Locating information	student-selected
93	Music/Musicians/Locating information	student-selected
94	Music/Musicians/Organizing information	student-selected
95	Music/Musicians/Writing first draft	student-selected
96	Music/Musicians Revising report	student-selected
97	Recognizing similies, metaphors and analogies	Recreational Reading books
98	Recognizing similies, metaphors and analogies	Recreational Reading books

Lesson	Topic/Focus	Resource
99	Using similies, metaphors and analogies	magazines
100	Categorizing similies, metaphors and analogies	library books, textbooks, basal readers
101	Population/Using maps and symbols reading map	Social Studies textbooks
102	Landforms/Using and Understanding maps	encyclopedias, atlases
103	Travel/Using scales and legends	road maps
104	Reading and using Maps	student-selected
105	Drawing A Map	school building/ grounds

Five-Day Integrated Lessons: Mathematics

Lesson	Topic/Focus	Resource
106	Mathematics/Time/world time zones	encyclopedias, Social Studies books
107	Mathematics/Geometric shapes/ architecture	magazines, Social Studies books, encyclopedias
108	Mathematics/Money	advertisement section
109	Mathematical concepts	magazines
110	Mathematical symbols	student-selected
111	Art/Fact or opinion	Art prints/books
112	Art/Fact and opinion	encyclopedias
113	Art/Fact and opinion	magazines
114	Art/Fact and opinion	interviews
115	Art/Fact and opinion	student-selected
116	Emergencies/Symbolism	phone books, first aid pamphlets, signs
117	Advertising/Symbolism	magazines
118	Symbolism	student/teacher-selected
119	Seasons/Inference	magazines
120	Outdoor Activity/Feelings/Inference	magazines
121	Emotions/Inference	basal readers
122	Authors', techniques/Tone, Mood	basal/Recreational Reading Books
123	Authors' techniques/Alliteration	(same as above)
124	Authors' Techniques/Imagery	(same as above)
125	Authors' Techniques/Purpose or Intent	(same as above)

Five-Day Integrated Lessons: Environment

Lesson	Topic/Focus	Resource
126	Environment/Recycling	magazines/ newspapers
127	Environment/Natural Resources	student-selected
128	Environment/Ecology	Science textbooks
129	Environment/Wildlife	student-selected
130	Environment/Food Chains	Science textbooks, encyclopedias
131	Autobiography/Time lines	teacher's example
132	Presidents/Time lines	encyclopedias, history books, biographies
133	Presidents/Time lines	(same as above)

Lesson	Topic/Focus	Resource
134	Storytelling/Recall/sequence	short stories and recordings
135	Storytelling/Recall/sequence	(same as above)
136	Storytelling/Recall/sequence	(same as above)
137	Storytelling/Recall/sequence	(same as above)
138	Advertising/Satire	magazines
139	Advertising/Techniques of persuasion	magazines
140	Advertising/Techniques of persuasion	TV Guide/commercials

Six-Day Research Project

Lesson	Topic/Focus	Resource
141	Authors/Selecting topic, resources	student-selected
142	Authors/Selecting resources, Locating information	student-selected
143	Authors/Locating information	student-selected
144	Authors/Locating information	student-selected
145	Authors/Writing first Draft	student-selected
146	Authors/Completing reports and sharing reports	student-selected
147	Bees/Relating information	science textbook
148	Pollution/Relating information	student-selected
149	First Aid/Relating information	student-selected
150	Oceans/Relating information	student-selected
151	Computers/Relating information	student-selected
152	Opera, musicals, broadway/Relating information	student-selected
153	Personal health care/Relating information	student-selected
154	Vacations/Relating information	student-selected

Six-Day Research Project

Lesson	Topic/Focus	Resource
155	Current world issues/Locating information	magazines/newspapers
156	Current issues/Locating and relating information	student-selected

Lesson	Topic/Focus	Resource
157	Current issues/Locating and relating information	student-selected
158	Current issues/Organizing information	student-selected
159	Current issues/Presenting information	student-selected
160	Current issues/Sharing information	student-selected

Ten-Day Research Project

Lesson	Topic/Focus	Resource
161	Real life issues/Problem solving	teacher/student
162	Real life issues/Becoming informed	student-selected
163	Real life issues/Gathering information	student-selected
164	Real life issues/Developing a plan of action	student-selected
165	Real life issues/Plan of action	student-selected
166	Real life issues/Organizing information	student-selected
167	Real life issues/Solving problems, preparing presentations	student-selected
168	Real life issues/Solving problems, preparing presentations	student-selected
169	Real life issues/Group presentations	student-selected
170	Real life issues/Group presentations	student-selected

Ten-Day Research Project

Lesson	Topic/Focus	Resource
171	Summer camps/locating information	newspapers, tourist guides
172	Summer camps/Designing a camp	student-selected
173	Summer camps/Planning a schedule	calendars
174	Summer camps/Planning a budget	Math books
175	Summer camps/Designing a brochure	student-selected
176	Summer camps/Advertising the camp	student-selected
177	Summer camps/Letters of invitation	Language texts
178	Summer camps/Planning a presentation	student-selected
179	Summer camps/Group presentations	student-selected
180	Summer camps/Group presentations	student-selected

Writing Sequence

Lesson	Mini-Lesson/Topic	Proofreading Focus
	Introducing Writing Process	
1	Selecting a topic	capitalizing titles
2	Beginning to write	simple sentences
3	"A monster came to school today."	simple subject
4	"Many people like sports."	verbs
5	"Many people are important to me."	*being* verbs
6	"I have a pet dinosaur."	complete subject/predicate
7	"My most embarrassing moment."	pronoun *I*
8	Editing and revision of selected writing	content clarity/complete, clear, sentences

Lesson	Mini-Lesson/Topic	Proofreading Focus
9	Editing and revision of selected writing	proofreading (Lessons 1–7)
10	Sharing Day	
	Five-Day Integrated Lessons: Machines	
11	Machines	adjectives
12	"Our bodies are machines."	subject/verb agreement
13	"Kim the Computer"	paragraph indention
14	Machines/Revision	selection of writing to revise

Lesson	Mini-Lesson/Topic	Proofreading Focus
15	Machines/Revision	complete revision
16	Dreams	use of vivid words
17	Exotic birds	present tense verbs
18	Favorite relative	past tense verbs
19	Special friends	past tense verbs with helping verb
20	"The Magic Race Car"	correct verbs
21	"The Magic Race Car"	s-form of verbs
22	Likenesses/differences	plural nouns
23	Comparisons/Animals	subject/verb agreement
24	Comparisons/Seasons	simple subject/ predicate
25	Comparisons/Sun/Moon	complete subject/ predicate
26	Comparisons/Transportation	run-on sentences
27	Proverb/"All work and no play makes Jack a dull boy."	expressing thoughts clearly
28	Proverb/"One picture is worth a thousand words."	(same as above)
29	Proverb/"The best things in life are free."	(same as above)
30	Proverb/"Business before pleasure."	paragraph indention
31	Editing and revision	sentence structure, subject/verb agreement, punctuation, capital letters
32	Editing and revision	(same as above)
33	Dialogue/Frogs	quotation marks
34	Dialogue/Being lost	use of comma in dialogue
35	Dialogue/Scary things	punctuation of conversation
36	Dialogue/talking trees	adjectives
37	Dialogue/Aliens	paragraphs in written dialogue
38	Dialogue/Pencils	(same as above)
39	Dialogue/Editing and revision	all elements of conversation
40	Dialogue/Editing and revision	all elements of conversation
41	Cinquains/Spaghetti	Cinquain form
42	Haiku/Nature	Haiku form
43	Free Verse/Country life or outdoor adventure	capitalizing lines
44	Limericks/Animals	rhyme and rhythm in limericks
45	Couplets/Seasons	couplet form, rhyming words
46	"A Special Gift"	adjectives
47	Picture/shape poems	similes
48	Humorous Poems	capitalizing lines
49	Editing and revision	poetry form and spelling
50	Sharing poetry	grammar, spelling, form
51	Letters of invitation	comma after greeting/closing

Lesson	Mini-Lesson/Topic	Proofreading Focus
52	Reply to invitation	commas separate city, state, day, and year
53	Friendly letter to relatives	periods after abbreviations
54	Letters of thanks	punctuation contractions
55	Friendly letters about school to students in another country	
56	Friendly letters about school to students in another country	descriptive words
57	Letters to the editor	use of *and, but, or*
58	Review letter writing	form, punctuation
59	Review letter writing	form, punctuation

Five-Day Integrated Lessons: Reading and Literacy

Lesson	Mini-Lesson/Topic	Proofreading Focus
60	Diaries	commas in series
61	Character attributes	adjectives
62	Story settings	adjectives
63	Making predictions	words that denote time
64	Fact and opinion	beginning sentences with *if, when, after, as*
65	Comparisons/Fruits or vegetables Musical Instruments	run-on sentences
66	Comparisons/Teacher/Artist	singular subject/ *being* verb
67	Comparisons/Seasons	capitalization/ punctuation
68	Comparisons/Computer/Brain	subject/verb agreement
69	Comparisons/Day/Night	adverbs
70	Editing and revision	review of proofreading
71	Anger	paragraph development: topic sentence
72	Foods or Hobbies	*ed* verb form
73	"Saturday is my favorite day."	paragraph indention
74	Rainy days	topic sentences
75	Movies	capitalizing titles
76	Mail, post office/employees	paragraph indention
77	Forests	proper punctuation
78	"Changing Myself"	use of suffixes *er, est*
79	Beauty	adjectives
80	Editing and revision	paragraph structure, indenting, topic sentences
81	Editing and Revision	(same as above)
82	Sharing Day	
83	Story settings	descriptive words
84	Story sequence and plot	sequence words
85	Characters	proper nouns
86	Story development	verb usage
87	Story endings	Words to denote time and closure

Lesson	Mini-Lesson/Topic	Proofreading Focus
88	Editing and revision	story development and flow
89	Editing and revision	(same as above)
90	Sharing Day	

Writing a Mystery

Lesson	Mini-Lesson/Topic	Proofreading Focus
91	Features of mystery	adjectives
92	Adding a character	character descriptions
93	Adding an animal	pronouns
94	Adding an object	prepositions
95	Writing a conclusion	sequence words
96	Editing and revision	previous proofreading suggestions
97	Peer-group editing	same as above
98	Rewriting story	neatness and spelling errors

Publishing a Book

Lesson	Mini-Lesson/Topic	Proofreading Focus
99	Selecting a manuscript/Title page	capital letters
100	Layout and illustrations	"dummy book"
101	Copying the manuscript	previous proofreading
102	Copying the manuscript	(same as above)
103	Copying the manuscript	(same as above)
104	Book construction	
105	Book publication completed	

Five-Day Integrated Lessons: Mathematics

Lesson	Mini-Lesson/Topic	Proofreading Focus
106	Everyday connections of Math	examples to support points
107	Geometry and nature or classroom	math terms
108	Money/Wages, salaries, budgets	money terms
109	Learning math concepts	pronouns
110	Math concepts and terms	proper punctuation

Short Stories

Lesson	Mini-Lesson/Topic	Proofreading Focus
111	"A Forest Fire"	contractions
112	"A Forest Fire"	*if* at beginning of sentence
113	"A Flock of Birds"	*When*
114	"A Flock of Birds"	verbs
115	"Slick and Slimy"	adjectives
116	"Slick and Slimy"	prepositions
117	"Prehistoric Adventures"	adverbs
118	"Prehistoric Adventures"	adverbs
119	Editing and revision	all Proofreading
120	Editing and revision	same as above
121	Rewriting the final copy Illustrations	neatness and spelling
122	Sharing Day	

Book Reports

Lesson	Mini-Lesson/Topic	Proofreading Focus
123	Outline and first draft	adjectives
124	Author's techniques	
125	Purpose of book reports	prepositions

Five-Day Integrated Lessons: Environment

Lesson	Mini-Lesson/Topic	Proofreading Focus
126	Recycling	subject/verb agreement
127	Beauty in nature	adjectives
128	Letter to the Editor: Ecological issues	correct letter form
129	Wildlife habitats	subject/verb agreement
130	Predator/prey relationships	pronouns
131	Similes	use of *as* or *like*
132	Human anatomy	use of *as* or *like*
133	Metaphors	correct spelling
134	Opinions and homework	topic sentences
135	Rights and responsibilities	possessive pronouns
136	Local issue and editorials	correct spelling
137	Honesty	*there* and *their*
138	Tall tales and exaggeration	*was* and *were*
139	Tall tales and exaggeration	*is* and *are*
140	Elements of science fiction	*do* and *did*
141	Wordless books	vivid descriptions
142	Wordless books	conversation punctuation
143	Wordless books	adjectives
144	Editing and revision	correct spelling
145	Rewrite story	all proofreading

Book Reviews

Lesson	Mini-Lesson/Topic	Proofreading Focus
146	Features of book reviews	capital letters, book names underlined
147	Book reviews	adjectives, adverbs, prepositions
148	Editing and revision	paragraph structure
149	Completing book reviews	handwriting
150	Sharing Day	
151	Autobiographies/Time lines	word to denote sequence
152	Autobiographies	commas in series
153	Autobiographies	proper nouns
154	Editing and Revision	all proofreading suggestions
155	Rewriting autobiography	neatness and spelling
156	Comparing books/Authors	
157	Comparing books/Authors	paragraph structure
158	Comparing books/Illustrators	
159	Comparing books	use of commas with conjunctions
160	Favorite books	Capitalize, underline book titles
161	"My Favorite Day in 4th Grade"	relative pronouns
162	"My Worse Day in 4th Grade"	adverbs
163	"My Best Friend in 4th Grade"	pronouns
164	"My Personal Improvements in 4th Grade"	plurals
165	Poetry: Teachers/Students	poetry forms

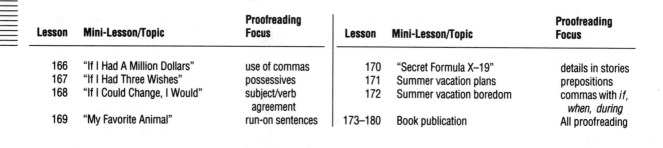
Lesson	Mini-Lesson/Topic	Proofreading Focus	Lesson	Mini-Lesson/Topic	Proofreading Focus
166	"If I Had A Million Dollars"	use of commas	170	"Secret Formula X–19"	details in stories
167	"If I Had Three Wishes"	possessives	171	Summer vacation plans	prepositions
168	"If I Could Change, I Would"	subject/verb agreement	172	Summer vacation boredom	commas with *if, when, during*
169	"My Favorite Animal"	run-on sentences	173–180	Book publication	All proofreading

Word Study Sequence

Lesson	Emphasis	Resources	Lesson	Emphasis	Resources
1	*as*/school opening	student handbook	39	*al*/freedom	Social Studies texts
2	*ea*/expectations for school year	student handbook, charts/posters	40	*cl*/taxes	newspapers
3	*or*/cafeteria	charts/posters	41	*ee*/careers	magazines
4	*us*/bus, traffic safety	health books, etc	42	*y*/music	Music texts, readers
5	*ar*/library	students' knowledge	43	*i*/medicine	newspapers
6	*oo*/classroom	observations	44	*e*/comedy	magazines
7	*ie*/subjects studied	textbooks	45	*a*/government	Social Studies texts
8	*es*/schedules, days or week	calendars	46	*o*/health	magazines
9	*en*/first six months of year	calendars	47	*u*/food	Health textbooks
10	*ai*/last six months of year	calendars	48	*aw*/disease	newspapers
11	*an*/machines	Science textbooks	49	*qu*/poverty	newspapers
12	*bl*/machines	encyclopedias, etc.	50	*er*/wealth	magazines
13	*gr*/machines	newspapers, etc.	51	*in*/literature	magazines
14	*bi*/machines	student-selected	52	*ur*/geography	atlas, maps, Social Studies textbook
15	*oa*/machines	Social Studies, Health texts	53	*ir*/love	student-selected
16	*pl*/people	magazines	54	*ss*/furniture	catalogues
17	*pr*/people	Recreational Reading books	55	*ment*/seasons	Science textbooks
18	*gl*/sports	newspapers	56	*milli*/mathematics	Math textbooks
19	*fl*/nature	newspapers	57	*ty*/Entertainment	TV Guide, newspapers
20	*sm*/money	magazines	58	*un*/failure	teacher-selected
21	*sc*/weather	Science textbooks	59	*ish*/strength	Recreational Reading
23	*sk*/travel	Recreational Reading	60	*tion*/unfamiliar words	same as above
24	*sp*/music	newspapers	61	*ness*/unfamiliar words	same as above
25	*st*/accidents	newspapers	62	*inter*/unfamiliar words	same as above
26	*dr*/time	Math textbooks	63	*ly*/unfamiliar words	same as above
27	*sw*/occupation/work	Health, Science texts	64	*ing*/unfamiliar words	same as above
28	*ance*/language	newspapers	65	*pre*/prefixes	newspapers
29	*dw*/technology	magazines	66	*un*/prefixes	magazines
30	*tw*/business	newspapers	67	*dis*/prefixes	any textbook
31	*tw*/astronomy	Science textbooks	68	*ful*/suffixes	magazines
32	*cl*/energy	any textbooks	69	*ian*/suffixes	Health textbook
33	*t r*/senses	food labels	70	*ed*/suffixes	Science textbook
34	*wh*/politics	newspapers	71	*ous*/anger	newspapers
35	*ch*/movies	newspapers	72	*un*/food, hobbies	magazines
36	*th*/theatre	newspapers	73	*in*/leisure	Health textbooks
37	*sh*/crime	magazines	74	*im*/weather	basal readers
38	*br*/aviation	newspapers	75	*dis*/movies	newspapers

Lesson	Emphasis	Resources
76	*ld*/postal service/mail	newspapers
77	*ga*/forests	Social Studies text
78	*t t*/foods	food ads, labels
79	*la*/populations	encyclopedias
80	*cc*/homes	magazines
81	*ss*/conversations	Recreational Reading
82	*spl*/synonyms	any textbook
83	*spr*/synonyms	Recreational Reading
84	*ses*/synonyms	basal readers
85	*em*/homonyms	Spelling books
86	*nd*/homonyms	newspapers
87	*ve*/homonyms	magazines
88	*ry*/compound words	encyclopedias
89	*r t*/compound words	dictionaries
90	*iz*/compound words	basal readers
91	*po*/multiple-meaning words	Spelling texts
92	*dy*/multiple-meaning words	newspapers
93	*gth*/multiple-meaning words	basal readers
94	*mb*/music	Music textbooks
95	*syn*/musicians	magazines
96	*hy*/body	Health textbooks
97	*iv*/safety	newspapers
98	*mp*/breakfast	magazines
99	*nt*/prehistoric times	Recreational Reading
100	*ey*/flying animals/objects	Science textbooks
101	*cy*/weather/seasons	Social Studies texts
102	*ap*/things that move/motion	newspapers
103	*sis*/families	magazines
104	*sne*/sleeping/night time	Health books
105	*url*/television	TV guides
106	*flo*/math/time	Math books
107	*opt*/math concepts/geometry	Science books
108	*exp*/business/money	newspapers
109	*eg*/numbers	Math books
110	*som*/math symbols	magazines
111	*spa*/forests, parks	Science, library books
112	*za*/radio	newspapers
113	*bom*/birds	magazines
114	hyp/*disease*	magazines
115	*nst*/mythology	encyclopedias
116	*ric*/prehistoric times	Science, Social Studies books
117	*ist*/time	newspapers
118	*ld*/movies	newspapers
119	*li*/publications	library books
120	*le*/unfamiliar words	newspapers
121	*ta*/eyes	Health books
122	*pa*/patriotism	Social Studies books
123	*la*/cities/towns	travel brochures
124	*ra*/acronyms	newspapers
125	*rp*/unfamiliar words	basal readers
126	*ma*/recycling	magazines
127	*ca*/natural resources	Science or Music books
128	*ri*/pollution	newspapers
129	*ct*/wildlife	library books
130	*p t*/food chains	encyclopedia
131	*ex*/deserts	recreational Reading
132	*est*/feet/hands	Health books
133	*un*/illness	newspapers
134	*ic*/homework	newspapers
135	*nom*/leadership	magazines
136	*cip*/college	newspapers
137	*fer*/magic	Recreational Reading
138	*sho*/exaggeration	basal readers
139	*eth*/furniture	newspapers
140	*own*/antiques	magazines
141	*ive*/hospitals	newspapers
142	*dem*/unfamiliar words	newspapers
143	*the*/prisons	newspapers
144	*van*/skin care	magazines
145	*ric*/cartoons	newspapers
146	*pon*/authors	Basals
147	*ect*/unfamiliar words	Recreational Reading
148	*sta*/investments	newspapers
149	*lop*/first aid	student-selected
150	*res*/oceans	student-selected
151	*don*/games	newspapers
152	*bra*/bravery, courage	basals
153	*min*/heroes	newspapers
154	*dre*/dogs, cats	student-selected
155	*con*/unfamiliar words	student-selected
156	*com*/art	encyclopedias
157	*cau*/world issues	newspapers
158	*try*/airports/trains/bus stations	student-selected
159	*gen*/food products	magazines
160	*sha*/unfamiliar words	newspapers
161	*mem*/fourth grade	Health books
162	*cin*/books	magazines
163	*rin*/friends	Recreational Reading
164	*tec*/writing	magazines
165	*lab*/imagination	Recreational Reading
166	*tri*/mountains	Social Studies books
167	*ild*/vegetables	Health books
168	*age*/birthdays	Recreational Reading
169	*der*/problems	student-selected
170	*vic*/boys	newspapers
171	*oth*/media	newspapers
172	*fer*/death/dying	Recreational Reading
173	*eau*/peace	magazines
174	*ser*/supermarkets	newspapers
175	*ink*/girls	magazines
176	*fic*/television	newspapers
177	*sim*/unfamiliar words	Social Studies books
178	*ear*/unfamiliar words	Health books
179	*sus*/unfamiliar words	Science books
180	*ary*/unfamiliar words	newspapers

Index

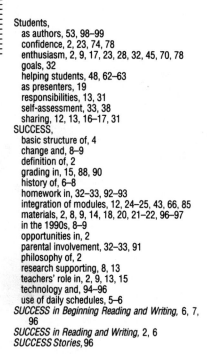